D1462349

LONG-RANGE GOALS

RELATED TITLES FROM POTOMAC BOOKS

Soccer's Most Wanted™: The Top 10 Book of Clumsy Keepers,
Clever Crosses, and Outlandish Oddities
by John Snyder

Soccer's Most Wanted II™: The Top 10 Book of More Glorious Goals,
Superb Saves, and Fantastic Fr ee-Kicks
by Jeff Carlisle

LONG-RANGE GOALS
THE SUCCESS STORY OF
MAJOR LEAGUE
SOCCER

BEAU DURE

POTOMAC BOOKS, INC.
WASHINGTON, D.C.

Library of Congress Cataloging-in-Publication Data
Dure, Beau.
  Long-range goals : the success story of major league soccer / Beau Dure.
      p. cm.
  Includes bibliographical references and index.
  ISBN 978-1-59797-509-4 (alk. paper)
  1. Soccer—United States. 2. Professional sports—United States. 3. Major League
Soccer (Organization) I. Title.
  GV944.U5D87 2010
  796.334'640973—dc22

                                                         2010000807

Printed in the United States of America on acid-free paper that meets the American National Standards Institute Z39-48 Standard.

Potomac Books, Inc.
22841 Quicksilver Drive
Dulles, Virginia 20166

First Edition

10 9 8 7 6 5 4 3 2 1

CONTENTS

PREFACE

In 1994, the World Cup came to the United States. As a young copy editor and sports columnist at the *Morning Star* in Wilmington, North Carolina, I decided to track down some information about a professional soccer league that was supposedly in the works around that time. I got back a packet of vague plans and lists of interested cities. It all seemed exciting and yet so distant.

In 2006, after several years of writing columns and features for *USA Today* and Knight Ridder Tribune News Service, I started to work in earnest on this book, realizing that no one had written a full-fledged history of Major League Soccer, the league that had once seemed so far off.

Not that it's really possible to write a full-fledged history of any league. Telling the stories of the great characters on the field and in the offices will require many books, not one. To give just one example of someone who will be mentioned only in passing: it's humbling to sit face-to-face with a man like Maykel Galindo, the Cuban striker who turned a short moment of opportunity into a great career with MLS, and hear him talk about the hardships he suffered along the way . . . with a smile on his face.

And the ending hasn't been written. The league is still in business. That's the story.

●

If soccer were a religion, then I had had an adult baptism. Like many kids who grew up in the 1970s, I was fascinated with the PBS show *Soccer Made in Germany,* but unlike the kids of Kearny, New Jersey, who would grow up to be U.S. soccer mainstays (such as John Harkes, Tab Ramos, and Tony Meola),

I didn't have the New York Cosmos next door to inspire me. I was vaguely aware of the Atlanta Chiefs' existence, but my family never made the trip to see them play. I played youth soccer and was a decent sweeper at the Under-14 level, but I switched to cross-country and chess in high school for reasons I've long forgotten. Although I was more curious about the game than most of my peers, to the point of asking my mother to send a clipping of the 1982 World Cup standings each day she wrote me at summer camp, it was still an idle fascination.

At Duke, I enrolled too late to see the men's team win a national championship, but I saw some good players and great games. Little did I know how much significance that opposing coach (Bruce Arena) and goalkeeper (Tony Meola) at the Duke-Virginia game would have in the years to come.

As thrilling and rowdy as Duke games could be, I didn't really get wrapped up in a soccer team's fortunes and misfortunes until MLS started. Yet MLS had little to do with the team I followed—the Carolina Dynamo, which played one level lower in the U.S. Interregional Soccer League (USISL) and the A-League, which merged with the USISL. I attended every game I could for a couple of years during which the Dynamo were the class of a rough-and-tumble league. It didn't matter that they played on a high school gridiron football field. Or that you could easily prove that they weren't the best team in the world. For that season, for me, they were.

But the Dynamo could have used more fans with such an irrational attachment. Too many fans at the games fit the "soccer mom" stereotype, driving our kids to a safe, well-organized activity, not responding to Yari Allnutt's call to turn up the intensity. At one game, while the crowd was wrapped up in the antics of "Dynamo Dawg" or whatever mascot the team employed at the time, I was one of the few witnesses to a spectacular goal by Brian Loftin, who would later have his own experience with league-building as commissioner of the indoor Xtreme Soccer League (XSL). A mini-ball was tossed out onto the field for Loftin to hurl into the stands. Seeing a one-man standing ovation, he pegged it right into my midsection, and it took all my amateur goalkeeping skills to hang on. By then, someone had alerted the kids that a goal had indeed been scored. Lacking hard-core fan support, the Dynamo eventually sold off their talented players—Allnutt, Loftin, John Ball, Scott Schweitzer—and dropped back to the amateur level, where the club is successful to this day on a modest scale.

I attended my first MLS game in 1996 in Tampa, Florida, watching the Tampa Bay Mutiny take on the Colorado Rapids. What I remember most about that game was that the suburbanites gathered near me were quite relieved to see the fans beating drums seated on the other side of the stadium, far away. That one moment showed me the problem MLS would have in uniting its fan base. Ultimately, to be a fan means to have that irrational attachment, one that makes you beat a drum or not particularly care that the person next to you is beating a drum.

Fast-forward to 2006 to see those irrational attachments in action. Before a pivotal late-season game against New York, D.C. United honored its 1996 championship team. Most—not all—fans warmly greeted 1996 coach Bruce Arena, though he was still under fire for his performance with the 2006 U.S. team in the World Cup and, not incidentally, was coaching the visiting Red Bulls. But the crowd awakened echoes in aging RFK Stadium upon greeting Raul Diaz Arce, the Salvadoran striker who had scored 23 goals in that first season. When Marco Etcheverry strolled out onto the field, the stadium roared. Somewhere in the space occupied by the Screaming Eagles and Barra Brava, the two largest United supporters' groups, fans waved a portrait of the Bolivian playmaker.

This league has fans. This league has players. And this league has history.

This book compiles much of that history from hundreds of newspaper accounts, MLS media guides, my own recollections, and exclusive interviews conducted in 2008. I also happened to find a videotape with something labeled "Great soccer"—which turned out to be the 6-4 Kansas City–Columbus game of 1996. But this history is far from complete. In 14 short years, too much has happened to compile in one book. Business students will want to explore the role Soccer United Marketing has played in reversing the league's bottom line. Lawyers are already examining the single-entity structure that MLS successfully defended in court. Fans and players have plenty of anecdotes that either I don't know or couldn't include. If this is the only MLS book on a bookstore shelf in 2011, that's disappointing.

There are already plenty of people to thank for their roles in keeping the league's history alive. The league itself does much of the work, with a communications department now led by Dan Courtemanche, Will Kuhns, and Lauren Brophy. On the unofficial level, David Litterer has been the keeper of U.S. soccer history online since the early days of the Internet. For pre-MLS history, Litterer works with two accomplished researchers. Colin Jose is quite literally a Hall of Fame historian, having been historian of the National Soccer Hall of Fame from 1997 to 2007. He and collaborator Roger Allaway, his successor at the Hall of Fame, have unearthed the forgotten records of the American Soccer League (ASL), among other accomplishments.

Among the other people to thank for their research, inspiration, and illuminating conversations:

Andrei Markovits and Steven Hellerman wrote *Offside: Soccer and American Exceptionalism*, explaining once and for all why this sport has had such a rough ride in this country.

David Wangerin picked up the torch from Markovits and Hellerman to write a compelling survey of the U.S. game, *Soccer in a Football World*.

Among the other great books on soccer and culture: *How Soccer Explains the World: An Unlikely Theory of Globalization* by *New Republic* editor Franklin Foer, and *Soccer Against the Enemy* (or *Football Against the Enemy*, depending on where you buy it) by Simon Kuper.

Documentary makers have picked up the story in the *History of Soccer* series and the disco-infused *Once in a Lifetime: The Incredible Story of the New York Cosmos*. The latter is also a book by Gavin Newsham.

Kenn Tomasch has kept meticulous data on various U.S. sports leagues.

The 150th pick in the inaugural MLS draft, Garth Lagerwey, is a fellow Duke alum who answered many of my questions and was happy to share his honest opinions. He should write a book like this one of these days, at least about his five-year playing career and current job as Real Salt Lake general manager.

MLS is well served by beat writers who have kept the daily news coming, starting with the dean of U.S. soccer reporters, Michael Lewis. We're also lucky in this sport to have the insights of *Sports Illustrated*'s Grant Wahl, whose 2009 book *The Beckham Experiment* shed light on the league's most famous player.

And MLS is lucky to have such a dedicated unofficial media. We have blogs such as the staggeringly comprehensive Du Nord and BigSoccer.com's tandem of Dan Loney and Bill Archer. Andy Mead travels more miles than most truck drivers to take professional photos and occasionally publish the lively *Emerald City Gazette*. The league's rivalries are intense, but the willingness of supporters to share information is truly admirable.

Many thanks to the following players, coaches, league officials, and interested parties for being so generous with their time for interviews: Mark Abbott, Freddy Adu, Jeff Agoos, Bruce Arena, Sean Bowers, Jimmy Conrad, Landon Donovan, Don Garber, Ivan Gazidis, Sunil Gulati, Garth Lagerwey, Alexi Lalas, Doug Logan, Richard Motzkin, Ben Olsen, Jim Paglia, Eddie Pope, Alan Rothenberg, Mark Semioli, and Eric Wynalda.

I'm especially grateful to everyone who helped bring this book to market. Allaway, an experienced editor as well as a soccer historian, read an early draft. So did Wahl, whose book provided vital material for the final chapters. My agent, Ian Kleinert of Objective Entertainment, provided expert guidance to a first-time author. At Potomac Books, Kevin Cuddihy saw potential in the book, Don McKeon and Bud Knecht gave the rough draft skillful edits, and Elizabeth Demers shepherded the book the rest of the way.

Also thanks to the many editors who have indulged my soccer interests over the years, particularly Deb Barrington, J. Michael Falgoust, Roxanna Scott, Don Collins, Steve Berkowitz, Janice Lloyd, and Adam Hirshfield at *USA Today*, Tom Peterson and Gregory Clay at Knight Ridder Tribune (now McClatchy-Tribune), Ann Alexander, Allen Johnson, and Cindy Loman at the *News & Record*, and David Brown and Scott Nunn at the *Morning Star*. Special thanks to Gary Kicinski and Monte Lorell for giving me time off to revive a dormant book idea and finish it.

Thanks to all those who argue with me at BigSoccer.com—and before that, at the North American Soccer mailing list—to help me see MLS issues from a variety of perspectives. Just remember that you're all wrong.

Thanks to the staff at Starbucks in Vienna, Virginia, and the Patrick Henry Library for providing great places to work.

And thanks most of all to my family. In 1996, MLS kicked off, and I met someone who was nice enough to consider a sports bar with a Premier League broadcast as a viable dating venue. I couldn't have imagined that we'd be taking our first son to a D.C. United reserve game 10 years later, or that I would start writing this book as our second son was born.

INTRODUCTION: PAST TO PRESENT

Taylor Twellman stood facing his locker, checking messages on his phone. The New England striker, temporarily forgetting the spatial awareness that made him one of the top goal-poaching forwards in MLS history, was oblivious to the post-game media throng that had crammed into the narrow space between rows of lockers at RFK Stadium, the aging Washington venue steeped in soccer history.

Before MLS Cup 2007, played November 18, Twellman had joked that he would give only quotes in the style of *Bull Durham*, the great baseball film in which Kevin Costner's savvy, world-weary Crash Davis tutored Tim Robbins's brash young Nuke LaLoosh on the finer points of feeding clichés to the media. Twellman is far too colorful to stick to the script. He never lacks for self-confidence, but like a good boxer hyping a fight, he balances arrogance with playful wit. Reporters know to seek him out.

Most people associated with MLS are grateful for any media attention. Like NASCAR drivers, they sense a responsibility to their core of fans. While most leagues shun bloggers, several MLS teams have given credentials to independent, amateur journalists who work alongside newspaper reporters. The league might limit access to a global megastar like David Beckham or a young phenom like Freddy Adu, who faced a legitimate concern of overexposure and overscheduling, but everyone else is easily approachable. Even Landon Donovan, whose media exploits include an appearance on MTV's *Cribs* with his TV-star wife and his notoriety as Mexico's nemesis, is generous in granting interviews and speaks openly in the locker room, shifting into

Spanish when asked. Bruce Arena, who parlayed early championships with D.C. United into an eight-year run as national-team coach, can intimidate reporters with his caustic wit but never shuts them off.

The media jockeying for position in that cramped space at RFK, which had been refurbished for baseball's latest attempt to usurp a stadium much better suited to "the world's game" than the one-time national pastime, would soon push the limits. The home locker room temporarily housing the Houston Dynamo was more spacious, but the New England Revolution occupied the visitors' space. Some of us stood only a few inches away from Twellman but gazed elsewhere, like commuters on a packed subway car. Twellman focused on his phone while we waited. Finally, he sensed one or two reporters were also focused on that phone.

Twellman whirled around and demanded a bit of privacy for another minute or two. The chagrined reporters, having nowhere to retreat, averted their eyes while Twellman went back to his messages.

His point made, Twellman took only a few seconds to turn back and open the floor for questions. A dozen reporters thrust forward tape recorders, then turned their eyes to me, the only one willing to break the ice and ask a few questions.

"I've got no emotion in me," Twellman said. "I've lost every final every which way we can. The way I look at it, we've got absolutely nothing to lose next year. Get back here, we should play four forwards and try to score 12 goals."

Twellman had managed to swing some sarcasm toward New England's critics, who often accused his team of playing too defensively in big games, but he was speaking out of heartbreak. For the third straight year and fourth of the past six years, he and the Revolution had played in MLS Cup. The Revs lost in overtime in 2002 and 2005, then penalty kicks in 2006. This time, Twellman's goal had given New England the lead for 41 minutes before Houston responded with the dagger of Joseph Ngwenya's scrambled goal and the axe of Dwayne De Rosario's powerful header.

No one would dispute New England's place among MLS elite over those six years. The annual runs through the playoffs were no fluke. Under the direction of Steve Nicol, the philosophical Scotsman who had a glittering career playing for Liverpool, the Revolution had left the struggles of its early years far behind. Nicol built a core of combative, fiercely loyal players—Twellman, fellow forward Pat Noonan, goalkeeper Matt Reis, midfield intimidator Shalrie Joseph, defender Jay Heaps, and playmaker Steve Ralston—and filled in gaps around them with shrewd draft picks.

The strategy worked. But it was working slightly better for Houston, which had kept a cadre of players together under different circumstances.

Dominic Kinnear, Scottish-born but raised in California, was saddened when his San Jose Earthquakes packed up and left the Bay Area for Texas in 2006. The move was unfair on many levels. The Earthquakes had trouble finding a suitable owner or stadium, but Houston had neither of these things. And the Bay Area's soccer lore was so strong that MLS had chosen San Jose's Spartan Stadium, narrow field and all, for its 1996 debut.

Upon moving to Houston, the franchise stumbled immediately. The club's original name—Houston 1836, taken from the year the city was founded—angered many Mexican supporters who remembered that the city's founding coincided with the defeat of Mexico's army. The team rechristened itself the Houston Dynamo.

Despite all the upheaval, many Earthquakes relocated to Houston with Kinnear. De Rosario had scored San Jose's winner in the 2001 final. Defenders Eddie Robinson and Craig Waibel, goalkeeper Pat Onstad, target forward Brian Ching, and winger Brian Mullan had been with the team for its second title in 2003. Two longtime Earthquakes had returned—Wade Barrett had spent a couple of years in Europe, and Richard Mulrooney rejoined his former teammates early in 2007 after a few years elsewhere in MLS.

The result of Houston's 2006 debut: another MLS championship, won in penalty kicks at the Revolution's expense at Pizza Hut Park in Frisco, Texas. Frisco was the home field for FC Dallas, not the Dynamo, but Houston's energized fan base made the trip in numbers.

The venue was part of the showcase that year, as it had been for four years. Players had put down roots with the Dynamo and Revolution. With venues like Pizza Hut Park, the league was also building roots, a literal foundation.

MLS has always sought to operate its own fields, controlling the revenue streams and creating an atmosphere more conducive to soccer than the cavernous NFL and college football stadiums it has shared in most cities. The first few years brought little success. The Miami Fusion, a 1998 expansion team, played in a cozy converted high-school football stadium but never drew enough people to stave off contraction from the league after four years. Lamar

Hunt, a pioneer owner in many sports and a holdover from the long-gone North American Soccer League (NASL) days, overcame political setbacks to get the league's first custom-built stadium in Columbus, Ohio, in 1999.

After the contraction of 2002, which eliminated the Fusion and the Tampa Bay Mutiny, the league stepped up the construction pace. Outside Los Angeles, the Galaxy's new ground became the centerpiece of a multisport complex called the Home Depot Center. The Frisco, Texas, complex—a stadium surrounded by many fields, suitable for youth tournaments—set the mold for several teams' proposals. Local politicians are always prone to make populist stands against subsidizing "billionaire owners," particularly when it comes to soccer rather than a more-established American sport like football or baseball, but adding much-needed facilities for youth recreation is a good way of getting the city or county to pay for the infrastructure upgrades.

MLS kept the spotlight on its shiny new buildings, putting the MLS Cup final in one of its venues five of six years. Columbus hosted in 2001, then Home Depot Center in 2003 and 2004. Pizza Hut Park hosted the next two.

By 2007, the ball was rolling elsewhere. Colorado moved into a new facility. Chicago had settled into its new place. The expansion team in Toronto packed its new stadium with rowdy, streamer-tossing fans. Salt Lake and New York started construction. Kansas City had plans in action. Only Washington, despite its loyal fan base and hosting duties for the 2007 final, had suffered a political setback, leading commissioner Don Garber to direct some uncharacteristically harsh comments toward local politicians in his annual State of the League press conference.

But the focus in 2007 was no longer on the concrete and steel. The league made international news for the first time in recent memory, splashing out substantial money to sign two megastars. From the Mexican league came Cuauhtémoc Blanco, a fiery forward from the massive Club America. From Europe came one of those rare figures whose celebrity transcends a sport— David Beckham.

Over the summer, the league reveled in the hype and hysteria. Blanco drew plenty of fans in his new home of Chicago and at road games, just as Mexican goalkeeper-forward Jorge Campos had in the league's first years. Beckham was omnipresent in the media, making the rounds on talk shows and having his every move chronicled on MLS broadcasts.

Real Madrid, Beckham's second and latest European club, accidentally fueled the mania. When Beckham confirmed that he would depart for MLS after Real's season, angry manager Fabio Capello threw a fit and banished him to the bench. Beckham responded with the good manners and good cheer Englishmen love to claim as endemic in their country. Capello relented, and Beckham played a pivotal role as Real surged to a surprising Spanish title.

Unfortunately for MLS and the Los Angeles Galaxy, Beckham also turned up injured.

The backlash that followed was grossly unfair but hardly surprising. Most people who had a casual interest in the game had long forgotten Beckham's humble beginnings. He was often cast as a pampered, preening celebrity, an image reinforced by his pop-singer wife, the former Posh Spice. The soccer world was often split between those who considered Beckham a brilliant player and those who thought his celebrity had surpassed his ability. Debating Beckham myth vs. Beckham reality was a popular European pastime, one that followed him across the Atlantic.

Beckham's MLS career began fitfully, with one injury leading to another. He and Landon Donovan—like Beckham, he was his country's most accomplished player but also a popular target for critics of his celebrity lifestyle—pulled the injury-riddled Galaxy into playoff contention with a late surge. The regular season ended with a showdown between Beckham's Galaxy and Blanco's Fire, with both teams trying to claim the last spot. The league's two hottest teams and two biggest stars somehow produced a dull finale, with the Fire taking the honors in anticlimactic fashion.

Blanco and the Fire proceeded to knock out D.C. United, which had the league's best record but seemed snakebitten over the two-leg playoff series, but the Revolution put a stop to the run in the league semifinal.

The backlash meme gathered momentum. Beckham and Blanco were out, as were the New York Red Bulls and marquee signings Juan Pablo Angel and Claudio Reyna. Dallas had failed to improve with the signing of Brazil's Denilson. Those five were the only players signed under the league's new "designated-player" rule, which let teams break the bank for one player—two, with an appropriate trade—without breaking salary-cap rules.

The big splash hadn't worked. Two exemplars of stability, neither of whom had a designated player, had advanced to the final.

While that wasn't fair to Beckham, Blanco, or Angel, all of whom had showed their class in every game they played, it was a perfect metaphor for soccer in the United States. Big splashes are easy. Building something strong and long lasting is far more difficult.

●

Soccer is known as the Beautiful Game, free-flowing and breathtaking. In the United States, the game's history has been anything but free-flowing and beautiful. The game has lurched forward and tumbled back. Several times, it has pushed its way to the forefront of the country's consciousness, only to fall into obscurity, forgotten and derided.

The conventional wisdom is that the United States has never known soccer in the past and is slowly but surely adopting it. The truth isn't so simple. Throughout the last century, the United States has seen boom times, but the game's roots have always been shallow, blowing away with the next drought.

The frustration of reading U.S. soccer history—at David Litterer's astoundingly deep online archive or in books such as *Soccer in a Football World* —is that it keeps repeating. A new league finds a warm reception and gathers momentum, then falls apart through internal disputes and overreaching.

Most Americans remember a time of a suddenly prosperous league with large crowds, glittering international stars, a few "Americanized" rules, and a free-spending giddiness that led the league to collapse as suddenly as it had burst onto the scene. But most Americans don't realize—and even fewer realized it before the work of the dean of North American soccer historians, Colin Jose—that the description applies just as easily to the American Soccer League of the 1920s as it does to the North American Soccer League of the 1970s.

The 1920s, hailed by Litterer as the first Golden Era in American Soccer, featured the strong ASL and some international exhibitions drawing more than 46,000 people. When that league fell apart in the '30s, the game labored in obscurity until new efforts to form a national league in the '60s. Those efforts led to the NASL, which drew plenty of attention in the late '70s and '80s with stars such as Pelé and large crowds in a handful of cities. The NASL imploded in the mid-'80s, leaving little in U.S. soccer but the college game and the then-thriving indoor game. From those ashes and a successful World Cup sprang Major League Soccer in 1996.

The miracle of MLS is not the occasional large crowd, such as the 69,255 fans who surprised the staff at Pasadena's Rose Bowl for the Los Angeles Galaxy's debut or the crowds over 90,000 for a couple of doubleheaders with MLS games and other marquee teams. It's not the strong contribution made by its players in the USA's run to the World Cup quarterfinals in 2002. The miracle is stability.

Most U.S. sports establishments wouldn't find simple stability as reason to celebrate. But most U.S. sports don't face ingrained hostility in the U.S. media and segments of the fan base. Americans love American things, and soccer is associated with the countries Americans left behind in their haste to assimilate. Academic works such as Andrei S. Markovits and Steven L. Hellerman's *Offside: Soccer and American Exceptionalism* (Princeton University Press, 2001) put that point in vivid detail. In *Soccer Against the Enemy,* Simon Kuper put it like this: "When immigrants from Europe landed in the U.S., their children were teased on the street for their funny accents, clothes, and parents. The last thing these children were going to do was play a funny European game on the streets and be teased again, so they took up baseball. This is why Americans don't play soccer."[1]

Today, in a rapidly evolving country, first-generation Americans may be more inclined to stick with soccer. But the older prejudices were handed down, and the sport is the frequent punching bag of sports columnists and talk-radio jackals. Sometimes, the hostility takes on semi-official status. Franklin Foer, the American author of the excellent hybrid of soccer and globalization theory *How Soccer Explains the World* (HarperCollins, 2004), unearthed a scathing comment in the records of a body that usually has better things to do than bash a popular pastime—the U.S. House of Representatives, where former NFL quarterback Jack Kemp urged American kids to play "real" football and shun a sport he likened to socialism. (Kemp later backtracked, not convincingly.) Legendary sportswriter Dick Young put it in language better suited for New York tabloids, telling young Cosmos beat writer David Hirshey that soccer is a sport for "commie pansies."

Beyond the hostility, there's apathy. Many Americans don't think their countrymen could ever enjoy the game, at least not in its traditional form. "Soccer is not a spectator-friendly game unless it's part of your cultural DNA or unless you have a really vested interest in the outcome." So says Jim Paglia, who bid against MLS for top-division status in the United States with a proposal that radically reinvented the sport.

Beyond the hostility and apathy lies a large but fragmented fan base. Doug Logan, the first MLS commissioner, describes the challenge:

This was probably one of the seminal issues that I had to face in the course of my nearly four years there. The issue was that we basically had three core audiences that were out there to really go after. Number one was the soccer purists of European ancestry—in New York, Boston, some other areas—people who knew what was going on in La Liga and the Bundesliga, people had a favorite team in the Premier League, people who scrambled to watch a soccer match on TV on the infrequent occasion that they could find one live. That audience really needed to be sold on the basis that this is a credible product. It's not the product we're used to, but it's credible.

The second audience which just was there for the taking was what I call New Americans. Basically Spanish-speaking, who were used to spending most of their Sundays either at a match or watching one on TV. They came out with their drums in droves. At the end of the first season, we had done some in-stadium surveys, which I announced pretty proudly to our board, indicating that some 35 percent of our in-stadium audience considered Spanish to be their first tongue. This is averaging in Kansas City, Columbus, Tampa . . . throughout the entire league, during the course of that regular season, 17,000-plus attendance in that first year, 35 percent considered Spanish to be their native tongue. I won't name any names, but at the board meeting that I announced that, I was told by a couple of board members, "Gee, we can't let that out. We can't let that be known."

Because the third core audience that we were going after was the soccer mom. A good number of our investors thought this should be a family sell, the same way that kids soccer is on playing fields around the country. I disagreed then, I disagree now. Soccer at its best is tribal. Soccer at its best in the stands has gotta be a little dangerous. I'm not advocating the thuggery that goes on. I'm just saying soccer at its best is very adult and is not the same as taking your kids to the circus or to an ice show. I thought that we were fighting ourselves at cross-purposes trying to accommodate that very audience that you described on your side of the field in Tampa.

To say the way to sell the league was to have seven-year-old kids come in their uniforms, boys and girls and parade the field really put a damper on what the match ought to be about. The product that MLS has always consistently put on the field has been a pretty aggressive, hard-hitting, fast brand of soccer that most players when they come from other leagues and other countries go into a period of shock about it. The skill levels were in the beginning and continue to be several notches below places where kids live with a ball at their feet 18 hours a day. The certain skills on a universal basis—I'm making some generalizations here—those are still a notch or two below, but from the speed of the game and the aggressiveness of the game, it's a product with a lot of bite to it.

At the end of the day, there has always been this yin and yang—if you go after one, you're denigrating the other and vice versa. Perfect example would be the huge crowds we used to draw at the Rose Bowl on a big match weekend, where the audiences were wonderfully divided between Mexican-Americans and soccer moms from Pasadena sitting not in different sections of the stadium but in the same row, watching a match but from two different lenses.[2]

Beyond that, the United States has casual fans with no exposure to the sport. European reporters tend to dig these people up to demonstrate American apathy during each World Cup, but they're not as numerous as the Europeans would like to believe. Still, the United States has a few people with a curiosity about a game they rarely see. And it's funny how many of them are employed as journalists.

And then there are the hard-core soccer bashers mentioned above and detailed in *Offside*. That cultural hostility has been handed down for generations, and with more American kids opting to play soccer instead of the all-American game (at least, as sanitized by various historians) of baseball, the flames are still being fanned, even as Major League Baseball accepts a steady flow of players from the Caribbean and Latin America.

Aside from the diverse audience, MLS is also unique among American sports leagues in that it is clearly *not* the best league of its kind in the world. The NFL is the only top-level American football league in the world, with a slight variant just north of the border in Canada. Few countries have baseball leagues, and Major League Baseball is easily the world's preeminent competition. Basketball and hockey are global, but the NBA and NHL supplement the deep North American talent pools by drawing the vast majority of the world's top players. In soccer, the leagues in major European countries are the best, while Brazil and Argentina have deep talent pools and a few great teams. Most good American players will pass through MLS at some stage of their careers, but the league occasionally loses mid-career players to teams in Scandinavia.

So MLS is dwarfed by other competitions in its country and in its sport. Yet over its history, it has survived and even started to thrive. The league hasn't suddenly skyrocketed in attendance or TV ratings, but its investors have figured out ways to make money off the game. Compare MLS at Year 15 to other U.S. sports leagues—from baseball's ancient National League to newer entities such as the Arena Football League or the country's dueling lacrosse leagues—and it stands on solid ground.

MLS teams have shown staying power not usually seen in other leagues. Of the original 10 teams, one folded, one moved, and the other eight remained in place as of 2010. One expansion team folded. Over the same period of time, NBA teams left Vancouver and Charlotte, NHL teams left Winnipeg and Hartford, the NFL's Houston Oilers moved to Tennessee, and baseball's Montreal Expos moved to Washington alongside D.C. United. Those leagues are several generations older than MLS; in their early days, teams came and went with the wind.

Soccer as a whole is even healthier. MLS has yet to capture all the country's soccer fans, though Garber has made that quest a priority of his leadership. In a nation of immigrants and an era of new media, it's easy to turn on the TV or scan the Web to follow soccer from Mexico, England, Spain, or elsewhere. Only the World Cup unites the whole group, which is one reason why Americans turned out in staggering numbers for the 1994 Cup and would do so in even greater numbers if FIFA (the French acronym for the International Federation of Association Football) were to put the tournament here again. The sport has its naysayers, but unless they're voting on stadium funding, they're irrelevant.

Nike, one of the companies fighting for a share of the soccer market, silenced the negativity in one effective ad leading up to the 2006 World Cup. While a talk-radio host droned through the usual soccer-bashing routine, saying no one cared about soccer in this country, the camera showed people of various ethnicities playing pickup games in all environments—streets, parched fields, anywhere. As the beat of Joy Zipper's "Go Tell the World" picked up, viewers saw Freddy Adu going through a dazzling series of tricks. Finally, the U.S. national team marched out into a packed stadium that roared as an American poked the ball into the net.

Yes, Americans care about soccer. And after 14 years of play, Americans care about MLS. That's why Taylor Twellman, minutes after another MLS Cup heartbreak, had several messages waiting while impatient reporters crowded into his personal space. The Beckhams and Blancos are important parts of the MLS story, but before they arrived, the league had players like Twellman. And the league is strong enough now that it's no longer a rash fit of optimism to suggest that there will be more Twellmans and Beckhams after they've hung up their boots.

We couldn't have said that in 1995. Or 2001. The league has needed more than a decade of successes and failures to reach this point. That's the story of this book.

1

Before Kickoff

April 6, 1996. More than a decade since the North American Soccer League's demise and almost 20 years since the heyday of Pelé and the New York Cosmos, a bona fide top-level U.S. soccer league was set to play. Major League Soccer was prepared to debut before a national audience on ESPN. Spartan Stadium, the home of the NASL's San Jose Earthquakes years before and now the home of the San Jose Clash, was prepared for its moment in the spotlight.

Or so thought Peter Bridgwater, the Clash's general manager.

By Bridgwater's request, an MLS logo had been painted in the center circle. That's a minor field decoration by American standards—ads are painted onto hockey ice, basketball courts are adorned with giant works of art, and even college soccer fields are heavily decorated for championship games.

When MLS's founder, commissioner, and deputy commissioner arrived in town with a couple of colleagues from FIFA, soccer's international organizing body, they said no. Some of the most influential names in world soccer would be present, and we weren't to start this league by violating Law 1, Decision 5—which governs field markings—in front of them.

And so Bridgwater's crew spent the first day of Major League Soccer's official history putting layers of green paint over the league's logo.

On its surface, the insistence on a green center circle was pointless. TV viewers would still notice a hazy outline at midfield. Later in the season, as American football teams moved back onto the fields they were renting to MLS, soccer games would be played on the football gridiron, with soccer markings scarcely visible amid the yard lines, hash marks, and odd squiggles along the sidelines. In future years, a couple of MLS teams would take up temporary residence on horrid artificial turf with the goal sitting in the middle of darkened football end zones that did more to deflate soccer fans' spirits than they did to raise those of football fans.

But even if the MLS officers didn't realize it at the time, they were taking a symbolic stand. MLS would not be just another fly-by-night U.S. soccer league that flouted international convention. This league would do things the right way, with few gimmicks, helping it do what no other U.S. soccer league has done—remain stable.

Not that "the right way" is easy to discern. And not that MLS has always gotten it right.

●

Throughout its history, American soccer has been pulled and stretched in every direction—amateur vs. professional, colleges vs. traditional amateur, indoor vs. outdoor, European style vs. Latin American style, and sometimes, just league vs. league.

After hosting the 1994 World Cup with spectacular success and record-smashing crowds, U.S. soccer at last had momentum. Youth soccer was booming, threatening to supplant Little League baseball as American kids' introduction to organized sports. The national team, virtually dormant since a 1950 upset over England in the World Cup, had earned its way into the 1990 World Cup and performed well at home in 1994. Cable networks dipped their toes into Europe to provide regular showings of professional leagues, filling a void left by the fondly remembered PBS show *Soccer Made in Germany.* The American Professional Soccer League (APSL), soon to change its name to the A-League, played at a reasonably high level, while the USISL was set to expand to 55 professional teams on top of a smaller amateur division even as the organization's name changed every few years.

The U.S. Soccer Federation had promised to start a bona fide professional league, classified as a "first division" league, in the wake of the World Cup. But once again, the way forward was disputed.

The U.S. Soccer Federation president was Alan Rothenberg, a veteran lawyer who had defeated incumbent Werner Fricker in 1990. He had experience in sports law and ownership, including a stint with the NASL's Los Angeles Aztecs, and a record of success in organizing the 1984 Olympic soccer tournament. FIFA, considerably more interested in U.S. soccer politics after awarding the 1994 World Cup to the country, had encouraged Rothenberg's candidacy. An Associated Press story years later would suggest that FIFA threatened to take away the Cup if Rothenberg didn't take over.[1]

One person working with Rothenberg was Sunil Gulati, an economist by trade who had organized two U.S. Cup tournaments and would be executive VP of the World Cup committee. "When Alan was elected, we started a committee to look at the development of a professional league," Gulati says.

> That group had a number of meetings. It's not what finally led to the startup of MLS. What really started formally the process of MLS was two, three, four of us who were at World Cup [the organizing committee for the tournament] started talking about putting a league together and what it would take to do that. . . . We really wanted to get a document put together, a business plan, and we needed to get somebody on board to do that. I said to Alan, do you have another young, smart Latham [& Watkins, Rothenberg's firm] attorney to join us.

Rothenberg recruited Mark Abbott to take a three-month leave from Latham & Watkins to draw up a business plan. "A bunch of us that were working on the World Cup were kind of doing this in between," Rothenberg says.

> I decided that we had to have somebody to devote undivided attention to it. Mark was an associate I had worked with at Latham [&] Watkins. I brought him over, and we put him on a full-time basis paid to write up the business plan. There was a bunch of us that had been brainstorming, figuring everything out. Everybody had a lot on their plates— I think their plates were overflowing—in trying to get ready for the 1994 World Cup.

Abbott was a lifelong fan, having been a ballboy and season-ticket holder for the NASL's Minnesota Kicks. "I had remembered the success of the [NASL] at that time and thought that if the league had been successful in certain cities for a period of time in the '70s, then given all the changes that had occurred from the late '70s to the early '90s that were positive for soccer, then there was a real opportunity for the league to be successful," Abbott says. "Seemed to me like an interesting project to write a business plan for the league."

But Abbott's plan would have competition. The USISL, which had many clubs that were only nominally professional, accepted its status. The APSL did not. It entered a bid of its own for Division I status. U.S. Soccer would vote, and as both bidder and federation president, Rothenberg was forced to walk a delicate line to avoid a conflict of interest.

Abbott emphasizes that Rothenberg was following procedures both domestic and foreign:

> At that time, there were very stringent procedures that were put in place to ensure that although Alan was the head of the soccer federation and leading the effort to make a presentation with respect to the league, he had been recused from the decision-making system in U.S. Soccer. There was a big meeting in December 1993 where we made our presentations. Alan was not part of the Federation board in making that decision.
>
> Also, and I think this gets overlooked, FIFA in awarding the World Cup to the United States did so very expressly for the purpose of using it as a springboard for a professional league. That's what he was supposed to be doing, using this event to help start the league.

The third bidder for Division I status went much further, proposing to use the Cup as a drastic reinvention of the game. Jim Paglia's League One America proposed dividing the field into zones marked with chevrons and limiting players to specific zones for an entire period. The color-coded uniforms—white for a striker, blue for players in the blue zone, yellow for the players in the yellow zone, and red for defenders—would include electronic signaling devices that would tell the referee when a player had veered too far, like an ankle bracelet for someone under house arrest.

FIFA expressed some interest in the plan, inviting Paglia to Switzerland to discuss it. Paglia says he was told not to discuss the trip, but FIFA spokesman Guido Tognoni spoke with USA Today's Roscoe Nance: "It is nice to see a private group put together a project. We're impressed. It is concrete. It seems they'll be ready in 1995. . . . But it would be best for them to join forces."[2] Whether FIFA was seriously interested in the plan or was simply trying to pressure Rothenberg and company to take care of business is anyone's guess.

Paglia, who had worked with the NASL's Rochester Lancers and with local World Cup organizers in Chicago, says the intent was to give spectators a chance to speculate on strategy:

> As much as I love the game, and I really do love soccer, I think it's really dull to watch unless you have a vested interest in the outcome because it doesn't promote spectator interaction. You can't sit there and talk to your friend about it like you would at a baseball game, where you can sit next to your friend, sipping a beer, the pace of the game is slower, there's more breaks in the action and you can say to your friend, "I bet he's going to throw him a curveball." And your friend can say, "Well I bet he's going to take on this pitch." And you can go round and round like that whether it's American football or American baseball. In the research we did, we concluded that the two games, American football and baseball, were virtually the same concept from a spectator perspective. It was territorial—first base, second base, third base. They're restrictive as well— the right fielder would never think to run to third base to cover a play. You have very limited territorial responsibilities. All those types of characteristics don't exist in soccer, and therefore they don't lend themselves to speculation. I can't sit there and say, "I bet he's going to pass to the right wing." Because in the time it takes to think it, it's over. The game is extemporaneous, it's improvisational. So we tried to revive the sport in a sense by revising it to make it more spectator-friendly.

Paglia's rules would give players and coaches—and therefore, fans— much more to think about during a game. Coaches would be required to change the lineup for the second period, reassigning players to different zones. Players' decisions to pass or shoot would be complicated by a multiple-point system—the farther away from the goal your zone was, the more your shot would count. The placement also could affect the scoring—the league would include a larger goal built around an existing soccer goal, with an additional half-point awarded for any shot squeezed between the two frames.

"The reason we did that is that the goals that exist today in soccer were essentially designed and constructed back in the 1700s, when the average goalie was 5-7 or 5-8," Paglia says.

Now they're growing, and they can cover that frame a lot easier. The average goalie today is over six feet tall. So we said why not make it more challenging for the goalie and more rewarding for the shooter who picks the post? If you can pick the upper 90 [a corner of the goal], you're going to get a better score out of it. . . . It was probably the most negative reaction we got from conventional soccer people, who really hated the idea that we'd be giving an additional half-point.

Spectators therefore had plenty of chances to speculate both during the game and in between each of the three periods. Paglia set up test games for players and spectators, who told him they both understood and enjoyed the new rules. Yet Paglia knew he had to brace for criticism, which is one reason why he reached out to Europe and managed to get the league's plans featured on British television:

> Our intent was that if we could convince the British that our approach to the game had some merit, then the criticism we would be drawing in the United States would be less severe. It's really difficult for an American to tell us you've bastardized the game when the British are telling us, in fact, our approach is revolutionary. And that's exactly what happened. We got tremendous feedback from all over Europe after that program aired. It was very well received. We got calls from all over Europe asking when we could bring our version of the game to Europe because they thought it had real merit.

Paglia's plan had two things in common with the plans Abbott drew up with Rothenberg and Gulati. First, he proposed a single-entity structure in which the league would own all the teams. "Sports lawyers had been thinking about that as a theoretical matter for a number of years," Abbott says. Rothenberg had a couple of decades of experience as a sports lawyer and asked Abbott to figure out a good way to implement the structure in his plan.

"I had thought of that years before when I was doing a lot of work with the NBA and other leagues and was a sports lawyer and commentator and saw all the day-to-day structural problems resulting from the way other leagues were created and felt that if I ever had the chance to start a league from scratch, that would be the right structure," Rothenberg says. "It would be pretty hard if not impossible to take existing leagues and switch them over. Starting with a blank slate, it made the most sense from a business standpoint."

Second, Paglia planned to build stadiums specifically designed for his league, though the stadiums would have other uses to maximize revenue:

> In my mind, it was critical that the physical facility be multipurpose. We couldn't have this big dormant bowl sitting there all week long for one game a week or two games a week. We needed to find a better use for the real estate. . . . I'd like to build something around the outside of this stadium that is a destination itself, and people will come for that purpose. And the stadium becomes a park-like setting when a game or an event isn't taking place. The real activity is going around the outside of it. When there's a game, the two worlds can peacefully coexist.

Paglia's stadium idea dated back to his days with the NASL's Lancers. It was part of MLS's long-term strategy, though it wouldn't be—couldn't be— the league's first priority. "It seemed very clear at the outset that one of the things that the league was going to need was soccer-specific stadiums," Abbott says. "The issue was that in addition to the capital requirements for the league, there would be significant capital requirements for the soccer stadiums. The very clear message was let's see if we can get the league going and get that on solid ground before we start to make investments in stadiums."

And so of the three plans put forward, MLS split the difference on the single-entity idea—Paglia's plan was more rigid, while the APSL had little interest in it at all. MLS hadn't yet specified its rules but was still offering the most traditional style of play, slightly more so than the APSL and much more so than League One America. MLS and League One America each sought stadiums, though the latter would be more aggressive in doing so initially.

Gulati recalls reaching out to the competitors:

> There were a lot of discussions with the APSL and with a number of their owners, virtually all their owners at one time or another, about joining MLS, putting the leagues together or whatever. . . . It became

clear in that process that the vision of what it would take to get a Division I league was very different. Some of the owners didn't like the single-entity model, but frankly, it was also a question of scale. Some of the people didn't want to take the risks associated with the business plan MLS was putting forward. In some cases, they were fully capable of taking it in terms of their net worth but didn't want to. Which is OK. But their thought was they should vie for that status. . . .

Alan and I met with Jim Paglia, but that was really, from everything I can remember, these sort of complexes—soccer stadiums and entertainment complexes. That didn't get anywhere near the sort of traction that Jim might have wanted for.

Paglia called it a "memorable and nasty discussion" in which he says Rothenberg invited him to control stadiums while the MLS crew controlled the soccer. Years later, in court, Gulati said he could not recall any such proposal, though he didn't recall whether he was in the room for the entire meeting. Rothenberg remembers very little of League One America:

The only other serious [proposal] was the existing league, the APSL. In our judgment it was just to take what existed as a clear minor league and try to relabel it major league, but nothing more than that. The other one was by a guy that just had an idea, no backing, nothing really of substance behind it. Sure, we met with him. We were looking at anybody that expressed a sincere interest. But having met with him, I just didn't think that anything serious was there.

The other two bidders went forward, but MLS had the inside track all along. Paglia had an innovative plan and the APSL had existing teams, but MLS combined a bold business plan with traditional soccer. "The other proposals were to really continue some status as minor league, and that's not what FIFA was looking for, that's not what the Federation was looking for," Abbott says.

The voters went with Rothenberg and the MLS plan. The league got 18 of 23 votes. The other five went to the APSL. "It came down to a feeling that this is the group that could best deliver its promises," board member and USISL commissioner Francisco Marcos told USA Today's Roscoe Nance.[3]

The APSL was free to continue as the country's second division. League One America had no sanction, and Paglia, who says several players were interested, quickly learned that meant doom. "We were told flat-out that there would be no access to players," Paglia says. "They would be expelled from the sport. And that really soured everything."

The APSL grudgingly took the second-tier status conferred upon it by the Federation, continuing to argue over the next year about how it should be allowed to promote itself. The indoor game maintained a few adherents who weren't ready to concede supremacy to some new outdoor league.

No more renegade leagues, no more infighting, no leagues floating under the radar. U.S. Soccer had picked MLS to step forward and put the United States on the professional soccer map.

That in itself was an improvement over past cycles, in which outlaw leagues insisted on continuing without the blessings of the U.S. and international overseers, usually annihilating any meager progress one group managed to make. Yet the resentment would simmer and boil over in court testimony a few years later when players sued the league, making the practically unsound but legally problematic argument that the United States would have been better off with *two* Division I soccer leagues, hammering away at Rothenberg's unique position as Federation chief, World Cup chief, and league organizer while also taking shots at the single-entity system.

So MLS stepped forward and began to hire more people, mixing its major league dreams with humble reality.

Ivan Gazidis, a South African–born lawyer who had played at Oxford University, gave up a partnership-track position in London after hearing from golf partner Mark Abbott that he could help start a soccer league. His colleagues reacted with a mix of envy and disbelief. Their suspicions seemed to be justified when Gazidis arrived in the league's Los Angeles office:

> The World Cup had two floors in the top of the twin towers in Century City. If you look at those towers, they have windows all the way up and then there's this sort-of silver band that goes around the top of each of those triangular towers. In that silver band, there are actually two floors that have no windows. I don't know what they're used for now, but in 1994, they were the whole of the World Cup offices. So I arrived in this

place that had no windows and asked to be shown to my office, and there was no office. Mark was in a fire closet, literally. There was a banner that said Major League Soccer; nobody knew what that was. I had a desk in a corridor of the main thoroughfare. I didn't have a telephone or a computer, and that's how I started.

●

Any soccer league that started with some fanfare in the United States would face skepticism within the soccer community and hostility outside it. They've seen it all before, or so they can claim. From the local level to the national, soccer has had no shortage of entrepreneurs with grandiose schemes and sales pitches. The vast majority of them have failed. That's a credibility problem, one that a new soccer league would have to fix. MLS would need to erase soccer's reputation as some sort of traveling medicine show that arrives in a city with great fanfare only to pull up stakes a couple of years later.

A sudden boom wouldn't do the trick. Putting together a big soccer event isn't enough to convince anyone—not the soccer bashers, not the Eurosnobs, not the Hispanic fans. Even a series of successful soccer events, from the Olympics to World Cups for each gender, has failed to convince anyone that soccer is any more than an occasional passing pastime. A league has to demonstrate staying power.

"You have to stay in business before you succeed in business," said Lamar Hunt in *Major League Soccer: A Celebration of 10 Seasons*, a coffee-table book produced by the league.[4] Hunt should know. He had been through the NASL's boom and bust, and he was a successful American football owner and pioneer. He was putting his money back into the game as one of the first primary investors in MLS, but his willingness to put his money back into soccer was tempered by NASL reality.

All MLS backers were well versed in the lessons of the NASL. In the boom time, the NASL had confused its occasional big crowds—driven by novelty and gimmicks—with a sustainable audience that would quickly grow to NFL proportions. The league expanded wildly, only to see those teams fold just as suddenly. In *Soccer in a Football World*, Dave Wangerin sums up the NASL's collapse: "Pro soccer seemed to have been a fad. Attending a match had always carried a certain novelty appeal, particularly when tickets were cheap and the atmosphere was festive. While the NASL produced a clique of native fans who warmed to the game, and even embraced it, the result wasn't nearly enough to fill big-league stadiums."[5]

By the 1994 World Cup, that clique was actually several cliques—some who had grown up with the NASL, some who had grown up with foreign teams, some who knew about soccer from the youth and college games. Putting those fans together for a short event of mammoth proportions such as the World Cup is just like getting warring factions of a family to play nice for a wedding. Getting them to cohabitate long enough to support a league? That's a tough task.

The league's most sophisticated soccer fans were determined to have their say in the culture and atmosphere. Determined to replicate the passion of foreign leagues without the sectarian, ethnic, and class divisions that fuel such fanaticism, they formed supporters groups—sometimes more than one per team—and brought drums, banners, and the occasional incendiary device to the games. The image of wild supporters is less awkward than some of the surviving photos of NASL players racing past cheerleaders who seemed oblivious to the game, as on the cover of Wangerin's book in the original British printing, but the typical sheltered suburban family might not be thrilled to see or hear it. Teams would have to find ways to placate all parties—and above all else, stay in business with a reasonable business plan.

MLS would reach out to Hispanic fans. The league worked out a deal with Spanish-language TV network Univision and would eventually have radio broadcasts in several languages. Fans and journalists would have an easy time finding league information in Spanish.

A league pitched to recent immigrants was nothing new in the United States, but there was no concrete precedent to predict whether it would or would not work. Wangerin dates such appeals back at least as far as 1890, when roughly 15 percent of the U.S. population was foreign-born. Various ASL incarnations had teams with ethnic names—Kearny Scots, Philadelphia Ukrainians, etc. Yet leagues had often sought to rein in those names, with the NASL only begrudgingly accepting the name "Toronto Metros-Croatia."

The NASL was marketed toward casual American fans, but the players hailed from all over the world. American players struggled to break into most teams' lineups. MLS would do the opposite, limiting the number of international players per team.

●

Beyond the demographic dilemmas, the new league's backers focused on one aspect designed to stop the cycle of boom and bust—cost containment. For that, they used the revolutionary single-entity structure that Rothenberg and Abbott had developed. The league would own all player contracts and spread investment capital throughout the teams.

Like the NFL and NBA, MLS would put a cap on player salaries. Various reports pegged the first such cap somewhere between $1.1 million and $1.3 million per team—hardly enough to pay for one half-decent player in other U.S. sports leagues.

"The single-entity ownership model came about because we wanted to avoid the problems that had helped sink NASL," Hunt said in the MLS10 coffee-table book. "In that league, some teams, most notably the Cosmos, were too top-heavy. Few other teams could carry the weight necessary to compete with them. In MLS, we strive for competitive balance and financial control that's reasonable."

What single-entity really meant was long debated among soccer fans and writers. The structure's details were described in greatest detail in court—specifically, an appellate court decision in the league's favor (against the players) in 2002:

> MLS has, to say the least, a unique structure, even for a sports league. MLS retains significant centralized control over both league and individual team operations. MLS owns all of the teams that play in the league . . . as well as all intellectual property rights, tickets, supplied equipment, and broadcast rights. MLS sets the teams' schedules; negotiates all stadium leases and assumes all related liabilities; pays the salaries of referees and other league personnel; and supplies certain equipment.[6]

The following excerpts are from the court's ruling (and are paraphrased if not in quotation marks):

▶ "In a nutshell, MLS recruits the players, negotiates their salaries, pays them from league funds, and, to a large extent, determines where each of them will play. For example, to balance talent among teams, it decides, with the non-binding input of team operators, where certain of the league's 'marquee' players will play." [Rules for allocating players would evolve, with teams eventually getting more control.]

▶ The operator/investors hire the commissioner, just as owners are ultimately responsible for naming league management in other leagues.

▶ The operator/investors of each team share the expenses and much of the revenues, though they are paid "management fees": "The sum of one-half of local ticket receipts and concessions; the first $1,125,000 of local broadcast revenues, increasing annually by a percentage rate, plus a 30% share (declining to 10% by 2006) of any amount above the base amount; all revenues from overseas tours; a share of one-half the net revenues from the MLS Championship Game and a share of revenues from other exhibition games."

The centralized structure would contain costs—at a cost. Parity also means it's tough to build strong teams that build fan loyalty—or compete in soccer's international competitions. And the single-entity structure would cause friction in the fragile soccer community. That was the reason later given in court for the APSL's reluctance to join forces with MLS. And MLS ended up in court in part because a group of players and their lawyers would claim the structure violated antitrust law.

MLS attracted bids from 22 cities in 1994. From that, the league picked a few cities: two teams in the New York area (New Jersey and Long Island), one in soccer-frenzied Los Angeles, one in Washington, one in Boston, and one in a city not known for major league sports—Columbus, Ohio.

Finding investors in the single-entity structure was more problematic, though Rothenberg recalls that it sank in over time:

The interesting story about trying to sell it—when I first got out trying to raise the money, I of course went to [Yankees owner] George Steinbrenner in New York, who looked at this thing and huffed that this is communism. About a year and a half later, somehow our investment book got to him through somebody else, and he called me, and it was in the midst of the baseball strike. Our business plan hadn't changed; it was still single-entity. And he said to me, this is brilliant! I sat there laughing. The same plan was communism one day, and a year and a half later it was brilliant.

But that kind of does tell you the story as far as what the reaction to single-entity was from various business people. It ranged from exactly that—communism to a brilliant concept.

The typical sports owner is a great entrepreneur type and generally a pretty strong individual. To introduce him to a concept that somehow restrains individualism to a certain extent was in some cases foreign to their way of doing business. (Doug Logan, later hired as commissioner, recalls that conversation taking place with Steinbrenner's business partner.)

In November 1994, Rothenberg announced the inevitable—the launch was pushed back from 1995 to 1996. Rothenberg says this wasn't necessarily bad news.

Was it frustrating? It wasn't for me. I think a lot of other people were probably disappointed. Our theory was that we had to do it right, not necessarily on a particular timetable. If we stumbled coming out of the starting gate, there'd probably be no forgiving us. We worried we weren't ready. We didn't have the total financing we needed, we were signing up sponsors but didn't have enough in place.

It's funny because a lot of people thought we lost momentum because of the excitement and the high attendance at the '94 World Cup. My view is the contrary, quite honestly, because I was afraid people would have unrealistic expectations for a league. Starting from scratch, we weren't going to be selling out 90,000-seat stadiums. And if people were dealing off the euphoria of the World Cup, 15 or 20,000 in the stands would be deemed a failure by the masses. If they had a year to settle down and view things realistically, it would make more sense. So I wasn't really that disappointed.

A false start would've been horrendous, would've been fatal.

Rothenberg wisely mixed in some good news, announcing that four investment teams had signed on:

▶ Lamar Hunt and family, who would take the highly unusual step of running two teams—Columbus and Kansas City

- Metromedia partners John Kluge and Stuart Subotnick, who would manage the New Jersey team eventually known as the MetroStars
- Los Angeles Soccer Partners, led by Marc Rapaport, which would take control in L.A.
- API Soccer, led by Kevin Payne, which would lead the charge in Washington

In the interim, the league named another city—Tampa—but combined the New Jersey and Long Island entries into one New York/New Jersey team.

The players started signing in 1995. Tab Ramos, a crafty U.S. playmaker who had suffered a gruesome elbow blow to the head against Brazil in World Cup 1994, went to Mexico in January to sign with Tigres, but Gulati convinced him to sign with MLS and be loaned to Tigres for the year instead. The first big-name international signing—marquee Mexican goalkeeper-forward Jorge Campos—was announced June 6. Gazidis recalls:

We were signing Tab when we didn't have investors. Tab made a very big leap of faith to be the first one to sign with the league. Campos was a similar type of thing. When Campos was signed, going back to the time line, we didn't formally close our financing until the end of 1995. So again, really he was taking a leap of faith. Very instrumental in that was Nike. They were very supportive of what we were trying to achieve. They helped us to put that deal together and provide the initial funding that was needed to get him committed to MLS.

Gulati was thrilled to get a flamboyant, charismatic goalkeeper who dabbled in playing forward:

That deal took a long time. I'd met Jorge, and we started a relationship, talking quite a bit. . . . He liked the idea of being a pioneer in the same sort of way that some of the American players coming back from Europe had. Jorge liked the idea of trying this. We signed an agreement. The idea was that he was going to play in both leagues, go back and forth. There would be some overlap problems [with Mexico's schedule, which kept teams busy most of the year aside from a summer break].[7] We finally got a deal done, signed at his uncle's apartment in Mexico

City. We worked out an agreement the same day that was signed with Pumas, which was his club at the time.

Along with the Campos announcement, MLS had a few other bits of business news in June: Budweiser's "official beer" sponsorship; the awarding of teams to Dallas, Denver, and Kansas City; and two more investors. One was the Kraft family, which owned the NFL's New England Patriots and gave the league two links—along with Hunt—to the wildly successful gridiron game. The other was a reclusive communications billionaire who would later prove vital to the league's survival—Philip Anschutz, who took the reins of the Colorado team.

The league had 10 teams and enough owner-investors to cover seven of them, including the two run by the Hunt family. Dallas, Tampa Bay, and San Jose would be run by the league. Next up—show off the team's names and uniforms. A few players would be nice as well.

"People talk about that period and ask what was the hardest part of it," Gulati says. "I say the hardest part was that we were doing everything at the same time. We were starting from scratch. We had logos and a TV contract and sponsors before we had any players or coaches. The sort of things that we had to do in that first year or two were almost impossible to believe."

Among those things: scouting all the U.S. players currently playing in the APSL, USISL, indoor leagues or overseas. Some weren't even active at the time. Then they had to find international players. A standard player contract —which Gazidis says took six months of intensive negotiation years later when a union was formed—was done on the fly, as were the processes for allocating and drafting players. All this in a league that had no model to follow. Other soccer leagues didn't have salary caps, and other U.S. sports with salary caps weren't operating in an international market.

"At the time we were signing many of those players, there were no general managers or coaches," Gazidis says. "These things were just being done at a crazy pace. That period of time was insane. We were working 24/7, just around the clock. There were no rules."

The good news was that American national-team players were often eager to return from overseas to join the league. Alexi Lalas, the quotable defender with the long red beard who had been playing in Italy, said players had dreamed about such a league for years while traveling to pursue their sport:

It made sense financially but even more so, as cheesy as it sounds, I wanted to be part of it from the beginning. And I had a recognition that many years from now, I wanted to be able to look back and be proud that myself and a bunch of other guys came back and helped establish the league. That did play into the decision. Not saying it wasn't an attractive offer and they didn't make it worth our while, but you have to understand that a lot of us were leaving potentially lucrative and high-powered situations over in Europe.

Marquee players—four per team—would be assigned by the league office to even out the star power. Easier said than done. Even in a single-entity structure—perhaps *especially* in a single-entity structure where the league makes the decisions—ticket sellers and general managers weren't going to be happy if they thought one team had more than its share of talent and celebrity.

To give just one example: From the World Cup in 1994, six U.S. players had stood out in the public eye—Lalas; Eric Wynalda, the goal scorer against Switzerland; Marcelo Balboa, the long-haired defender who barely missed the Colombian goal with a spectacular bicycle kick; John Harkes, a mid-fielder who had made a splash in England; Ramos; and Tony Meola, the goal-keeper from two World Cup teams who had dabbled in football and drama. The first three were easy to scatter across the league's teams. The last three had all grown up in Kearny, New Jersey, watching the Cosmos in Giants Stadium, which would now be the MetroStars' home. Putting so many of the league's thin base of legitimate celebrities on one team in the New York metro area would surely bring back unpleasant memories of chasing the Cosmos in the NASL.

And so the "MLS Unveiled" gala—October 17, 1995, at the Palladium in New York—was big on uniforms and short on players. Ramos had long been assigned to the MetroStars. Campos was the big name for the Los Angeles Galaxy, all the better to draw fans of Mexican soccer. Fellow Mexican Hugo Sanchez, an aging legend who had a brief stint in the NASL, went to the Dallas Burn. Colorado picked up the only other player with NASL experience—U.S. national teamer Roy Wegerle, a South African–born, South Florida–educated forward who had spent most of the past ten years playing in England. Lalas and World Cup teammate Mike Burns went to the New

England Revolution. Kansas City got Mike Sorber, a national-team midfielder who had been playing in Mexico.

Harkes marched out in a D.C. United uniform, then told the *Record*'s Frank Giase he was unsure of his team assignment.[8] Eventually, the Metro-Stars would get two of the Kearny three, with Meola joining Ramos. Harkes would relent and accept his role with United, while the MetroStars would eventually be assigned another star—Italian national-team midfielder Roberto Donadoni.

Gulati says he had been talking with Donadoni's representative for a while:

> I think in Roberto's case, it was a lot about the possibility of coming to New York. Also, at that time, he was thinking it would be at the end of his career. As it turns out, his last game in that stint at Milan they won the Serie A championship and he played a critical role. He came here for a few weeks and then went straight to Euro 96 as one of the key players in the Italian team. The last year or the last six months of his play at Milan were even better than expected. He was thinking of it as a good way to wind down his career, then in fact, he played here for a while and then went back because he was still clearly a top international player at that time.
>
> I think he had a spirit of adventure in him, wanted to learn the language. All the right reasons.

The Donadoni signing was a rare but important exception to the league's conservatism. The MetroStars would not be the Cosmos, an assemblage of talent that only a handful of elite European clubs could match. Donadoni was one of a small band of top-level international players that also included Campos, Sanchez, and Colombian playmaker Carlos "El Pibe" Valderrama, assigned to Tampa Bay.

Most of the foreign talent also hailed from Latin America, not Europe, reflecting a shift in U.S. demographics that MLS hoped to turn to its advantage. Italian Giuseppi Galderisi, who would join former Padova teammate Lalas in New England, was the only European besides Donadoni among the 40 original allocated players. Yugoslav-born midfielder Predrag Radosavljević, who went by "Preki," was assigned to Kansas City, but he had played for several years in American indoor leagues and would later join the U.S. national team. Latin American players made up more than one-quarter of the allocations, with Dallas and Los Angeles taking three players each. Four allocated players hailed from Africa.

●

With player signings inching along in November 1995, the league got a new public face. Rothenberg remained as chairman but the day-to-day governance would go to the league's first commissioner, 52-year-old Doug Logan, a sports and entertainment promoter.

Logan—who, like the NASL stars of yesteryear, had partied with Mick Jagger—says the whole thing started with a random phone call from a headhunter who called him while he drove along the California coast toward a golf weekend in Pebble Beach. He had a majority interest in a San Diego basketball team along with some hockey and entertainment interests at the time and immediately told her he wasn't interested.

A couple of hours later, a lunch with close friend Tony Tavares, the president of the NHL's Mighty Ducks and baseball's Angels, changed his mind.

"In the middle of this lunch, I happened to relay to him the fact that I received this phone call and that I'd said no," Logan says. "As only a good almost best friend can say to you, he said you just made a big mistake. I said why. He said because your entire professional life has been a dress rehearsal for that job."

Logan reconsidered and called back to declare his candidacy, then learned the league had 105 résumés. "I thought, well that shouldn't take long, I'll probably get eliminated somewhere along the line," Logan says.

A couple of weeks later, Logan got another phone call to learn the field had been cut to 10, and he was still in it. After a few more weeks, he was one of four finalists who had been called to interview October 10.

Logan flew to Dallas/Fort Worth International Airport to prepare for a Tuesday interview at a neighboring hotel, where he would be the last of the four interviewees. He flipped on *Monday Night Football* and was surprised to see Lamar Hunt, one of the panelists scheduled to interview him the next day, in the Kansas City Chiefs owner's box.

"I said, well, there must be some mistake, this guy's not going to be at this interview because he's at this football game," Logan says. When the Chiefs won in overtime and Hunt once again appeared on camera, Logan was convinced he wouldn't be meeting the great sports pioneer the next day.

The next day, Hunt was the first person Logan met in a small, stuffy room "with the detritus of coffee and donuts and all sorts of stuff, the remnants of lunch lying around," in Logan's words. Perhaps not the best environment for a man who had flown overnight from Kansas City and had already been through three interviews. Logan explains:

> After some introduction, they asked a question that required a certain amount of talking. I start giving them my best stuff. I'm about seven minutes into it, when I notice to my right where's Lamar's sitting, he's folded his arms and fallen fast asleep. He wasn't dozing—he was *asleep*. I immediately thought three things. Number one, you have just put America's preeminent sportsman to sleep. Number two, you're not getting this job. Number three, I'm going to treat the rest of this as an exercise in poise. Let me see if he can throw me off my game.
>
> They had me there for a little over two hours. I made eye contact with everybody, including Lamar. Lamar woke up three times during the course of the interview and each time asked a question I had answered already. I didn't say I'd answered it already; I answered the question again. I finished up . . . when I finished I had this incredible smile on my face having just gone through a 2½-hour exercise in futility, right? I shook hands with everybody. I remember calling my wife, and she says, well? And I say, don't pack anything.

But Logan was immediately summoned to New York to meet the rest of the governors. He then came face to face for the first time with Rothenberg, whom Logan says he had been asked not to contact during his candidacy. Why? Logan says Rothenberg had been spurned by his own league:

> There was a negotiation that took place between Rothenberg and the group of people that were putting the league together and the investor/ owners where Rothenberg made a proposal to be CEO/commissioner, and they were unable to reach an agreement. And he had made a pretty aggressive offer with what both the terms of his employment were to be and his portion of equity. They asked him to leave the room, and they decided that they were going to go out and do a search to find their own CEO. The resulting search that ultimately selected me was a consequence.

Rothenberg says he wasn't interested in being league commissioner, having tired of travel from his World Cup days and preferring to stay with his firm in a secure position, working toward retirement. He also says he thought the league should be based in New York, and he had no interest in leaving Los Angeles.

Logan says he was actually the one who raised the issue of moving the league headquarters to New York and that the decision wasn't made until June 1996.

By the time Logan was called back to reconvene with the governors, he was the commissioner-elect, pending 10 days of negotiation to hammer out a deal.

The new commissioner had no prior soccer experience but had plenty of experience in sports business. One other talent that couldn't have hurt: Logan was legitimately bilingual, spending part of his childhood in Cuba.

By this time, Logan had mounted a moving train. He says he had little time to influence a major decision: the league's rules.

Rules had long been the biggest flashpoint in the battle between the traditional way (in other words, the European way) and the Americanized way. For much of the world, the Laws of the Game are written in stone, but international organizers FIFA have often approved or even encouraged a bit of experimentation in the United States.

Experimental rules had become part of U.S. soccer's history. The NASL declared that the offside rule would only apply within 35 yards of the goal, and tie games for several years were decided by a "shootout"—not the usual tiebreaker of stationary penalty kicks but a more dynamic one-on-one confrontation in which a player dribbled toward the keeper and shot. The NASL and other U.S. leagues also tinkered with the standings to give bonus points for goals. Even the old leagues didn't leave the game alone—historians claim the strong St. Louis leagues played 30-minute periods at one time and that the old ASL experimented with hockey-style "penalty boxes."

College soccer has done everything shy of putting down ice and handing out hockey sticks. The indoor soccer game that thrived in the '80s wasn't the current international standard of futsal but a game that's basically hockey with a soccer ball and fewer fights. More recently, the USISL was a laboratory for all sorts of tests—kick-ins instead of throw-ins, larger goals, a clock that stopped when the ball went out of play, a shootout attempt when the other team fouled too often.

Had the APSL won Division I status, the United States might have continued to be the land of novelty points systems—six points for a regulation win, four points for a shootout win, one point for each goal (maximum of three) and so forth. League One America proposed novelties not even seen in any American league to date.

Concerned about the state of the game after a low-scoring World Cup in 1990, FIFA was open to changes and was urging to give offensive players the benefit of the doubt wherever possible. MLS paid for the bigger goals used as an experiment in the USISL. "Serious soccer people" suggested that MLS should play in quarters rather than halves, Abbott says, to give players a quick breather and give TV advertisers two more windows per game.

"[FIFA] have always been pretty accommodating with regard to letting places that they considered second- or third-tier locations to try rules out," Logan says. "There are parallels in other leagues, too. The NBA did not go to three-point goals until that was pretty thoroughly vetted not only with the ABA but at the minor league level with the CBA. Leagues are prone to do that. The critical issues that were being considered at that time were larger goals, shootout, a limited amount of kick-in vs. throw-in from the sideline—something which did not get a whole lot of support—and of course the infamous clock-up vs. clock-down to sort of Americanize the product to a degree."

But the league decided not to be a laboratory, certainly not when it was new and trying to establish credibility. "We said we're never going to take the lead on something like that," says Abbott, whose three-month leave from Latham & Watkins had carried over to official status as MLS's first employee.

The game itself would look recognizable, with only a couple of subtle changes. The first change viewers would notice: the clock would count down instead of up, a minor change from convention. "The clock was widely misunderstood—the referee still controlled the time, he just told the clock guy when to stop the clock as opposed to adding the time at the end," Abbott says. "The clock didn't really change anything, but it changed people's perceptions."

The only MLS novelty that involved an actual change to the game's laws was a quirk in substitutions. Teams could use four substitutes rather than the standard three as long as one substitute was a goalkeeper. One fringe benefit of this rule: the Los Angeles Galaxy would occasionally use the fourth substitute to bring in a backup goalkeeper and move goalkeeper Jorge Campos up to forward, a crowd-pleasing move but not one that brought the Galaxy a lot of extra offense. At least Campos is likely to hold for years to come the career record for offside calls against a goalkeeper. "It always helped Campos," Logan says. "It facilitated some excitement in getting him as a field player."

The most controversial inclusion was the tiebreaker. As in the NASL, MLS decided that Americans simply wouldn't want ties. A game deadlocked after 90 minutes would end in an NASL-style shootout, with five players from each side lining up to dribble in on goal from 35 yards out. With the league insisting on a time limit for each shooter, each stadium was compelled to have a large shot clock that would be wheeled out of the tunnel as needed.

Each team could therefore report a simple record of wins and losses. But it didn't necessarily reflect reality. A regulation win was worth three points in the standings, the international norm. A shootout win was worth one. A team with a 12-10 record could be ahead of a 15-7 team in its division. The muddled standings only made the sport known as the "simplest game" that much more confusing to a U.S. audience. And though the shootout received the blessing of former European and NASL stars such as Johan Cruyff and Rodney Marsh in the documentary *Once in a Lifetime* and technically wasn't a rules change, many fans still saw it as an affront to the purity of the game. Logan recalls:

> I will tell you from a personal standpoint, these advances were going forward the entire time. To a very large degree, I am personally a real purist when it comes to leagues. I believe that authenticity sells. If a game is structured in a particular way and has the kind of following throughout the world that certainly soccer has had. To this day, I can't stand the designated hitter in the American League. A manager in the National League is very different than a manager in the American League.
>
> From that standpoint, I had significant reservations with regard to instituting some of these changes. The ones that were adopted were strictly the shootout and the clock. What is interesting is every person of any note from any league who came into the country . . . everybody was very excited about the shootout. They liked it. I'm talking about Mexi-

cans, Italians, Englishmen. But the core fans we had, the traditional soccer purist fans just rejected it out of hand, as well they probably should
have from the very first moment. What was interesting was that on an
international basis, we were not looked down upon as somehow sully-
ing the game but as being pioneers and trying to inject something which
was exciting and provided some interest.

Some Eurosnobs might dislike the league's insistence on settling the championship through a playoff system, though Mexico and other Latin American
leagues use similar schemes that are often much more complex. Less easy to
defend was the league's insistence on taking 8 of its 10 teams into the playoffs,
essentially using a 32-game regular season to eliminate two teams.

On the plus side for the traditionalists, MLS would participate in the U.S.
Open Cup and CONCACAF (Confederation of North, Central American,
and Caribbean Association Football) tournaments that the NASL ignored.

The shootout—along with the backwards clock and the substitution rule
—would disappear over the years in tacit acknowledgment that such Amer-
icanizations weren't bringing more fans into the stadium. Neither were the
flashy uniforms and trendy postmodern nicknames—"San Jose Clash," "Dallas Burn," "Kansas City Wiz"—which only provided fodder for jokes, particularly when the Wiz and Burn would play each other.

Even with the shootout, the clock, and the "Wiz," MLS had stepped boldly toward the traditional.

●

The allocated players fell into place in January and early February. By
late January, nine teams had at least two players on the roster. The exception
was Columbus, whose lone early allocation was Doctor Khumalo, a celebrity
in South Africa and a key cog on a national team that won the African Na-
tions Cup in January. Tampa Bay picked up Valderrama, rising U.S. forward
Roy Lassiter, and Mexican-American Martin Vasquez. San Jose got Michael
Emenalo, later to be joined by fellow Nigerian Ben Iroha, along with a prized
American star—Eric Wynalda.

Most of the players who weren't allocated went through a process familiar to NFL fans but surely strange to most soccer players—a "combine" lasting nearly two weeks at the University of California–Irvine in preparation
for a two-day, 16-round draft. Teams watched more than 250 players culled

from the ranks of the APSL, USISL, and indoor leagues go through a series of physical and mental tests. Americans who had bounced around in Mexico and Europe came home for the grueling audition as well.

Several of the allocations were finalized just before the draft—Balboa and young South African Shaun Bartlett to Colorado, Juan Berthy Suarez to D.C. United alongside fellow Bolivian Marco Etcheverry, Ecuador's hulking forward Eduardo "El Tanque" Hurtado to Los Angeles along with one of the prized players in the pool, Salvadoran playmaker Mauricio Cienfuegos.

Coaches weren't always happy with the decisions, Gazidis recalls. "Marco Etcheverry arrived in D.C. as an allocated player, and Bruce Arena said for the first few weeks, 'Well, what have you given me here? This guy is damaged goods, he's got a bad knee.'" Said Arena, "He was still not close to being recovered from surgery. . . . He had come in heavy, had not played in a long time, was really unfit, overweight, and really needed time to adjust to a new country, a new style of play, a lot of things—adjustments that, if you follow the history of MLS, are probably no different than any other foreign players. It was a transition period, and Marco needed time."

The teams gained a bit of control with the draft. The order had some subjectivity involved—the weaker your allocations were perceived to be, the higher your pick. Columbus, with Khumalo surrounded by Uruguayan forward Adrian Paz and low-profile Americans Brian Bliss and Brian Maisonneuve, was given the first choice in the draft. The Crew chose wisely—Brian McBride, a St. Louis University grad who had been playing with Wolfsburg in Germany. The hard-working forward would be a mainstay of the U.S. national team for the next decade and the public face of the club until his departure for England's Fulham made front-page news in Columbus in 2004.

The first round would be heavy on veterans of various U.S. indoor and outdoor leagues—proven scorer Jean Harbor to Colorado, APSL midfielder Ted Eck to Dallas, defender Robin Fraser to Los Angeles, Canadian national-team defender Iain Fraser to New England, CISL Rookie of the Year Mark Chung to Kansas City, goalkeeper Mark Dougherty to Tampa Bay, Bay Area mainstay Paul Bravo to San Jose, and indoor defender Matt Knowles to the MetroStars. D.C. United bucked the trend with the last pick, taking Salvadoran forward Raul Diaz Arce.

A month later, the league had a supplemental draft for players who hadn't gone through the first time, starting with Italian defender Nicola Caricola to the MetroStars. Future U.S. star Chris Armas went to Los Angeles with the seventh pick, while Columbus waited until the tenth pick to nab the scorer of the most important goal in recent U.S. history—Paul Caligiuri, a defender based in Germany whose long-range effort in Trinidad had secured U.S. qualification for the 1990 World Cup after a 40-year absence.

Finally, the league had a more traditional draft—at least, one that was more familiar to football and basketball fans—of college players. Kansas City took Matt McKeon first, giving traditional power St. Louis University the honor of having a player picked first in two of MLS's 1996 drafts. D.C. United then took North Carolina defender Eddie Pope, who would have the most distinguished career of the 1996 collegiate pool. Three third-rounders were still prominent players in 2009—D.C. selection Jesse Marsch has remained in MLS, San Jose pick Eddie Lewis moved on to England and played in two World Cups before returning to MLS, and Los Angeles pick Ante Razov was one of the league's top career scorers in the first decade.

While the player pool was mostly American with a mix of Latin and African flair, the coaches were rooted in Europe and the old guard of U.S. soccer. One-time U.S. coach Lothar Osiander took charge in Los Angeles. Five coaches were NASL holdovers—Ron Newman (Kansas City), Laurie Calloway (San Jose), Timo Liekoski (Columbus), Bobby Houghton (Colorado), and Eddie Firmani (MetroStars). Thomas Rongen (Tampa Bay) was a former NASL player from Holland who had stuck around to coach in the ASL. None had more experience than Newman, the Hall of Famer who coached the better part of 15 years in the NASL and kept coaching right on through the indoor years. Firmani was a former Cosmos coach seen in the documentary *Once in a Lifetime* lecturing German great Franz Beckenbauer on the importance of passing to temperamental forward Giorgio Chinaglia.

The only coach with no U.S. ties was another European—Frank Stapleton (New England), the former Irish captain and veteran of England's leagues just a couple of years into his managerial career at age 39.

Only two coaches were American-born. D.C. United hired Bruce Arena, who won five national championships at University of Virginia and wasted little time adding his former college players to the roster. Dallas took advantage of Dave Dir's expertise in the talent pool—he had coached many future MLS players with the APSL's Colorado Foxes and spent two years as the embryonic league's director of player development. They would be the only two of the original MLS coaches to win a trophy with their original clubs—Dir in the 1997 U.S. Open Cup, Arena in the 1996 and 1997 MLS Cups as well as the 1998 CONCACAF and Interamerican Cups.

Everyone associated with the league preached patience. They expected to lose money at the outset. They expected average attendance to be five figures, but not much more than that—maybe 12,000. By U.S. soccer standards, that was an exceptional goal. For all the fond memories of 60,000 fans turning out to see the Cosmos, the NASL rarely averaged more than 14,000—and not much more—in a given season. By the standards of a start-up league, the expectations were high. The NBA spent more than two decades averaging less than 10,000 per game. Baseball attendance boomed after World War II, 70 years into its history. Only the NFL, built on the back of a sturdy college game, had done so well so quickly.

And so the league that kicked off April 6, 1996, cast its net as widely as possible. For the traditionalists, the rule bending of past leagues had been tossed aside for the most part, and one club—D.C. United—even sported a nickname suggesting a European rather than an American pedigree. Hispanic fans were courted aggressively. The uniforms and other branding were taken straight out of the fashion of the time—at least, what was *thought* to be the fashion of the time. Most players were American, but a handful of marquee players from overseas were set to wear the uniforms and take part in the shootouts. It was soccer with American style rather than an American game loosely based on soccer. The most important Americanization was one not seen on the field—the single-entity structure designed to keep the league afloat in an indifferent or hostile country. Aside from the most hardened soccer bashers in the country, most people seemed willing to give the league a chance. In fact, more people than MLS expected.

2

The Launch

At the opener in San Jose in 1996, the crowd—listed at a healthy total of 31,683 people and announced as a sellout—saw a game marked by the inconsistency you'd have to expect with two teams that barely knew each other after being formed just a few weeks earlier. Each team featured one legitimate American star—World Cup goal-scorer Eric Wynalda with the host Clash and John Harkes, fresh from a successful stint in England, with D.C. United.

United also had defender Jeff Agoos, one of the last players cut from the 1994 World Cup roster, and goalkeeper Jeff Causey and midfielder Richie Williams from the Open Cup champion Richmond Kickers. The attack force was all South Americans, with Salvadoran striker Diaz Arce running with Bolivians Juan Berthy Suarez and Marco Etcheverry. Suarez, though, would be one of three United players making both his first and next-to-last appearance with the team—the others: defenders Said Fazlagic and Thor Lee.

San Jose was slightly ahead in team chemistry, building around the backbone of players from the APSL's San Francisco Bay Blackhawks, who had not coincidentally been coached by Clash coach Laurie Calloway. Defenders John Doyle and Troy Dayak were solid anchors, and Paul Bravo would be a good complement to Wynalda. San Jose also had a good young player who would go on to success in England and in the 2002 World Cup—89th-minute sub Eddie Lewis.

"As I look back on it now, a pretty bad soccer game for all," Agoos says. "Electricity was in the air. . . . Going into that game, I think both teams had been through a few weeks of preseason, nobody knew what was going to happen, what it was going to look like. It felt like a bunch of people running around for 90 minutes. There wasn't a whole lot of good soccer."

The first yellow card in league history went to Diaz Arce in the fifth minute. United's Shawn Medved blocked a close-range effort from Victor Mella. Causey made four saves, two in quick succession on a powerful swerving Wynalda free kick and a rebound effort. The action wasn't bad, given the hasty construction of each team, but the teams found themselves a few minutes from the league's worst nightmare—a scoreless tie. That's not a popular result in most of the world. In the United States, where the popular mindset ranks ties with "kissing your sister," a 0-0 finish would be a public relations disaster.

Wynalda rescued the league from such a fate. He took a pass down the left side from Ben Iroha and found himself matched up against Agoos. He drove toward the end line, then abruptly cut back. For a split second, he had a good angle to shoot far post, particularly if he had a little bit of bend on the shot. Wynalda might not have had the most speed or aerial ability among U.S. forwards, but few Americans have ever matched his finishing ability. Causey could only wave at the shot. In the 88th minute, Wynalda turned and flipped his shirt off to celebrate (these were the days before such celebrations drew automatic yellow cards), and the league had a much-needed defining moment to show its would-be fans.

Even Agoos concedes that the goal helped the league: "There happened to be a dramatic goal at the end. In the end, I thought it was probably better there being a goal at the end than being a 0-0 tie. There was a lot of scrutiny, the league was under the microscope at that point."

A couple of people who most would've wanted to see the goal missed it. Clash general manager Peter Bridgwater told the *San Jose Mercury News* he was on his way down to the field for the shootout.[1] Ivan Gazidis, who had helped Sunil Gulati stock the league's player pool, was elsewhere.

"I remember it was the 89th minute of the game, it was nil-nil, it was a total disaster, it was clearly going to a shootout," Gazidis says. "I decided I want to see the shootout, so I went to the bathroom. As I came back from the bathroom, I heard this huge roar, so I sprinted out, and as I came out, someone threw a beer on me. That was my whole experience of the Eric Wynalda goal."

Doug Logan was more fortunate:

I saw it. I saw it from field level. By that time, I'd gone down on the field. I had an incredible view of it. The claim was made that Wynalda saved the league, that had we wound up being in a 0-0 situation and going to a shootout that the demise of the league would've come very quickly thereafter. I disagreed—the fact that people were talking about us was the most important thing. . . . What young leagues have to do is continue to be in the crosshairs of people observing it.

So San Jose was ensured of at least one week as the best team in MLS, with a 1-0 victory in the inaugural game. Wynalda, the brash Clash forward, found himself in the position of denying that he would be heading back to Germany, where he had spent a couple of seasons before and after the World Cup. United coach Bruce Arena, fresh from his successful run at the University of Virginia and a couple of years away from an eight-year tenure as national-team coach, began to reevaluate his team.

"The team that we started with at D.C.—I think in the first 10 games we went 2-8," Agoos said, missing by only one (United was 2-7, then 3-7). "The team we started with and the team we ended with in 1996 were completely different animals that were put on the field. What we started with at San Jose was nothing like what we looked like versus LA in the final."

THE FIRST FULL WEEKEND
Things got worse for United the next week in Columbus. D.C. defender Thor Lee became the unlucky answer to a trivia question as the first player to score a goal for the Crew, knocking in an own goal in the 18th minute before an opening-night crowd of 25,266 in Ohio Stadium, Ohio State University's football venue. Then top draft pick Brian McBride announced his presence with authority—a goal, an assist, and a second goal nominated for Goal of the Year. Goalkeeper Bo Oshoniyi, using the cozy confines of the track-encircled field to the Crew's advantage, punted the length of the field to the target man, who flicked the ball with his head and then volleyed to finish off a 4-0 rout of Arena's team.

Home teams fared well on the field and at the gate. Tampa Bay got goals from Ivan McKinley, Roy Lassiter, and Steve Pittman in a 3-2 win over New England before a crowd announced at 26,473. Zimbabwe striker Vitalis "Digital" Takawira, soon to be famous for the "Digital Crawl" celebration, scored twice as Kansas City ran over Colorado 3-0 in front of 21,141. The league's first Sunday game also saw the league's first scoreless draw and therefore the first shootout, with the host Dallas Burn riding Mark Dodd's shootout saves to a "win" (one point in the standings) over San Jose. The finish may have disappointed some in the crowd, or perhaps Dallas's first games were scheduled too close together—the Burn drew 27,779 for the opener and only 9,405 for its second game four nights later.

The biggest opener was in Los Angeles. And it was far bigger than anyone anticipated.

Two days before the game at the giant Rose Bowl, only 15,000 tickets had been sold. The *Daily News* gave the estimate for the walk-up crowd: "Galaxy officials expect to sell out their downsized capacity of 28,000 at the Rose Bowl and will then open extra sections in the stands as needed, which could mean a crowd of more than 30,000."

Then the crowd kept coming. And coming. Waves of people. The total crowd doubled the estimate. The number of people who tried to get in the stadium may have tripled it.

Galaxy officials raced around the Rose Bowl to remove tarps that had been put in place to turn empty seats into scenery. The box office staff scrambled to accommodate the crowd.

The final tally was 69,255, and it easily could have been higher. Many were turned away when police closed some streets. Not all of the seats were available, tarps or not—some had been roped off for a fireworks display.

For star power, the Los Angeles Galaxy had two players whose claims to celebrity couldn't be more different—Jorge Campos, the Mexican goalkeeper/forward, and *Melrose Place* actor Andrew Shue, who had just enough of a soccer pedigree to lend legitimacy to his place on the roster.

Those looking to Campos for entertainment value weren't disappointed. Campos took off beyond midfield with the ball at his feet, racing upfield while Galaxy defenders Robin Fraser and Dan Calichman—both accomplished veterans of various U.S. leagues—scrambled to cover against possible disaster.

Shue got into the game with the Galaxy up 2-0 in the 65th minute behind goals by World Cup veteran Cobi Jones and Arash Noamouz. The MetroStars cut it to 2-1 on a Giovanni Savarese goal—the first of many from the unheralded Venezuelan player in the opening season—but got no closer.

The Galaxy had another player who would inspire a fan base—Mauricio Cienfuegos. Gazidis learned quickly of the Salvadoran playmaker's support:

I was sitting behind a Salvadoran fan, just sitting in the crowd, and I was looking around thinking this is unbelievable. There was such a great atmosphere in the stadium. The Salvadoran guy turned around and he's so excited after one of the goals. He literally grabs me—doesn't know me from Adam—grabs me by my T-shirt and says, "You see that guy over there, you see that guy, that little guy there." I say, yeah, Mauricio Cienfuegos, I signed him. He says, "He's little but he's BIG! You know, he's BIG!"

Shue may not have been an attendance draw in his own right, but he played exclusively in front of big crowds. May 12 in San Jose: 31,728. June 1 in Tampa Bay: a respectable 19,717. June 9, he tallied his lone career assist on the last of the Galaxy's four goals in rout of the MetroStars before 53,250 at Giants Stadium. He then played in front of the biggest crowd in MLS history until 2006 —92,216 fans for a June 16 doubleheader with a USA-Mexico game—and was on the field for Galaxy's tying goal against Tampa Bay.

That was his last MLS appearance. Banged up his first season and an afterthought in his second, Shue played a total of 96 minutes in five games.

Galaxy teammate Mark Semioli still speaks highly of Shue's contributions:

Andrew was my first roommate in MLS. I remember picking up the phone, and it was Elisabeth Shue, my childhood idol.

Andrew was awesome, he was one of my favorite teammates. He loved soccer more than I did, more than most people that played in MLS did. He was a tremendous asset to our team, he got us a lot of publicity, he was an above-average player. He won our [fitness] tests, when you have to run two miles. He smoked everyone. He loved soccer. So any time we used to spend time outside of the field, we didn't do any Hollywood stuff. He always wanted to know about soccer, he always wanted to talk soccer.

He was a tremendous asset to our league. He's an amazing guy, he's doing some great stuff now with his foundation. A lot of people look down on him like he was the actor who wanted to play soccer, but nobody wanted to do more for the sport than Andrew Shue.

Credible player or not, Shue's appearance was a tradeoff for the league—publicity for the casual fans, ammunition for the league's critics. But it was Campos, not Shue, who gave the league headaches. The colorful goalkeeper was happy to play in MLS but unwilling to give up his career in Mexico. That meant the Galaxy would share a player not only with the Mexican national team but also with a Mexican club in the MLS off-season.

As a goalkeeper who never seemed to tire, Campos reveled in playing as much as possible. In that June 16 doubleheader, Campos played both games, including a brief stint at forward for the Galaxy. In September, MLS arranged for a charter jet to ferry Campos from a World Cup qualifier in Honduras to the Galaxy's season finale in Dallas. The league drew the line at a flight to France for a friendly game in September.

Closer to the ground, Campos decided he was in position to make a few demands. Specifically, a Ferrari. Gazidis recalls, "I remember it as being the Monday after the game. Campos' advisor comes into our office and says, 'Now, let's talk about Jorge's contract.' We said, 'Yes, we have it in a drawer. We signed it with him and we're very pleased that he's playing in Major League Soccer.'"

But Logan concedes that the league had made a few promises: "It was a part of the original deal to get him to come. What we did was we dragged our feet in getting it for him. As a consequence of the 69,000 that [were] there, we could no longer drag our feet. . . . Had we had a more modest crowd, we would've tried to keep from leasing the car for as long as we could." Gazidis picks up the story: "The guy says, 'There were 70,000 people at the game. How many of them do you think were there to see the Los Angeles Galaxy, and how many were there to see Jorge Campos.' So one of the things we needed to address was his desire to drive a Ferrari in Los Angeles. It was Mark Abbott that was dispatched to buy a Ferrari. Campos had gone the day before and told them which car he wanted."

Abbott then got a crash course in Ferrari's way of doing business:

I called up the Ferrari of Beverly Hills dealership. I said I've been assigned to buy this Ferrari. I said I don't know much about buying Ferraris. The guy said it's very easy—we tell you the price and you pay it. I said I'm the top negotiator for the league here, and I'm going to come in and negotiate, he says, "Good luck with that." . . .

I said, "Well, I'd like to pay a little bit less than that. I'll offer you this." He said, "I'll tell you what I'm going to do. You seem like a nice guy, I'd like to close the deal here . . . I'm going to throw in the AM/FM radio for free."

The good news was that Campos and the Galaxy would prove to be the league's biggest draw. Not only did the Galaxy take a comfortable lead in home attendance—helped by that debut and the doubleheader—the team was the league's best road draw at 21,638 fans per game. Campos surely deserved some of the credit for those figures, though it helped that the team won its first 12 games.

And even the players who didn't have Ferraris were pleased with the opportunity. Semioli, a veteran of other leagues, felt he had taken a step up just as he thought his career might be ending:

> While [the APSL] was a professional league, there was no doubt that the standards and level of competition were not the same as what MLS became. It was sort of a step up in every sense of the word, from the level of competition to the media attention to the way that the players were treated, even the amount that the players were paid, it was more of a structured league that was recognized as being a Division I league and a business more than anything. Players, owners, coaches, and administrators were all treated a little more professionally.
>
> I had already played six years professionally in the APSL and maybe a year in the USISL. It was almost like restarting a career. I thought maybe it would be time to move on, this opportunity to came up. . . .
>
> Being drafted and to be able to play in Los Angeles was an unbelievable opportunity that, for many of us, we thought would never come. It was like a revival of a career that was coming to an end.

HIGH SCORING

With Campos, Shue, the shootout, the outlandish uniforms, and the occasional doubleheader, MLS could be accused of some gimmickry. Yet the league had much more going for it in the first season. First up was the novelty factor, which gave the NASL a temporary boost when it suddenly got hot and would give MLS (and later, the women's professional league, the WUSA) a solid start at the box office. Beneath all the curiosity factors, though, was another feature. On the field, the teams may not have been the best in the world, but few could deny that the games were entertaining.

For one thing, they were higher scoring than most top-flight leagues around the world. Call it enthusiasm for a new league, call it a commitment to attacking soccer, call it tactical naïveté, or call it an inability to defend against the simplest of deceptive moves—the goals kept flying into the net.

One of the earliest televised games was a May 2 barnburner between the Kansas City Wiz and Columbus Crew, a whirlwind introduction to MLS for much of the national TV audience on ESPN and for new Wiz player Mo Johnston, who had just joined the team for practice the day before. Johnston was perhaps too famous in Scotland, where the Catholic had crossed Glasgow's great sectarian divide by going from Celtic, supported largely by Catholics, and signing with the fiercely Protestant club Rangers. In Kansas City, where he would go on to play for six years, Johnston was still getting used to the heat and other oddities of his new home.

"It was something different," he told soccer writer Michael Lewis years later. "All the music in the background and they had all the razzmatazz. For me, it was comical at first because the day before I must had taken like 40 shootouts because the coach—Ron Newman—had come to me and said the game might go to a shootout. I didn't know what it was."[2]

The first half seemed innocent enough, with Mark Chung opening the scoring on a precise medium-range shot and McBride answering with a header. The second half started with a quick pair of goals—Johnston expertly poaching in the box after Preki's right-footed shot rattled the crossbar, quickly leveled by Todd Yeagley's alert finish amid a confused Wiz defense.

The real fun came in the last 26 minutes:

64th minute: Columbus maintains possession after a corner kick and works it to the right. Billy Thompson crosses to Michael Clark, who heads it down and crumples to the field as he scores, leveled by a collision with Tommy Reasoner. The countdown clock stops as Clark gets attention. 3-2 Columbus.

65th: Doctor Khumalo steals the ball a few seconds after the kickoff and plays it left for McBride. Reasoner's misfortune doubles, as his effort to clear McBride's dangerous cross sails right past goalkeeper Pat Harrington.

Beautiful shot if he's at the other end of the field; at that end, it's called an own goal. 4-2 Columbus—a lead that's usually safe at this stage of a game.

67th: As Kansas City heads the other way, Columbus defenders get mixed up in the box, and a handball is called. Preki steps up to take the penalty kick. Oshoniyi, who had saved a penalty against Tab Ramos the week before, tries to get the upper hand by moving early. Preki sees him moving to his left and dinks a low-power shot into the net. 4-3.

70th: A long ball down the right for Takawira. His cross is headed back to him, and he heads it right back in. Johnston, wide open 10 yards in front of the goal, whips his right leg around on a side volley and slaps it in at the right post past a frozen Oshoniyi. 4-4.

77th: Mike Sorber, a starter on the 1994 World Cup team, lets fly from 30 yards out and finds the upper corner. 5-4 Kansas City.

87th-88th: Columbus gets a couple of close-range chances to tie it on a free kick, with Sorber blocking one shot. Takawira leads the counterattack and slashes across the field with defenders scrambling back. He dribbles next to Preki, who takes the right-footed shot himself and curls it around Oshoniyi, who comes up holding his hand and grimacing. 6-4 Kansas City, final score.

The ESPN crew handed Johnston a headset for a postgame interview. Clearly a bit bewildered and winded, Johnston was also gracious. "I'd just like to thank the American public for making me welcome here. . . . Your stadium is second to none, the lads are very skillful, and I think your league will be a major success."

Oshoniyi regained his composure to shut out Dallas 10 days later, only to lose in the shootout. He conceded MLS's first hat trick May 15 to D.C. United's Steve Rammel and would later compete for playing time with Harrington, who wound up in Columbus after losing his spot in Kansas City.

With 539 goals (3.37 per game) in one season, the league was particularly brutal for goalkeepers. Campos led the league with a goals-against average of 1.20 that would be middle of the pack in most of the rest of the world. English veteran Chris Woods limped to a 1.87 figure with Colorado.

Harrington lost his job in Kansas City to Garth Lagerwey, the last goalkeeper selected in the inaugural draft. Jim St. Andre, one of New England's allocated players, split time with A-League call-up Aidan Heaney. Harrington would move to Columbus, only to find himself benched alongside Oshoniyi when U.S. national teamer Brad Friedel suddenly became available, the victim of one of English soccer's periodic fits of declining work permits to undoubtedly qualified players. Harrington and Oshoniyi were waived at the end of the season.

Oshoniyi persevered, working his way through the A-League. He returned to MLS with Kansas City, site of that free-for-all in 1996, winning an MLS title as a backup in 2000 and starting in MLS Cup 2004. Harrington, Woods, and St. Andre didn't play in MLS again after that first year.

Coaching casualties also piled up through the season. In New Jersey, former Cosmos coach Eddie Firmani lasted only eight games—3-5, with two shootout wins—before leaving the MetroStars, claiming he was fed up with the revolving door of players joining and then leaving for international duty. Carlos Quieroz took over for the rest of the season. In Columbus, Timo Liekoski departed with a 6-16 record, with only four of those wins in regulation, only to see Tom Fitzgerald post a 9-1 record after the switch. Bob Houghton was unable to see out the season in Colorado, with Roy Wegerle serving as player-coach in the finale.

The league's top goal scorers were a good mix of American and international players, known names and rising stars. Leading the way with 27 goals was Tampa Bay's Lassiter, a classic goal poacher paired with one of the league's top playmakers and the eventual 1996 MVP, Colombian Carlos Valderrama. Lassiter, who played college ball at N.C. State, had played well enough in Costa Rica to earn a call to the U.S. national team. Getting his name in the paper in 1995 had one drawback—police in North Carolina were waiting with a warrant from a 1992 theft. He spent 30 days in prison but was cleared to start his MLS career.

With Lassiter and Valderrama, next to Alexi Lalas the most recognizable player in the league thanks to a blonde frizzy mop of hair resembling that of Sideshow Bob on *The Simpsons*, Tampa Bay led the league in scoring with 66 goals (2.06 per game) and claimed the league's best record at 20-12. Most remarkable was that the Mutiny compiled that record with little help from the shootout, in which the team was a surprisingly woeful 1-3. Indeed, the shootout had little effect on the standings—New England won six of its eight tiebreakers but failed to make the playoffs.

In this league, missing the playoffs was like missing the broad side of a barn with a 10-yard shot. For the most part, MLS had avoided the American megasport delusions that hung like an albatross around the NASL's neck, but the league went overboard in its desire for playoff excitement. The NFL—which overlapped with MLS through owners Hunt and Kraft—has one of the more reasonable U.S. playoff systems, taking 12 of 32 teams after a regular season in which most teams are not able to play each other. The NHL is often ridiculed for taking 16 teams to its playoffs, but at least that tournament has tradition and folklore behind it. The NBA playoffs, also a bloated bracket of 16, take an eternity to play but are well tolerated by league fans.

Even by those standards, taking 8 of 10 teams to the playoffs after a 32-game regular season is rather extravagant. Yet that's exactly what MLS did. Tampa Bay cruised to the playoffs with several games to spare, as did most of the teams in the West.

Just as Tampa Bay soared in the East, the Colorado Rapids sank in the West. Wegerle, the U.S. international and English league veteran who served as interim coach in the finale, scored only twice. The bright spots were Jean Harbor, who carried over his APSL and indoor form with 11 goals, and Shaun Bartlett, a young South African who would work his way through the European leagues to be a solid player in England's Premier League.

Behind the Galaxy, who didn't maintain their fast start but held on for first, came the Dallas Burn. Goalkeeper Mark Dodd and defender Leonel Alvarez were selected to the league's Best XI—an All-Pro team, in terms NFL fans would understand. The Burn drafted well—APSL veteran Dodd hadn't been selected until the sixth round of the inaugural draft, and fellow Duke alumnus Jason Kreis, picked one round earlier, began his prolific career with 13 goals.

Kansas City matched the Burn's record but finished third on goal difference after conceding a league-worst 63 goals. The team's offense almost kept it even with 61 goals, with Preki's 18 goals and 13 assists at the center of a quadruple threat with Takawira, Johnston, and Chung.

San Jose finished a close fourth, with goal-minded Wynalda finishing with a surprising 13 assists to tie Preki for third in the league. Dave Salzwedel took over goalkeeping duties and was second in the league with a 1.31 goals-against average. Doyle, one of the many former APSL Blackhawks on the roster, took MLS Defender of the Year honors.

In the East, D.C. United shook off its rough start with a methodical in-season makeover. Midfielder Tony Sanneh, goalkeeper Mark Simpson, and scorer Steve Rammel were plucked from the indoor and USISL ranks. Defender David Vaudreuil joined in June. When the disappointing Suarez departed, United picked up another Bolivian forward—Jaime Moreno, who had been in the Premier League with Middlesbrough. The other three allocations lived up to expectations—Agoos was a reliable defender, Harkes steadied the midfield, and Etcheverry led the league with 19 assists.

Arena's early concern over Etcheverry's fitness was ancient history. "Once Marco got fully into the swing of things, I would argue that he was the best player in the history of the league," he says.

The MetroStars struggled for continuity, changing coaches and fielding 35 players. The defense, with former national-team forward Peter Vermes as the anchor in front of revitalized goalkeeper Tony Meola, emerged from the chaos to allow the fewest goals in the league. Roberto Donadoni, a Best XI pick, played well enough to earn a callback to play for Italy in the Euro 1996 tournament. The offense was erratic, with Savarese's 13 goals more than doubling the tally of any teammates.

The race for fourth came down to the final game September 21 between the Crew and Revolution in Foxborough, Massachusetts. Columbus came into the game up a point in the standings and got an early break when New England's Mark Watson was sent off. McBride followed up with his 17th goal of the season. Friedel made 11 saves to make the goal stand up. The Revolution fell short of the playoffs, squandering the 11 goals Joe-Max Moore scored in just 14 games. The Crew were 9-1 under replacement coach Tom Fitzgerald, thanks in no small part to Friedel.

The Revolution drew a crowd of 38,633 to that final game, but the league as a whole lost momentum as the novelty wore off. By late summer, the league was no longer the primary occupant in its stadiums. Football lines were painted on the grass—for the last season at Washington's RFK Stadium, where the Redskins' departure to the Maryland suburbs would leave United as the main tenant for several years. In Giants Stadium, the MetroStars would finally have something in common with the Cosmos besides Firmani—the grass was removed, leaving artificial turf in its place.

MLS's average attendance of 17,406 had benefited from the occasional doubleheader, including the June 16 pairing with a USA-Mexico game that drew 92,216. The All-Star Game, set up as a doubleheader with a matchup of "FIFA All-Stars" against the mighty Brazilian national team, drew 78,416 fans, announced as a record for a sporting event in Giants Stadium—yes, even more than Pelé and the Cosmos ever saw. Valderrama set up Tab Ramos and Steve Pittman for goals—the former an emphatic blast from the top of the box, the latter a dazzling, slashing winner in the 88th minute—as the East beat the West 3-2.

A bullish Logan touted the need to put MLS in more markets. At half-time of the All-Star broadcast, he said the league was actively seeking expansion: "We're going to do it a calculating way. The optimum size for our league is going to be 16 teams but not for a while yet."

The playoffs would see no groundswell at the gate. Kansas City opened its series against Dallas at home in front of an announced crowd of 4,466. The Wiz won that game 3-2 on an 89th-minute Preki goal, putting the Burn under pressure in the league's unique playoff format—one game at the lower-seeded team's home, followed by two home games for the higher-seeded team, which had home-field edge but no margin for error. The Burn responded with a 2-1 win in Game 2 before giving up the ghost in a fashion that purists feared—a shootout after a 2-2 regulation tie, with Lagerwey besting Dodd in the tiebreaker.

The curious format also forced Los Angeles to the brink of early elimination. Wynalda set up Tayt Ianni for the lone goal in San Jose. The Galaxy were seven minutes away from a do-or-die shootout in Game 2 before a wild finish—a goal from unlikely scorer Robin Fraser, red cards to Wynalda and Clash teammate Oscar Draguicevich, and a clinching goal from Eduardo Hurtado on an assist from front-running Campos. With two players out, including Wynalda, the Clash put up little resistance in a second 2-0 loss in Game 3. Los Angeles drew the best crowds of the first two playoff rounds—27,833 and 30,231.

Tampa Bay took a different route through the first round, winning 2-0 at Columbus on two Lassiter goals set up by Steve Ralston, the league's Rookie of the Year, then dropping Game 2, 2-1. The Mutiny restored order with a 4-1 win in the finale before a thin crowd of 6,871.

The other first-round matchup planted the seeds for a great I-95 rivalry between D.C. United and the MetroStars, starting with a bizarre first game in Giants Stadium. Diaz Arce pounced on a Meola mistake far from his own goal and lobbed the ball into the net. The teams traded goals before Savarese, on the field less than two minutes, tied it in the 75th minute.

The ensuing shootout would be one of the strangest moments in league history.

United waited until the last minute to swap goalkeepers, preferring Jeff Causey to Simpson in the shootout. He stopped only one of the regulation five shots and managed to foul Donadoni, who was awarded a less-taxing penalty kick that he converted. Meola could do no better stopping shots, and the teams played on, trading conversions and misses through five more rounds. Meola himself shot wide in the ninth round. Causey, last on the United list, shot and missed in the 11th.

Vermes had come up limping during the game but had not been replaced. As he stepped up to take his shot in the 11th round, United protested. The next five minutes were little more than televised confusion. Finally, referee Esse Baharmast let Vermes shoot, and he converted for a MetroStars victory.

The next day's *Washington Post* explained the problem. Vermes had been listed eighth on the shootout order, chosen at the end of regulation, but had not taken his turn. In United's eyes, Vermes had forfeited his turn. The *Post*'s Steven Goff described the postgame festivities: "After the game, Logan, deputy commissioner Sunil Gulati, and MLS senior vice president Bill Sage met with enraged United Coach Bruce Arena and D.C. President Kevin Payne behind closed doors in the United locker room. Ten minutes later, Arena came out fuming, and Gulati slammed the door closed as the coach exited."

United needed a second-half goal from Etcheverry in a 1-0 Game 2 win that saw Moreno ejected for a retaliatory swing on the MetroStars' Nicola Caricola. Rammel put United ahead in Game 3, but Donadoni set up Antony De Avila for an equalizer in the 86th. With a shootout looking likely, a fateful foul decided the series—Rob Johnson brought down Etcheverry in the box. Diaz Arce's penalty kick sent United to the next round as some in the crowd of 20,423 stormed the field to celebrate.

The conference finals seemed anticlimactic in comparison with the three-game thrillers of the first round. Diaz Arce had a hat trick in a 4-1 romp over Tampa Bay, which had lost Valderrama to Colombian national-team duty. The playmaker returned for Game 2 at home, but Diaz Arce ended the Mutiny's season with a chip in the 82nd minute for a 2-1 win.

The West final was closer, with defender Greg Vanney the hero for the Galaxy. His long-range blast sealed a 2-1 home win in Game 1. He fouled

Preki in Game 2 to give up a penalty kick, which the Wiz playmaker converted on the rebound, but he atoned with another long-range effort to tie the game. In the shootout, Vanney again found the net, helping the Galaxy close out the series.

That left two teams whose fortunes had reversed during the season to face each other in the final. United had tinkered throughout the summer to find the right players. The Galaxy followed up its 12-game winning streak with a 4-13 mark over the next 17 games, including only two regulation wins. Three straight wins in September gave the team a boost heading into the playoffs.

MLS Cup 1996 was set for the neutral site of Foxborough on October 20. By the morning, MLS and its remaining two teams couldn't be blamed for wishing the game were in sunny Florida or just about anywhere else. Rain that poured before and during the game turned the field into a quagmire, and the gusting wind simply blew the rain around. A bad day in England or Scotland is drizzle and breeze by comparison. Games are routinely postponed in less horrid conditions, but nationally televised championships are not easily rescheduled.

"There was a lot of talk that the game was going to be canceled," Semioli says. "It was a monsoon, mini-hurricane, one of those nor'easters. The field was absolutely flooded."

That talk wasn't coming from Logan. "Absolutely not. No lightning. Had there been lightning, there would've been some question mark."

The Galaxy weren't at full strength on defense. Big defender Dan Calichman was suspended, and Fraser, Jorge Salcedo, and Mark Semioli played through nagging injuries. But Eduardo Hurtado put the Galaxy ahead 1-0 in the fifth minute, and Chris Armas doubled the lead early in the second half.

Etcheverry's set-piece wizardry turned the game. First, he found Sanneh rising above a crowd for a near-post header in the 73rd minute. Then Shawn Medved pounced on a rebound from another Etcheverry kick and stabbed it home.

Unlike the regular season and other playoffs, MLS Cup would go to sudden-death overtime. It wouldn't last long. Etcheverry's corner kick sailed to Eddie Pope, a young defender who would use MLS's debut season as a springboard to a long national-team career. Pope headed it home, and United's players gave the league a signature celebration, sliding en masse through the soaked grass.

Logan, calling the game a "great exclamation point on an incredible season," marveled at Etcheverry's precision in the conditions:

Marco goes to the corner, places the ball in 3 inches of water and delivers a corner kick right onto Eddie Pope's head and they win the game. I go down to the dressing room, and I said, "Marco, this is one of the most remarkable things I've ever seen in my life. How were you able to control the ball coming out of the water that way with such accuracy?" He said he had a coach who once a week would bring out buckets of water to the field and would flood the lowest point in the field and make him kick balls out of water. And I said this is the difference between an American player and a South American player.

Semioli says the Galaxy had been confident that they had the best team in the league:

It was very disappointing. At the same time, we thought with the team we had in L.A., it would be a year later and we'd be right back where we started. We had tremendous players. We had a good mix of young and old. I felt at that time that we'll be back, there was no way we wouldn't be back in the championship the following year. Unfortunately, it did not happen that way.

It was a still a tremendous honor to be able to play in that first game. I'll never forget it. I still have my uniform from that game. I still talk about it all the time. It was a tremendous honor just to be able to walk onto that [pauses here to find the right word] puddle and be able to represent MLS and American soccer on a very special day.

As it turned out, United was the team best placed to move forward, in part because Bruce Arena was the early master of the evolving art of acquiring players. Agoos said, "If you stand back from it now, it just seemed like the Wild West. Nobody really knew the rules well, and there seemed to be a lot of loopholes. Bruce was very good at that part of it. He understood what the loopholes were and how to use them effectively. I think that's what helped make D.C. as good as we were; we used the way MLS was set up to our advantage."

Arena, looking back, doesn't really see loopholes. He sees the freedom he needed to overhaul the squad on the fly:

> The rules were a lot simpler then than they are now. Over the last six to seven years, the rules of player transactions have become much more complicated.
>
> We started out very poorly in the league in 1996. We had a very poor roster opening day, our 18-man roster at the time.
>
> What we were able to do is make quick changes and understand that we had weaknesses in certain areas and were able to acquire players and make those changes. It wasn't due to the fact that we knew the rules better. It was just an example of understanding what our team needed, understanding what players were available and going to get them.

Ten days after MLS Cup, United did the "double," winning the U.S. Open Cup final at home against the A-League's Rochester Rhinos. The Open Cup, a competition for all U.S. teams regardless of league, had an 80-year history behind it but had been ignored by NASL teams. With USISL teams joining in 1995 and MLS teams in 1996, the Cup had a complete mix of amateur and pro teams for the first time since the ASL days.

With that, MLS completed a first season that had exceeded anyone's expectations. Best of all, the league had taken teams that existed only on paper months earlier and made fans care about them. Jeff Bradley, who would eventually leave his position as a MetroStars public relations director to become a staff writer at ESPN's magazine and one of the deans of online column-writing, recalled his amazement: "I remember saying to Filip Bondy of the *New York Daily News*, as I looked at D.C.'s fans as they bounced and sang, 'Can you imagine people caring so much about a team that's been around such a short time?'"[3]

That's an accomplishment. Outside college sports and the Big Four of the NFL, NBA, NHL, and Major League Baseball, players and teams tend to be transients. Minor league players with any substantial talent move quickly through the ranks. Arena football and lacrosse leagues have been slow to move the spotlight from the game to the players, in part because most players weren't full-time employees until recently. And arena football has proved to be less than stable.

In 7 of the 10 cities, the league was a hit. The two major population centers led the way in attendance—28,916 in Los Angeles and 23,898 for the MetroStars. Traditional hotbed New England was next at 19,025, followed by a town that more than justified a leap of faith in landing a small-market team—Columbus, with 18,950. San Jose and Dallas, both of whom would struggle in later years, had solid debuts—17,232 and 16,011, respectively. D.C. United, later known for one of the most solid fan bases in the league, was only seventh at the gate in the first year with 15,262.

After that, it was a drop to the bottom three—Kansas City (12,878), Tampa Bay (11,679), and Colorado (10,213). That was perfectly in line with league projections, but each team clearly had room for improvement.

Logan thought that improvement was sure to come. After averaging 17,406 fans in the league's first season, far above the projected 12,500, the commissioner boldly aimed for 20,000 in Year 2. That would be a mistake.

3

After the Boom

MLS's debut had drawn raves, with attendance far exceeding expectations and *SportsBusiness Daily* naming the league its 1996 Sports Industrialist of the Year. Little wonder the league was bullish heading into Year 2.

In April 1997, MLS announced its first expansion teams. Ken Horowitz would take a team into South Florida. Philip Anschutz would join Lamar Hunt as a two-team operator, adding a Chicago franchise to his Colorado holding. In May, Logan told Seattle that they'd be next, as long as the state passed a referendum for a new stadium to be shared by the NFL's Seahawks and an MLS team.

Television options improved with the debut of the Shootout package, making regional broadcasts available nationally in a pay-per-view package akin to the NFL's successful Sunday Ticket. Between the Shootout, ESPN's networks, and ABC, 87 percent of the league's games were available in English. MLS already had games in Spanish on Univision, where Andres Cantor's epic "gooooooooallll" call had earned a bilingual following even before the league's debut.

To replenish the talent pool, MLS launched Project-40, aggressively enticing talented young players to give up a year or more of college eligibility to go pro. The program offered tuition money as well as salary, though few players took up the educational offer. Carlos Parra, the first signee, joined the MetroStars. The debut class of 11 players was not a rousing success—Parra played 57 games but faded over a four-year career, while some of his classmates started fewer than five games. Still, Brian Dunseth, Joey DiGiamarino, and Eric Quill had long, fruitful careers, and the program improved over the years.

Yet all the steps forward couldn't stave off a sophomore slump on the business end.

The league had early warning signs that the attendance bubble was bursting. Kansas City, rechristened the Wizards instead of the Wiz, drew 10,198 for a March 29 opener, with 8,406 the next week, and 6,272 April 18. Dallas was worse—11,063 for the opener, then 6,195, and 5,911. Both teams would average fewer than 10,000 fans a game for the season, with Tampa Bay and Colorado slightly higher. Los Angeles (20,626) and attendance champion New England (21,298) balanced the scales if not the budget, but Logan's hope that the league would average 20,000 would be nowhere near fruition. As a whole, the league dipped below 15,000.

"We were surprised by the drop the second year," says Mark Abbott. Says Logan:

> Every entertainment and sports parallel that I've ever gone through shows a modest sophomore slump. I wasn't overly surprised by it or its magnitude. It wasn't very great—people made a whole lot more to it than it actually was.
>
> I was the one who took the hit for having said our goal next year is to increase by 10 percent. You always want to have a goal to increase. That was somehow turned into that I had predicted a 10 percent increase in attendance. Which was not the case at all, but that's all right—I'm a big boy, I can take that.

MLS also couldn't make much money off those fans as long as it remained a tenant in giant NFL venues. In Columbus, Lamar Hunt made the first attempt to change the physical and financial landscape, pushing the league's model of a soccer-specific stadium. The local MLS team wanted to become its own landlord, controlling its own schedule and revenue in a reasonably sized venue. The process tested Hunt's persistence. In May, Franklin County voted against a tax increase to fund an arena and stadium. Nine months later, another initiative would fail in the suburb of Dublin. It would take a year of false starts before Hunt's dream would come close to reality. The Crew would eventually open the league's first MLS-focused stadium, but its efforts showed just how tough it would be to put the idea in concrete.

Most teams didn't even have adequate training facilities. The exception was D.C. United, which took over a suburban complex the NFL's Washington Redskins had abandoned.

"It had everything," says Eddie Pope. "It had our offices upstairs, downstairs we had our lounge, we had our training room, we had a basketball court, we had locker rooms and a weight room, then we could walk right out the doors and there was a turf field and a grass field. At that time, it had to be the best setup in MLS."

"In terms of the idea behind it, it was ahead of its time compared to what the other teams were doing," says Jeff Agoos. "It was by no means state of the art, it wasn't new, it was an old training facility used by the Redskins years ago, but in terms of what we needed to use it for, it was ideal. You had the office there, you had the players there, everything was under one roof, it made a whole lot of sense. I think the idea behind it was a key to our success over the first four or five years."

Other teams were practicing any place they could find. "When I was with the Revolution, we were training at Babson or Brandeis or at the old psycho ward out in Foxborough—it was an abandoned psychiatric hospital that had fields around it," says Alexi Lalas. "If there was a patch of green grass, we would find a way to train on it. More often that not, it wasn't even a patch, it was scattered blades of grass that we made into a training facility. The Galaxy was training outside the Rose Bowl in the parking lot, what on weekends would be used as actual parking. It was the Wild West to say the least, on and off the field."

"We were nomads," says Garth Lagerwey, who would move from Kansas City to Dallas in 1997. "Public parks, community colleges, we'd get places where we'd get a lease for a month and then move on again. We trained indoors for a month at a time. You name it, we tried it. . . . Dallas was a bit better—we were in temporary buildings at a middle school. It was an absolutely rock-hard field, it wasn't clear that it was maintained at all. Two double-wide trailers crammed in. Looking back, just tough conditions. You made the best of it. If anything, I think in Dallas it brought us closer together as a group and as a team because it forced us to adapt and survive."

But at least MLS had one advantage over other U.S. leagues. "The big difference between the USL and MLS was that MLS did your laundry," Lagerwey says. "If you were with the USL, you had to do your laundry for the next practice. MLS had equipment managers, and equipment managers were the greatest thing that ever happened to me. They would wash your gear. I'm not joking—you want to feel like a pro, you have someone else wash your clothes. For me, that was the greatest thing in the world."

Beyond the facility issue was another problem, one much more common to American sports leagues than European leagues. The players, encouraged by the surprising success of the league in Year 1, were ready to take action.

A strike? No. Strikes and other labor stalemates can be detrimental, sure to raise the ire and perhaps laughter of the braying media, but every major U.S. league has weathered one. The legal-minded players among the U.S. talent pool decided to form the MLS Players Association as a trade association rather than a union. That meant the players could sue the league.

"I got served with the lawsuit on February 14, 1997," Logan says. "So it was my own private little valentine."

Lagerwey insists the obstinate league office backed the players into a corner:

> I would say it was the only option that we had at the time as players. Did it accomplish anything? No, it didn't. It did nothing for the labor movement, it did nothing for the players. I think ultimately it was a failure. But I know having sat in the meetings when the decision was made to pursue litigation that it was the only choice we had. If we unionized, the only threat we had was to strike, and that wasn't a credible threat. . . . So the only mechanism we had to try to achieve a labor agreement was the threat of litigation. Any time you try to address a problem by suing somebody, it's probably a bad idea. It's not the best way to mediate a solution, it's not the best way to solve a problem.
>
> I wound up being a corporate lawyer because I saw how destructive the litigation process was, and I didn't want any part of it. But having said that, the impression that we had—rightly or wrongly—was that the league was not going to negotiate with us under any circumstances. As a result, we felt that this was the only path that we had. Folks are entitled to their own opinions and hindsight is 20-20, but I can tell you unequivocally that was the impression that we had, that we simply had no other choice. Not only was the league not going to negotiate with us, but they were not going to speak to us.

Sunil Gulati, the league's primary contract-maker as the deputy commissioner, saw a little bit of room but not on the issue of single entity: "About structural issues, the league and the investors had a strong belief that the only way to get stabilized and get soccer in the United States was in the structure that had been forwarded. So from a structural issue, I don't think there was a lot of room for discussion. On economic issues, there's always room, keeping in mind there were huge investments at that time."

Eric Wynalda didn't agree with the suit but understood the players' concerns:

> When the league started, there was an enormous amount of animosity among the American players who were given "take it or leave it" contracts. I think Alan Rothenberg's quote was "if they don't like it, they can go back to washing cars." There were a lot of pissed-off players. They recognized it was a huge opportunity, but Sunil Gulati, Alan Rothenberg, Doug Logan, Ivan Gazidis, they leveraged that on the emotions of those players and essentially got everybody to sign up for, in my opinion, a pretty raw deal.

Mark Semioli, the Galaxy's player representative, voted against taking the association/lawsuit route. But a meeting in which players were treated "extremely unprofessionally" helped to push the players into the legal arena, and he says he felt an obligation to put his name on the suit to represent his teammates as they had voted:

> After season one and in the off-season, many players and many agents who are still involved with the game today felt that MLS was less than honest with some of their players. . . . Through discussions with my agent—and this happened with other players—we were told that if you do well, if you show that you're worth more, after the first year, we'll renegotiate your contract. This promise was made not only to myself but to many players. Many of them.

Besides, the lawsuit could go on while players remained on the field. Semioli continues:

The options were to either strike—which really was not going to happen, an unrealistic option—keep the status quo or sue under antitrust law and let the court handle the situation while soccer goes on. In my opinion and in the opinion of many, it was a way to keep soccer moving forward and hopefully redress any of the grievances, inconsistencies, and inequities that were placed upon some of the players. . . .

The decision was to go the antitrust route. Figured the game could still go on. If the collective bargaining process doesn't pan out, you could be stuck with a choice between a strike and the status quo.

A preliminary skirmish went to the players. Paul Caligiuri, the 1990 World Cup qualifying hero, had sought to play for Los Angeles. The league declared his original contract void and moved him to Columbus instead. After one season with the Crew, Caligiuri won an arbitration decision allowing him to move to L.A. at last, but he sat out several games while the Galaxy and MLS figured out how to address the salary-cap issues his move created.

One problem with the MLS Players Association, from the league's perspective, was the specter of labor strife in the past, aided and abetted by an outside party. In the NASL days, a player named John Kerr had participated in a players' strike with the assistance of the National Football League Players Association. Kerr went on to work for the NFLPA. Though his son, John Kerr Jr., had returned from England to play in MLS, the senior Kerr also signed on with the fledgling MLSPA. League execs weren't happy to face the hired muscle from the giant American sport of gridiron football. "It's the NFLPA lawsuit—they've [the NFLPA] conned a few [MLS] players into being a part of," D.C. United president Kevin Payne told *Washington Times* writer John Haydon in a 1999 feature for *SoccerTimes*.[1]

Jeff Agoos had plenty of questions about the NFLPA's involvement:

A lot of people I knew really didn't want to go the lawsuit route. There was no stability in this league, we were all sort of in this together, and we wanted to make sure that the league was viable and that there was a place for players who came after us. The NFLPA really turned the screws. I think John Kerr Sr. was involved at the time at heading the thing up with [the NFLPA's president] Gene Upshaw.

I always question why the NFL really were involved in this. If you look at it, we're really competing against one another. We weren't as big as the NFL, and I don't see us being as big as the NFL in the coming years for sure. It just seemed like the NFL were trying to protect their own interests. I really question why they would want to represent us. I know they weren't doing it out of the goodness of their hearts. I had serious questions as to what they were in it for, and I just didn't agree with the lawsuit.

The NFLPA had competition in its bid to represent the players. John Harkes, in his book, *Captain for Life*, recalled that an independent New York law firm wanted to help the players form a union rather than an association. The competing offers left the players confused and uncertain. Harkes recounts, "One day, the D.C. United players voted overwhelmingly in favor of the law firm, and the next day voted 11-10 in favor of the NFLPA. No one seemed able to make up their mind. After at least two league-wide votes and a lot of confusion, the players sided with the NFLPA."[2]

Wynalda, who says he had a nasty argument with Upshaw about associating the "milk-and-cookies" sport of soccer with the battered image of NFL players, says the first vote was rather lopsided against the NFLPA, but that a second vote—taken while national-team players were in camp and out of the loop—barely favored the association.

The players' suit would argue that American soccer would be better off with competing leagues. Coincidentally, the A-League—which had vied for Division I status—merged into the less ambitious USISL for the 1997 season.

Meanwhile, the centralization at the heart of the players' suit was evolving. In the frenzied startup of the league, Gulati and Gazidis had acted as general managers for the entire league's talent pool. Now that each team had a full staff and a year of play under its belt, those teams had more say in signing players. Gulati recalls:

For the most part early on, we weren't stocking teams per se, we were stocking the league. Individual coaches and general managers were picking the players. That was true in most cases. We were signing players without having coaches and general managers—Jorge, Tab, and many others were signed before. Clearly teams got more freedom over time. The league still makes the final decision to this day on players, but after the first year or two, that process started to change. Even in the first year, when we had people running teams, that process changed.

While the process evolved, so did the talent pool. Some players later claimed the league retaliated for the labor strife with low offers. Other players simply hadn't panned out as planned.

Most of the marquee players divided so carefully among the league's teams had turned in solid debut seasons. The biggest international stars—Jorge Campos in L.A., Carlos Valderrama in Tampa Bay, Roberto Donadoni with the MetroStars—showed their class throughout the season, as did lesser-known Bolivian Marco Etcheverry with D.C. United and Salvadoran midfielder Mauricio Cienfuegos in L.A. Of that quintet, all but Campos made the league's Best XI squad. The names known from the USA's 1994 World Cup team—Eric Wynalda, John Harkes, Marcelo Balboa, Cobi Jones, Tony Meola, Alexi Lalas—didn't make the Best XI but were impact players. Beyond that top tier, some players didn't live up to expectations.

New England in particular had bad luck with its original allocations. Italian Giuseppe Galderisi lasted only four games in 1996 before being waived, later to resurface with Tampa Bay. Goalkeeper Jim St. Andre couldn't nail down the starting job and didn't return for Year 2. American forward Joe-Max Moore returned from Europe in the middle of the 1996 season to shore up the offense, and the Revolution reached overseas for another Italian, colorful goalkeeper Walter Zenga.

Coaches started to rotate quickly through jobs. Carlos Alberto Parreira, who coached Brazil to the World Cup in 1994, took over the MetroStars from Carlos Quieroz, who announced his departure for Japan's Nagoya Grampus Eight before the end of the 1996 season. Frank Stapleton left New England, with Thomas Rongen moving north from Tampa Bay to replace him. That left five clubs with their original coaches—D.C. United, Los Angeles, Dallas, San Jose, and Kansas City.

By the end of the season, it was down to three—Bruce Arena in D.C., Ron Newman in Kansas City, and Dave Dir in Dallas. Laurie Calloway would depart San Jose with a 5-10 record, not much excelled by successor Brian Quinn as the Earthquakes failed to make the playoffs. Lothar Osiander was out in Los Angeles after the Galaxy's 1997 start was as bad as their 1996 was hot—seven points through 12 games.

Columbus strengthened its side with national teamers Thomas Dooley and Mike Lapper.

But the changes that would pay off down the road were in Colorado, where the Rapids hired coach Glenn "Mooch" Myernick, added U.S. veteran Peter Vermes, and put a rising young player named Marcus Hahnemann in goal.

Defending champion D.C. United was the hottest team, not losing in regulation until Kansas City brought them down to earth with a 6-1 pummeling June 21. Despite that glaring blotch on the record, United finished with a league-best 55 points (21-11) and league-high 70 goals. Jaime Moreno and Raul Diaz Arce finished 1-2 in the league's goal-scoring race with 16 and 15, respectively.

Carlos Valderrama led Tampa Bay to second place, leading the league in assists with 19 and taking MVP honors for the second straight year in the All-Star Game. The Colombian midfielder had a goal and two assists in the East's 5-4 win, a stat matched by the curiously rejuvenated Galderisi, Valderrama's teammate in Tampa Bay. A few weeks later, Galderisi was traded back to New England, where he would later serve as assistant coach.

Another international star, the MetroStars' Roberto Donadoni, left after the 1997 season. The Italian midfielder had played well enough to earn a call back to his national team for Euro 1996, and he took advantage of an opportunity for one more season with AC Milan after the MetroStars failed to make the playoffs. He conceded that artificial turf, which replaced the grass in Giants Stadium when NFL season rolled around, factored into his decision.

The turf also affected coaching decisions. Said Tobias Xavier Lopez of the *Fort Worth Star-Telegram* of a September game: "The Dallas Burn defeated the MetroStars 1-0 on the Giants Stadium turf when former Burn coach Dave Dir fielded a lineup of former indoor players with turf speed. Despite the victory and tactical adjustment, league officials berated Dir because he did not use the older, slower marquee players."[3]

Another conflict: international scheduling. The league's refusal to schedule around national team dates came to a head in the playoffs, as the Galaxy limped through a game against Dallas without Mauricio Cienfuegos and Jorge Campos. And Campos's time-sharing between two clubs—the Galaxy and Mexico's Cruz Azul—looked more awkward when those clubs faced each other in the final of the Champions Cup run by CONCACAF, the regional federation. Campos played for the Galaxy, switched to forward in the second half and scored a goal, but Cruz Azul won 5-3.

Still, the year ended on an upbeat note. MLS set the playoff final for October 26 in Washington's RFK Stadium and was rewarded with a sellout when United reached its second straight championship game against Colorado, which had missed the playoffs in 1996 but scraped in as the fourth seed this time around.

Once again, the weather refused to cooperate. The rain wasn't of biblical proportions as it had been the year before in Foxborough, but it was steady and cold. The fans stuck it out to see the league's most consistent team face a scrappy, streaky one. Colorado had endured a six-game losing streak late in the season, then swept through two best-of-three playoff series with four straight regulation wins, starting with a 3-0 rout at top West seed Kansas City. While United had the Moreno–Diaz Arce–Etcheverry magic triangle working to perfection, Colorado had no player with more than eight goals, having parted ways with the 1996 tandem of Shaun Bartlett and Jean Harbor early in the season. Leading scorer Paul Bravo departed the final in the 27th minute, leaving a makeshift strike force of Wolde Harris, David Patino, and former United forward Steve Rammel. At the back, the Rapids had veterans in Vermes, Balboa, and Steve Trittschuh, clamping down to allow only three goals in four playoff games.

But United simply had too much flair for the Rapids to contain. Tony Sanneh, whose goal started the United comeback in the 1996 final, played a cross that Diaz Arce dummied for Moreno. The league's leading goal-scorer didn't miss, giving United a 1-0 halftime lead. Sanneh doubled the lead in the 68th minute, slipping past the Rapids' back line for a wide-open header off a Harkes cross.

The Rapids pressed the rest of the way, with Balboa mimicking his near-miss bicycle kick from the 1994 World Cup with a powerful overhead shot that United keeper Scott Garlick smothered. Substitute Adrian Paz placed a perfect shot into the upper corner to cut it to 2-1 in the 75th minute, but Garlick protected the lead, finishing with nine saves. United remained MLS's only champion after two years.

But United finally lost a trophy, failing to score in the U.S. Open Cup final and losing that title to Dallas on penalty kicks. At last, an MLS team not in Washington had a trophy of its own.

Preki took MVP honors after leading the league in "scoring"—an Americanized stat awarding two points per goal and one point per assist—with 12 goals and 17 assists. Friedel nosed out Zenga and Campos in goalkeeping stats with a 1.21 goals-against average and took the Goalkeeper of the Year award. Preki, Valderrama, and Etcheverry were the only repeat players in the Best XI.

Logan gamely answered questions on attendance, saying on the MLS Cup broadcast that the league had "consolidated our core audiences."

1998

The MetroStars were a team in perpetual transition. The team used 51 players in its first two seasons, far and away the most in the league. The third MLS season started with the fourth MetroStars coach as Parreira left to coach Saudi Arabia in the World Cup. Alfonso Mondelo, his replacement, didn't make it through the season, replaced by former U.S. coach Bora Milutinovic.

Semioli, who had been traded to the MetroStars in 1997, recalls that Parreira's departure was more significant than the other coaching changes:

Unfortunately, there was a lot of interference at the league level with the way the MetroStars did things. Not because they were being nefarious. They were trying to help the MetroStars become a strong team because, as we all know, even in the major sports, it helps when the New York team was doing well.

They had some smart people there, and they never really got it together. Because of that, every year, a different idea was tried, a new player was brought in. The quick fixes—it reminds me of the modern-day [NBA] Knicks. It has to be done in the short term because of the fixation that New York has to be good or else. If there's anything MLS can be proud of, it's that they've thrived without New York doing well. It's shown tenaciousness in being able to slowly but surely grow. . . .

I was there for a couple of good years, had some great coaches. But some circumstances occurred that led to coaches having to leave. I know we had a great coach in Carlos Alberto Parreira. He brought me in. I had trained with the Brazilian national team [in 1994] in their two-month stay at Santa Clara. I knew him from that time. He had seen me play during that period of time. That's I think one of the reasons I got brought in to New York. If he had stayed there and not gotten plucked by the Saudi Arabian national team, I think we were going in the right direction. He had brought in some players that were going to make a difference, and I felt like that next year, we were really going to make a move. And then he was gone.

That was unfortunately a turning point in the franchise's history. He knew what he was doing. He had a plan, he was a great man, intelligent, organized, experienced, and I really felt we were going to turn the corner with him. He left, and we had to start over with a new coach, and it sort of became a cycle since then.

Marquee players were on the move, too, with a three-team deal sending Raul Diaz Arce to New England, Alexi Lalas to the MetroStars, and a bunch of draft picks to D.C. United. World Cup vet Lalas may have been the headliner, but the deal was heartbreaking for D.C. United, which made no secret that the salary cap forced the deal. "Ultimately, we had no choice," United president and general manager Kevin Payne told the *Washington Post*. "We tried every avenue imaginable short of completely gutting our team. This was the only step available to us."[4]

The deal also soured United's relations with its sizable Salvadoran fan base, which turned out several times over the next few years to cheer against the home team whenever Diaz Arce's team or Mauricio Cienfuegos's Galaxy turned up at RFK Stadium.

United managed a great trade early in the season, though, dealing the fading Roy Wegerle for Roy Lassiter. Marco Etcheverry proved as adept at setting up Lassiter goals as Carlos Valderrama had in Tampa Bay.

Expansion Chicago, coached by longtime Arena lieutenant Bob Bradley, snared a marquee player by trading for Jorge Campos, but he failed to nail down the starting job. Also in that deal, the Fire picked up Chris Armas, who would anchor the Chicago midfield for the better part of a decade. Outside the existing MLS ranks, the Fire tapped into the Eastern European talent pool with Czech defender Lubos Kubik and the Polish triple threat of Jerzy Podbrozny, Roman Kosecki, and Peter Nowak.

The Galaxy re-acquired Kevin Hartman, Campos's backup, whom the Fire had picked in the expansion draft. Hartman kept the Los Angeles job for the next several years.

Goalkeeper Brad Friedel finally got his work permit straightened out to begin a long career in England. Columbus replaced him with another veteran of English play, Juergen Sommer, and revved up the offense with two Caribbean players, Stern John and Andy Williams.

Young players signed through Project-40 got more of a chance to play as MLS formed a team—sort of a reserve team for all 12 MLS clubs—to play in the second-tier A-League. Project-40 already provided several advantages to young players who were capable of making the leap. For one thing, they could stay closer to home.

"We didn't go into the draft," says Ben Olsen, who joined D.C. United as part of the 1998 Project-40 class. "Because I think there was this push and this excitement from the league to get Project-40 up and running, and also because the guys were younger, the thought process was that it was an easier transition to get them near their hometowns."

Olsen, who had been playing at the University of Virginia, also had a chance to join ex-Cavaliers coach Bruce Arena in an atmosphere built around Virginia alumni. Olsen recalls:

Probably the main factor in leaving was Bruce Arena. I trusted Bruce, and I still trust Bruce's decisions. He basically told me it was time to go. He said you've passed the college game, if you're serious about wanting to become a professional soccer player, we can make it work so you can come to D.C. United. . . .

D.C. United probably had a bit more of a family thing, especially early. It was a real tight group, probably because Bruce was that way and the camaraderie surrounding all the UVA guys. At one point I think we had, what, 10 guys that went to UVA? Probably more than not. We all knew each other, we'd all played with each other, the families knew each other. The early days of D.C. United, the first four or five years, the team's family sense was huge. Everybody really got involved.

Arena sees a link between the family atmosphere and United's advantage in having something other teams lacked:

The reason we were able to do that was because we had a training facility. We had a place where our entire organization came every day. Not only players, coaches, and technical staff—our entire front office, we were all together in that building. That created a family atmosphere.

I could tell you the extreme of that. When I was in New York the last year and a half, it was the furthest thing from that. You can't build a team and a close-knit group when your facilities and your whole concept of how to build a club isn't there.

Almost our entire team [United] and staff lived within a radius of 10 miles of that facility. We were always together, we could do things at work and away from work. So it created a very good environment.

The league had made some progress on stadiums, at least. The Miami Fusion, who acquired Carlos Valderrama from Tampa Bay, showed off a new type of MLS atmosphere in its televised debut at Lockhart Stadium, filling the cozy venue with 20,450 enthusiastic fans for a difficult matchup with D.C. United. The two-time champions won 2-0.

Another intimate venue was finally approved in Columbus, where the Crew got a favorable lease at the Ohio Expo Center. Gov. George Voinovich signed off on the deal June 9, and the Crew broke ground August 14. Construction moved quickly, and the 22,555-capacity stadium—with a fan-friendly concourse overlooking one goal—was finished early in the 1999 season.

The Galaxy—dominant early in the first year but strugglers early in 1997—once again stormed out of the gate, winning their first 15 games on the way to a 24-8 record. L.A. won 22 in regulation to finish with 68 points and showed off its dynamic offense in a 7-4 win over Colorado in May.

But in 1998, international competition took the spotlight. It didn't go well.

A few weeks before the World Cup in France, shocking news emanated from the U.S. national team. Steve Sampson, the former Santa Clara collegiate coach who had taken over the U.S. team for a successful run at the 1995 Copa America, cut John Harkes from the team. Harkes, an English league veteran and cornerstone of two-time champion D.C. United, had been Sampson's "captain for life." He later wrote a book by that title, detailing the schism on the team.

Sampson made a few other surprising moves, adding MLS players Chad Deering and Brian Maisonneuve to the mix out of nowhere. The two midfielders had scant national-team experience before 1998. Also new: defender David Regis, a Martinique-born Frenchman who had married an American and rushed through his citizenship process in time to join the team. Jeff Agoos, the long-suffering defender who had burned his uniform after being cut from the 1994 team, lost playing time to his heretofore unknown teammate.

Lacking proper preparation, feuding, and playing an unconventional six-midfielder formation (3-6-1), the USA lost its opener to powerhouse Germany. The crushing blow came a few days later.

Most Americans knew little about Iran beyond the long-simmering feud between the two countries since Ayatollah Khomeini deposed the U.S.-backed shah in 1979 and took hostages in the U.S. embassy for more than a year. The soccer team, apart from a couple of players based in Europe, was relatively unknown as well.

What the USA found was a team that may not have been as talented across the field as the Americans but had a shrewd counterattack. The USA pressed the attack throughout the game and hit the woodwork countless times. But Iran scored a first-half goal against the run of play, then burned the U.S. defense on a counterattack in the second half. Brian McBride managed to scramble a ball into the net late, but Iran held on for a 2-1 win.

Harkes's national-team career, as it turns out, wasn't quite over. Sampson's was. He coached the Cup finale, a dreary 1-0 loss to Yugoslavia, then resigned before heading home from France.

The MLS All-Star Game—which stretched into an All-Star weekend that included a "skills challenge" and other gimmicky events—gave U.S. players a slight measure of redemption. Opting to play American stars vs. international stars instead of the usual East-West approach, MLS watched the USA win 6-1 in Orlando.

That game proved little, but MLS teams would win some international honors and respect. D.C. United beat Mexico's Toluca in August to claim the CONCACAF title. Then in December, United topped Brazil's Vasco da Gama to take the erratically contested Interamerican Cup. Vasco was burned out from playing international competition all over the world, and the Brazilian club's "home" leg took place in Fort Lauderdale, but the excuses mattered little as a three-year-old American club claimed the title of best team in the Western Hemisphere.

Harkes responded in *Captain for Life*, describing the second leg in Fort Lauderdale:

> There was talk in the media about how tired Vasco was after traveling four days earlier from Japan after a 2–1 loss to Real Madrid in the Toyota Cup, the world club championship. But tired or not, there was no way that a squad like Vasco wanted to lose to us—an American club team—and they came at us with all they had. In fact, they had even more at stake after losing to Real Madrid since they did not want to return to Brazil empty-handed. They made only one change to the lineup that played in the Toyota Cup, which showed they took us seriously.[5]

United lost the home leg 1-0 in Washington. In Fort Lauderdale, where only 7,000 fans turned out at the Fusion's Lockhart Stadium, Tony Sanneh and Eddie Pope—both of whom had a history of timely goals—scored in a 2-1 aggregate victory. Logan lashed out at the U.S. media for failing to notice United's accomplishment.

Brazilian fans noticed, says Eddie Pope:

> The biggest thing I recall about it was how unknown it was in the U.S. For us, it was such a huge deal. In other countries it was a big deal as well. It was a big-time tournament. For us, no one really understood it, no one understood the importance of it, no one understood how big the exchange we had with Vasco da Gama was. I think that part was sort of unfortunate. For me it was an amazing tournament. That's certainly one of the championships that I'm extremely proud of. I hope it's something that D.C. United fans remember and hold dear to their hearts. It was a very difficult accomplishment to say the least.
>
> One of the things I remember is that once we beat Vasco da Gama, we heard the streets were packed with their rival teams. Everyone's out in the streets in Brazil partying. We were sort of just getting on a bus in Miami, not a whole lot of fans at the game. That was pretty amazing to hear that story.

Arena noticed the lack of U.S. media attention and heard the excuses, but he sees it as an impressive early step for the young league:

> To me it simply said, for the league in its early going, there's a team able to put together the quality to play against a very fine club team with a reputation worldwide. We were successful. To counter that, one would say Vasco da Gama had to travel over to Japan for another competition. Both games were played in the United States. But at the end of the day, it still demonstrated that in the first three years of the league, the league was able to have a couple of clubs that built a team with quality. It gained the league respect around the world.

United did not, however, win the MLS title. Nor did any of the nine teams that had chased United for the league's first two seasons. That honor went to the expansion team from Chicago.

While United had once again dominated in the East, the Fire's success wasn't a shock. Chicago finished 20-12, 12 points behind Los Angeles but comfortably second in the West. American forward Ante Razov meshed well with the Eastern Europeans running the offense. Campos found he couldn't dislodge big, young American Zach Thornton, who led the league with a 1.17 goals-against average.

The Fire also drew well at home, with knowledgeable fans who bucked the trend of low playoff attendance by turning up in force in the Western final against Los Angeles. Before a crowd of 32,744, the Fire saw off the Galaxy in a shootout.

The final once again drew a solid crowd of 51,350 as the weather cooperated for once for the October 25 game at the Rose Bowl. Nowak, who would later have success coaching D.C. United, was the Fire's sparkplug. He and Lubos Kubik undid the United defense with quick passes back and forth, leaving Nowak alone against goalkeeper Tom Presthus. Nowak passed up the easy finish for an easier finish by Jerzy Podbrozny.

Just before halftime, Nowak struck again with a shot that deflected off teammate Diego Gutierrez. Presthus was left agonizingly wrong-footed. The goal was mildly controversial, as Ante Razov was clearly offside in front of Presthus but didn't touch the ball.

United fired away through the game, outshooting Chicago 22-10, but Thornton made eight saves to become the first goalkeeper with a shutout in a final. Nowak claimed MVP honors.

Chicago also won the U.S. Open Cup, knocking out defending champion Dallas in the semifinals and beating Columbus in extra time to match D.C. United in taking the "double" of league and cup.

The other expansion team didn't fare as well. Despite a strong debut, Miami averaged only 10,284 fans for its first season. The Fusion picked up 14 points in 19 games before firing coach Carlos "Cacho" Cordoba. With Ivo Wortmann at the helm, the Fusion slipped into the playoffs ahead of weak Tampa Bay and New England. Paired against D.C. United, from which it had snared three players in the expansion draft, the Fusion put up a good fight and dropped both games by a single goal. Diego Serna combined well with fellow Colombian Valderrama to score 11 goals. Valderrama had sulked after the coaching change and seemed likely to leave, prompting a barrage of questions for Doug Logan on the All-Star Game broadcast.

The revelation of the season was Columbus forward Stern John, who had bounced around in the A-League before slipping to the Crew in preseason. He scored 26 goals, one shy of Roy Lassiter's 1996 total, to overshadow a fine 19-goal, 13-assist campaign by Cobi Jones. Etcheverry, who led the league with 19 assists, was the league's MVP and the first three-time Best XI honoree.

With a smooth expansion year and stadium construction underway in Columbus, MLS seemed solid and stable after three years. Attendance dipped only slightly from 1997, though it would still be perceived as a steep drop from the novelty year of 1996.

The talent pool, always a concern when a league adds teams, had been replenished from unexpected sources—Eastern Europe provided the Fire's spark, while Stern John hailed from Trinidad and Tobago. Young players such as Thornton and Columbus's Brian McBride were gaining experience. Project-40 was turning up better players—future national-team mainstays Tim Howard, Ben Olsen, and Josh Wolff played in 1998, followed by Chris Albright and DaMarcus Beasley in 1999.

Yet the league had lingering problems. Three teams—Dallas, Tampa Bay, and San Jose—still had no owner-investors. Miami's Ken Horowitz was the only new investor the league had lured in three years.

One prospect was Alan Rothenberg—the same Alan Rothenberg whose name adorned the MLS championship trophy, a tribute to his work in starting the league—who had a deal with Japanese advertising giant Dentsu to share owner-investor rights in San Jose, but the deal fell through.

"My primary financial partner was out in Japan, and the economy in Japan went south, and with that, so did my financial partner," Rothenberg says.

The labor situation was still volatile, with a lawsuit that would eventually force MLS to say it had lost a lot of money through the early years. Fans still griped about the shootout and player transactions that seemed arbitrary and sometimes unfair. Year 4 would bring change.

4

Concrete Steps and Change

Sunil Gulati doesn't look like a major power broker in the sports world. He looks much more like a college professor who has worked for the World Bank. He, however, is all three.

While each MLS team had gained some autonomy in selecting its own players as the league settled from its frenzied start, deputy commissioner Gulati had stocked the talent pool. He would be a pivotal figure in the player lawsuit. A more powerful personnel manager might not exist in any sports league in the free world.

In February 1999, Gulati lost his job. "Sunil Gulati was stripped of his post as deputy commissioner last month, supposedly over renewing the contract of midfielder Tab Ramos without consulting the MetroStars," reported the Associated Press's Brian Trusdell. Several news reports at the time concurred that MetroStars investor Stuart Subotnick had pushed to have Gulati removed, though the final decision rested with commissioner Doug Logan.

Neither Logan nor Gulati, who later took Alan Rothenberg's old post as the head of U.S. Soccer, would discuss the ouster for this book.

"Sunil is an extraordinarily gifted executive," Logan says. "It was a heart-wrenching decision for me to reach that conclusion, and I would not have done so frivolously. I'm happy that at the end of the day he has found his niche with the Federation. I gave people my word that I would not comment on the details."

With Ramos's renewal, the MetroStars had run into salary-cap trouble and made a startling trade—marquee attractions Tony Meola and Alexi Lalas for two solid but lesser-known players: dependable winger Mark Chung and goalkeeper Mike Ammann.

While Lalas moved to his third team in four years, the New Jersey–bred Meola lashed out. "I'm OK, but the ones who are really hurt are the fans, who are loyal to teams and players and then get treated like this," he told Trusdell.

Raul Diaz Arce also was on the move again, heading to San Jose via the MetroStars in a complicated deal that saw MetroStars fan favorite Giovanni Savarese head north to New England. The MetroStars ended up with the MLS equivalent of IOUs—a player allocation and future considerations.

Little wonder the MetroStars ran into trouble. A 6-0 loss June 20 at Kansas City left the team 4-9, with eight points. A shootout win followed a couple of weeks later, but a league-record losing streak of 12 games wiped out any hope of contending.

United was once again a different team, thanks to the salary cap. Captain John Harkes was traded to New England. Tony Sanneh took a more lucrative offer in Germany. Scott Garlick and Mario Gori also left D.C. On the flip side, United was able to stock up in 1998 on more young talent in addition to Ben Olsen. The previous year's trade of Roy Wegerle for Roy Lassiter would turn out to be one of the most lopsided deals in league history, and then in 1999, Chris Albright joined the club.

The most successful coach in the league's brief history also was out. Bruce Arena left D.C. United to replace Steve Sampson as U.S. national-team coach. Thomas Rongen, the former NASL player who had already coached in Tampa Bay and New England, took over at RFK Stadium.

The Galaxy kept up a trend of starting quickly in even-numbered years and poorly in odd years. As in 1997, they fired their coach, replacing Octavio Zambrano with Sigi Schmid, the longtime UCLA coach who was reunited with many of his former players.

Meola and Lalas couldn't help Kansas City avoid an atrocious start. Meola injured his ACL (anterior cruciate ligament) in preseason. Coach Ron Newman lost his job, replaced by former U.S. coach Bob Gansler. The Wizards started 1-10, an impossible hole even in a league that takes so many teams to the playoffs.

The Rapids went in the other direction, adding to the attack Sweden's Andres Limpar and Panama's Jorge Dely Valdes, who celebrated goals by dialing a number on an imaginary cell phone. Goalkeeper Marcus Hahnemann was sold to England's Fulham partway through the season and replaced by former Revolution keeper Ian Feuer, a 6-7 giant who also had played in England. The Rapids started 12-4.

The league also lost an investor. L.A. Soccer Partners sold its rights to the Galaxy to Philip Anschutz, who already owned the Rapids and Fire. The Kraft family joined Anschutz and Lamar Hunt as multiple-team operators, taking over the league-owned San Jose Clash with an option to buy down the road. Lynne Meterparel, a 30-year-old executive with the Revolution, was installed as Clash president/general manager in place of the old guard of Peter Bridgwater.

A FIELD OF THEIR OWN

The league's biggest change was in Columbus, and it had nothing to do with the roster.

Twice, the Columbus Crew had lost a vote on public money for a stadium. In May 1997, Franklin County voted against a 0.5 percent tax increase for a downtown stadium and arena. In February 1998, it was Dublin's turn to say no.

Lamar Hunt regrouped quickly, casting his eye on some land on the state fairgrounds. He offered to pay for the stadium construction. Ohio reciprocated with a reasonable 25-year lease—$50,000 a year, plus some sharing of parking revenue. "A fair deal for both parties," Rick Frenette, general manager of the Ohio Expo Center & State Fair, told *USA Today*'s Peter Brewington.[1]

That passed the Ohio Expositions Commission by a 6-2 vote May 15, 1998. Gov. George Voinovich signed off a couple of weeks later, and the Crew broke ground August 14.

Nine months, one day, and $28.5 million later, the Crew played the Revolution in their first "home" game. No longer would Columbus squeeze into Ohio State's narrow football field while the fans rattled around the massive stands.

Stadiums were always part of the league's philosophy. "From the beginning, there was the idea to invest in soccer-only stadiums, but not until Columbus built one did we follow through," Hunt said in the league's tenth anniversary book. "I'm not sure we adequately gauged the difficulty of playing in overly large American football stadiums."[2]

Rothenberg says the league felt "trapped" at the beginning. The big stadiums offered several disadvantages—a lack of control over revenues and scheduling, a lack of atmosphere, and the clutter of American football markings. But the alternative had been high-school or small college stadiums "with wooden bleachers, getting splinters in your butt and going to outhouses for toilets." Rothenberg continues:

> As we first test-marketed the business plan, we had investors who said . . . this has failed so many times, I'm not going to put all those extra millions into a soccer-specific stadium, and find out that if the league fails, I'm stuck with a white elephant. So we got resistance. We said we've gotta get the league launched, and it's unrealistic to do stadiums. Fortunately, in there from the start with us was Lamar Hunt, who fully agreed with that concept, and he got to work right away with what he did in Columbus. And while it was a very Spartan-type stadium that he built, it proved a point. And God bless him, Phil Anschutz jumped on the bandwagon, and the rest, as they say, is history. So that was the soccer-specific stadium part.

As Rothenberg says, Columbus Crew Stadium was neither overly large nor overly extravagant. The capacity was listed at 22,555, though the crowd that first night was announced at 24,471. The stadium feels open, with its concourse overlooking both the field and the fairgrounds. The stadium would see other action, hosting state high-school soccer championships, all-star football events and concerts, but it was the Crew's home, christened with a 2-0 win. Jeff Cunningham scored the first goal in the new stadium, with extraordinary scorer Stern John adding the second. It would also host memorable U.S. national-team games, giving Mexico a dose of cold weather in World Cup qualifying.

The Crew had come into the game on an unlikely roll. Saddled with a seven-game road trip to start the season, Columbus won five. What could have been a disaster—imagine a 2-5 team stepping onto the field in May—turned into an opportunity as fans celebrated their first chance to see not only a new stadium but a hot team as well.

The simple but effective stadium also benefited from a quirky promotion later that summer—"Buck a Brat" night, in which the price of bratwurst was slashed to $1. The cozy stadium was a hit, and the Crew led MLS in attendance at 17,696 per game, just ahead of Los Angeles and D.C. United.

Logan reveled in the attention the league earned with the bold move. But that would be his last great moment in the job.

CHANGE IN COMMAND

With its single-entity structure, the MLS front office was always going to be a lightning rod for controversy. Gulati, whose hand seemed too heavy for many in and around the league, had been pushed out.

In April, Logan courted controversy with a move beyond Gulati's longest reach. Seeing a long-standing feud between Carlos Valderrama and Miami coach Ivo Wortmann, Logan resolved the impasse with a "reassignment." With a simple announcement from the commissioner, one of the league's best players moved back to Tampa Bay.

"It has become clear in the past days that an irreconcilable impasse has been reached between the Miami Fusion and Carlos Valderrama with regard to his continued participation with that team," Logan said at the time. "At the same time, it has become apparent that there is no possibility of a trade materializing within any reasonable time-frame that would be satisfactory both to the Miami Fusion and to another MLS team. I have therefore today decided, under the powers vested in me as Commissioner of MLS, to reassign the services of Mr. Valderrama from the Miami Fusion to the Tampa Bay Mutiny effective immediately."[3]

SoccerTimes called it "a transaction that could only happen in Major League Soccer."[4] Among the Internet communities growing around the game, the Valderrama move and other questionable player transactions drew comparisons to "Calvinball," the improvised pseudo-sport with malleable rules from the comic strip *Calvin and Hobbes*.

Logan defends the move today. He had an unresolvable clash between a playmaker who had gained world renown with a certain style and a coach trying to change that style:

> Carlos at that time was an expensive player, probably getting the third or fourth highest salary of any player in the league. To see him sit over a prolonged period of time on the bench and not be utilized to me was the squandering of an asset. I had a discussion with the investor-operator, I had a discussion with the coach. It didn't look like there was going to be any movement on either side, and this was over the course of several

weeks. I then indicated that the most prudent thing would be, for the benefit of the entire league, was to go ahead and trade the player to somebody who might want to use him. They went out into the trading market, and it became pretty rapidly known that they were trying to extract an extraordinarily high price for this player. But at the same time, they were sitting him. At a certain amount of time after researching the powers that I had, what I did was I forced a trade with Tampa. As I recall, Miami wound up getting significant value for Carlos. . . .

I would do it again the same. I admit the fact I did it in a heavy-handed kind of way, but I would do the same thing all over again.

Tampa Bay, winless at the time, won its next game over the MetroStars and went on to reach the playoffs as the third seed in the East. Miami scraped into the fourth spot. Both teams were eliminated in two games by D.C. United (over Tampa Bay) and Columbus (over the MetroStars), the only teams in the East with winning records.

Logan faced a few other problems. Grant Wahl spelled them out in a June *Sports Illustrated* column:

▶ Attendance was still below 15,000.
▶ ABC and Univision were broadcasting fewer games.
▶ Only one of the three league-owned teams had been sold.
▶ The Gulati ouster had angered several league managers, according to Wahl's anonymous source.
▶ The pronouncement that the league would aim for an average attendance of 20,000 in 1997 hurt MLS in the media.

Wahl's conclusion: "It has become increasingly clear that commissioner Doug Logan should go."[5]

Logan quipped to *SoccerTimes* writer Gary Davidson, "The last person who said 'Logan must go' was Uncle Sam who told me I had to go to Southeast Asia. But I survived that one, too."[6] He took a more direct approach with *Soccer America*'s oft-curmudgeonly columnist Paul Gardner, who had found the entertainment value of MLS games on the decline, using MLSnet, the league's official website, to issue a response.

Gardner and Logan, coincidentally, were neighbors in New York. Logan says he liked Gardner personally and took him out for a meal after a family pet died. But Gardner, described by Logan as a "fan and personal friend of Sunil's," had always been rough on Logan in print.

"He was someone who reached a conclusion and then took his pad out and found out the facts to validate it," Logan says. "But he is probably the most knowledgeable soccer journalist in the United States, but I was never able to reach a point of him approving anything that I did."

In this particular case, Logan says:

> Somebody asked me why goals were hard to come by, and I indicated the fact that, as I recall, goal scoring went up as the temperature went up in the warmer months of the summer, and that had occurred the prior three seasons. He wrote a column that just made fun of that. And I responded by getting the facts out, and sure enough, we looked at goals scored . . . and June, July, and August were the highest number of goals scored. I have no idea the reasons why—I just knew there was a historical antecedent for it. He made some sort of remark in a column about me, I made a sort of remark that was probably scatological in nature about him. It was blown up, it was something that I shouldn't have done. I should've bit my tongue. It was done with my tongue in my cheek. It came as a consequence over this relatively minimal disagreement we had over the reasons why goal scoring went up in the summer.

By then, MLS was sharing the soccer spotlight, if not being nudged completely out of it. The Women's World Cup had come to America and was a stunning success, at least in venues where the charismatic U.S. team was involved. Three years after winning Olympic gold on home soil, Mia Hamm was already American soccer's most prominent advertising star. The country also saw plenty of talkative midfielder Julie Foudy and uninhibited defender Brandi Chastain. As in 1994, the country fell in love with soccer and packed a California stadium—this time, the Rose Bowl—for a pivotal U.S. game. No one seemed to mind that the game was tentative and scoreless when Chastain settled the penalty shootout with a strong strike and whipped off her shirt to celebrate, burning the image of her sports bra in the minds of millions.

Two years later, MLS All-Stars paid homage to Chastain by tossing away their shirts to reveal sports bras after scoring goals. Perhaps they should've done it in the 1999 game, only a few days after the women's final, when Chastain's image was still fresh in everyone's minds. The ageless Preki, not usually one to participate in such shenanigans, scored two goals and took MVP honors in a 6-4 West victory in San Diego, which didn't have an MLS team but produced a respectable 23,227 fans who unfortunately rattled around in oversized Qualcomm Stadium.

As the women's team made the talk-show rounds, they made a few teasing references to being more popular than their male counterparts. Teasing or not, MLS needed to figure out a way to make the rising tide of soccer attention lift their boat along with the women's team.

Logan wouldn't be around to answer the challenge. By August, he was out.

SoccerTimes veteran columnist Robert Wagman saw a long chain of events leading up to Logan's ouster. Robert Kraft, the Revs and Quakes owner-investor, had been agitating for a move since the end of the 1998 season, Wagman said. Gulati's ouster raised the Hunt family's ire. The Anschutz group, which controlled one-fourth of the league's teams, was miffed when Albright wasn't assigned to the Galaxy and when MLS couldn't figure out a way to get the 1999 MLS Cup to Chicago. When the All-Star Game turned into a "marketing disaster," in Wagman's words, Logan's time was up.[7]

Logan describes his departure:

> When I took the job I anticipated getting fired within the five years of the contract. As a result, I negotiated hard and got a very acceptable exit negotiated into my contract. I was fired without cause, and they chose to go in a different direction. By the time that occurred, I had reached a point of losing the confidence of my board.
>
> [NHL commissioner] Gary Bettman called me a day or two after it happened and he said to do this job correctly, you will always have seven or eight people with a knife in their hands wanting to cut your throat. [Bettman has] a board of 28 guys, [I have] only got a board of seven or eight, which I thought was amusing. . . .
>
> My last words in my parting press conference were the following four phrases: "I had no bitterness, I had a wonderful time, I did my best, and I have no excuses." To this day, I still reiterate the four. It was a difficult year. We did not have a very successful All-Star Game in San Diego, for which I took responsibility. We had a few other things go wrong,

and not by way of making excuses, but that entire year, I was biting my tongue and walking on five stress fractures, three in one foot and two in another—so maybe my level of patience was not the best in the world. But I never took a day off of work for them. As a consequence, I maybe did and said some things that I would do differently today. But that's the past.

In fact, the wheels had been turning for a while. At an NFL owners meeting earlier in the year in Atlanta, Kraft asked league executive Don Garber what he knew about soccer, Garber says. Garber recalls his response: "Not a whole lot, but I've been exposed to it over in Europe. I like it. I've attended a bunch of games. Why do you ask?"

Once word reached Logan, he didn't want to wait around until the end of the season or whenever the ax was scheduled to fall:

> I found out about it—I was down in Mexico with the national team. I got a phone call during the national anthem. . . . That was on a Saturday, and I made a couple of phone calls and was able to confidentially verify that. I came back to New York on Monday, called Subotnick and said we need to talk. Apparently they were either going to do it at the end of the season or something short of it, but once I got wind of it, then the plans unfurled at that time. I said let's settle this thing.

The official announcements came quickly—Logan out, then Garber in. Logan went back to his multiple interests in sports and entertainment.

"Somebody asked me one time what my professional goals were, and a very flippant answer came out of my mouth that's still valid to this day," Logan says. "'I want to make a few friends, make a little money, and make a little history.' Out of my experience there, I did make some really good friends, I did make a little money, and I think I made a little history."

●

The new commissioner, by his own admission, hadn't grown up with the game. Like a lot of parents of his generation, he was pressed into service as a coach for young kids. Yet through his NFL ties, including a stint as senior vice president of the league's international operations, he had found himself attending games that any soccer fan would be thrilled to see—the 1994 World

Cup final as a guest of Coca-Cola, a Real Madrid–Barcelona game, a Rangers-Celtic derby in Glasgow. He was getting hooked.

Also in Kraft's favor—NFL commissioner Paul Tagliabue was a fan of the game and a one-time counsel for the NASL. Tagliabue gave his blessing and encouragement as Kraft courted Garber for a likely vacancy, Garber says.

Many journalists noted the similarity of his old and new jobs—taking a sport popular in one part of the world and trying to establish it in another. That was one angle. The other was far less kind to Garber. U.S. soccer fans and journalists are usually skeptical of outsiders. The game hasn't always had the best custodians in this country, and its niche status imposes a bit of insularity among its fans and backers.

Garber recalls his introduction to the job:

> It was a rude awakening for me. Here I thought I was riding into the soccer world on the wave of 16 years of success at the NFL and I'd be embraced by the soccer community because I had been successful and here I was putting my career on the line, if you will, to try to grow the sport professionally. And I go to the opening press conference, and I got lambasted by everyone. . . . Filip Bondy had bought my house in Montclair, New Jersey. I thought he'd at least give me a hall pass, and he killed me. He just said "the wrong guy at the wrong time." So I remember going home with my wife and scratching my head and saying, "Man, I hope I did the right thing." But we hit the ground running.

Garber didn't step into the front office and immediately try to turn MLS into some sort of hands-free NFL. He listened and quickly grasped the complexities of the U.S. soccer marketplace. MLS had not won over all of the fans who showed up to cheer the national team or watched overseas action on cable or satellite. The fans who preferred European and Mexican soccer to their local teams were both MLS's best opportunity and toughest obstacle.

Within a couple of months of taking the job, Garber told the *Washington Post* he wanted a better relationship between MLS and the U.S. Soccer Federation: "How do we do things together so the league is not competing with its federation? It's our big challenge. We've cut up an already small market. That makes no sense to me."[8]

Garber's first big move was aimed squarely at the game's traditionalist fans: the shootout tiebreaker would be eliminated. He recalls it as a simple decision to align the U.S. sport with international protocol:

> I think any product has to be authentic. Authenticity is a requirement in creating believability. I didn't understand when I came in—without knocking the founders or my predecessors in the league office—how you could try to sell a sport whose core equity was that it was part of the most beautiful, popular game in the world and not at least play by the same rules. . . . There was no agenda—I wasn't trying to win over anybody. It was pure logic to me. I'd go to games, and it was different rules than the kinder-kickers I coached in Montclair.

Garber recalls hearing right away from people within the league that the shootout should go. Especially one guy: "One fan came running up to the sideline rail and yelled, 'Garber, what's the matter with this damn league? Who cares about shootouts? This is what's wrong with Major League Soccer! I'm never coming to another game again.' Instead of walking away with the agony of defeat, he walked away angry at the league."

The issue jumped near the top of Garber's priority list:

> I spent the next couple of weeks calling other coaches and speaking to Sunil Gulati, who I have tremendous respect for and a close relationship with, meeting with Mark Abbott and Ivan Gazidis at that time and made the decision.
>
> I remember the press conference where we announced the changes in the MLS conference room. . . . All the soccer writers finally feeling excited that we're making the right move and taking this step in the right direction. That adoption of the international rules of the game and our understanding that it is simply about connecting to the broader aspects of the world's most popular sport would be a key part of our positioning, that in fact it has been our teams that have branding ourselves that way, supporters clubs have been celebrating the games the way they do in other parts of the world. And it gives us a point of difference in a very crowded and competitive sports landscape.

He made it official before MLS Cup 1999 in November, along with a few other changes:

▸ Ten minutes of sudden-death overtime instead of the shootout, with no further tiebreaker.

▸ No longer would the game time be kept on a stadium clock counting down from 45:00 with a horn abruptly stopping play at 0:00. The referee would keep official time, as it's done elsewhere in the world. This change was already in effect at MLS Cup.

▸ A new broadcast package would go into effect, with a weekly "Soccer Saturday" game on the ABC and ESPN networks. ESPN2 would have a weekly highlight show called *MLS Wrap*.

▸ In a less traditional move, the league would split from two divisions to three.

For decades, the power brokers in American soccer had been traditional soccer guys, often British, who imposed untraditional rules in an effort to Americanize the game. Several NASL bigwigs still defended the practice in the documentary *Once in a Lifetime*. Now, four years into its existence, MLS had a commissioner who had not grown up with the game but believed that the path forward was to respect and follow the game's internationally accepted practices.

Would that work?

UNITED AGAIN

While Garber settled into his new office, D.C. United took care of business on the field. After a 3-3 start, United raced to a 23-9 record, winning the East by 12 points over Columbus. Lassiter, the 1996 goal-scoring champion with Tampa Bay, tied Stern John and Dallas's Jason Kreis for the 1999 crown with 18 goals.

Kreis became the first MLS player with 15 goals and 15 assists as Dallas finished a close second in the West behind Los Angeles, where Mauricio Cienfuegos continued his playmaking mastery and goalkeeper Kevin Hartman gave up less than a goal a game. Chicago and Colorado, which cooled considerably after its fast start, tied for third.

In the last year of the shootout, San Jose's record showed just how bewildering the artificial tiebreaker could be in the standings. The Clash—

featuring a good crop of first-year players in goalkeeper Joe Cannon, defender Jimmy Conrad, and midfielder Richard Mulrooney—finished 19-13 but were 11 points behind Chicago, which wound up 18-14. At one point early in the season, the Clash were 5-2 but had yet to win in regulation. They failed to make the playoffs, as did the woeful Wizards, who rebounded slightly from their 1-10 start to an 8-24 finish.

The league's balance of power had shifted to the West, leaving the East open for at least one mediocre team to make the playoffs. Tampa Bay had plenty of offensive talent in Valderrama, MLS assist leader Steve Ralston, and the well-traveled Diaz Arce, but only Scott Garlick's goalkeeping heroics kept the team from leaking too many goals. Miami acquired inconsistent scorer Welton and Wynalda, who had been injured playing with Mexico's Leon in the off-season, in a complex four-team trade that paid off when Wynalda's goal in the season finale pushed the Fusion past New England for the last playoff spot.

The Revolution had a colorful season with Italian goalkeeper Walter Zenga also taking on coaching duties, but he spent much of the year feuding with officials and fans before issuing a "take it or leave it" ultimatum to the team with two games left. The Revs took him up on his offer and replaced him with Steve Nicol, the longtime Liverpool great, who won his two games in charge but was not given the permanent job. Not yet, anyway.

The MetroStars, who kept trading players for future allocations that never quite arrived, were never in the race. Eccentric Serbian star Sasa Curcic was the best player the MetroStars could acquire, but his arrival produced too little, far too late. Bora Milutinovic, often hailed as a miracle worker for his World Cup exploits with the USA and other national teams, was out after a 7-25 season with only four regulation wins.

In August, the MetroStars learned that help would be on the way next season. German Lothar Matthäus, easily the biggest European star the league had ever signed, was allocated to the team for the 2000 season.

While the MetroStars waited for their marquee player, D.C. United and Columbus once again rolled to the East final, with United again sweeping Miami. Los Angeles swept past Colorado with little trouble as the Rapids finished the season on an epic streak of 679 minutes without a goal.

For the first time since 1996, a first-round series required all three games, and it was the most eventful matchup the league had seen, stirring up a rivalry that would be commemorated with a new trophy.

The Dallas Burn scraped past defending champion Chicago 2-1 at home. In Chicago, the Fire put a nasty beating on the Burn, chasing goalkeeper Matt Jordan from the game. Mark Dodd, the league's early breakout star who had lost his starting job to the young Jordan, stepped in as the Fire finished off a 4-0 rout. In the process, fiery Chicago midfielder Dema Kovalenko viciously fouled Dallas's Brandon Pollard, breaking his leg and all but ending the career of the promising defender, who returned for only half of the 2000 season before retiring.

In Game 3, with Dodd in goal again, Chicago took a 2-0 lead over the hosts. Dallas responded with a stirring comeback to tie it 2-2. In the 86th minute, the Burn got a winner from Ariel Graziani, the potent scorer whom Dallas had picked up from New England in a fleecing of a trade after he had played only three games for the Revolution.

By 2001, supporters of each team bought a trophy to be awarded to the winner of the season series, dubbing it the Brimstone Cup to keep up the theme of the teams' incendiary names.

Both conference finals required three games. Columbus put five goals, three from Stern John, past D.C. United in Game 2 but couldn't break through in RFK in Game 3. Dallas won the last shootout in league history to take Game 2 but couldn't win on the road. The home teams won all six games, setting up a rematch on November 21 of the first MLS Cup between D.C. United and Los Angeles.

Once again, the game was in Foxborough, though the weather was considerably better—a warm 63 degrees, perfect for the halftime gyrations of Christina Aguilera and some dancers in United and Galaxy garb. Once again, D.C. United took the trophy, its third MLS title in four years.

The Galaxy suffered a massive blow early with an injury to captain Robin Fraser, the league's Defender of the Year and a three-time Best XI selection. Jaime Moreno poked home the rebound of a Lassiter shot in a cluttered six-yard box for a 19th-minute goal. Just before halftime came a moment of madness—Kevin Hartman, the league's Goalkeeper of the Year, coped with a bad hop on a backpass to elude the pressing Roy Lassiter but failed to clear it with his next touch. The wounded duck of a clearance landed right at the feet of Ben Olsen, who swiftly fired into the open net. The Galaxy managed little offensively after a first-half flurry and tamely lost 2-0.

Olsen had found himself in the right place at the right time, in more ways than one:

> It just capped off those two great years—winning the Cup and then scoring a goal and helping the team out in that way. I wasn't a very good soccer player, I don't think, the first two years, at all. I was just a guy who worked my ass off and fit into a great team. That team needed a guy out wide that could just run forever and fight and be kind of a young role player. The goal—I always still give Kevin a little shit every now and then. It's unfortunate—the field that day was terrible, absolutely terrible. The game wasn't that bad for the field conditions. I think the Patriots had really beaten that field up. It looked OK on TV because it was all spray-painted up. But when you're actually playing out there, it was tough to connect a pass. Kevin got on the wrong end of a bad field, and I felt kind of bad for him. I benefited from it.
>
> As much as I'd lost at that point, it was just nice to win a final. I'd lost at that point two years in a row in the finals [Virginia in 1997, United in 1998]. I was starting to think I had a little jinx. Winning that whole deal was more relief than joy.

The upsets were saved for the U.S. Open Cup. The sparkling franchise of the A-League, now incorporated into the USISL, was the Rochester Raging Rhinos, which often drew five-figure crowds and talked of a new soccer stadium. The Rhinos had a few MLS-caliber players on the roster, including future MLS Goalkeeper of the Year Pat Onstad, and carried a scrappy underdog mentality in Open Cup games. They shocked defending champion Chicago, knocked out Dallas in extra time in the quarterfinals, and eliminated Columbus 3-2 in the semis. The Crew's loss stung because the Open Cup had been renamed in honor of team owner Lamar Hunt, and Columbus would host the final. Only 4,455 fans showed up to watch the Rhinos complete the parade of upsets with a 2-0 win over Colorado.

Four years after the A-League had asserted its own claim to Division I status, a team had beaten MLS opposition to win a tournament with a history dating back to 1914 and built in the old American Soccer League's golden years. But MLS wasn't about to fight old battles. At least, not until they were forced to do so in court. The lawsuit would hang over the 2000 season, Garber's first full year in charge.

MLS AT Y2K

With former NFL executive Garber in charge, MLS was ready for its first season with a more traditional approach, replacing shootouts with a 10-minute sudden-death overtime that usually produced ties. The league had more of a presence on ESPN's networks with the highlight show *MLS Extra Time*, featuring a surprising commentator—Alexi Lalas, who had hung up his boots before age 30. At least for the moment. He explains:

> It's a long story, but as is the case with most of these good long stories, there's a woman involved. Lucky for me, that woman ended up becoming my wife and the mother of my kids. I also had gotten to a point in late 1999 where I'd been burning it pretty hard on and off the field, both ends of the candle. It had taken its toll physically and mentally. I got up one day and said this is not what I want to do, and it's not fair to anybody for me to continue doing it. I moved out to California and spent a sabbatical year, if you will. I got to do some TV and more importantly got to spend some time with a young lady who would become my wife.

While Garber's arrival and Lalas's departure pushed the league into the future, San Jose reached back to the past, dumping the "Clash" nickname in favor of "Earthquakes," the name of San Jose's team in the old NASL.

For all the soccer tradition on display, the league borrowed an idea from baseball, sending all 12 teams to Florida for spring training. The league held a February tournament, giving D.C. United yet another trophy.

MLS moved away from baseball in another respect, effectively but not yet officially eliminating temporary call-ups from A-League affiliates. The relationship had never really worked and sometimes created awkward situations in the U.S. Open Cup.

A-League players featured in the new "SuperDraft," which combined the college and supplemental drafts into a single event that would also include Project-40 players, who had previously been assigned by the league office.

Each year's college draft had produced some funny results in retrospect. The first-round picks in 1997 virtually disappeared, while Kevin Hartman—

the first goalkeeper with a goals-against average under 1.00—was a late third-rounder. The 1998 draft had a better first round—Chris Klein, Clint Mathis, Mike Petke, Jeff Cunningham, and Wade Barrett were just a few of the solid players involved—but future midfield anchor Pablo Mastroeni slipped to the second round. In 1999, few picks beyond the first seven had any sort of substantial MLS career.

The first two rounds of the SuperDraft turned up several productive MLS players, though the first overall pick—UCLA's Steve Shak to the Metro-Stars—would end up rated as a bust.

D.C. United took three youngsters, picking up local products Sergio Salas and Micah Cooks in the later rounds and leading off with 16-year-old Bobby Convey as the 12th overall pick. The three-time champions surely could not have realized at the time that Convey would prove to be one of the few bright spots of the season. Years of dismantling the roster to comply with salary-cap rules would finally catch up with United, which tumbled to last place in the four-team Eastern Division and the second-to-worst record in MLS—8-18-6. United appeased its Salvadoran fans by reacquiring Raul Diaz Arce, but with his scoring output slipping steadily, he wasn't able to offer much beyond a few glimmers of yesteryear.

Olsen recalls the team losing talent and chemistry as United headed into their darkest period:

> We had a lot of big names and a lot of success. When you're kept with a certain salary cap, and you've got guys that are big names who want money, you can't have them all. You can't do it. A lot of people had to leave and go other places because of financial stipulations. We had a great team chemistry the first couple of years. It was like clockwork, the way they played. They had a similar core that stayed through those first four years. When you break that up sometimes, and it's been there for so long, it takes a while to figure out your next core. Who are the guys you want to rely on and build your team around again? Marco [Etcheverry] was getting older. . . . Jaime [Moreno] had some injury problems. It was just a whole bunch of things.
>
> I'm glad I went through that, though. I was like, what's going on right now? I come here, all we do is win? Is this how professional soccer is—you just go and win every year? The next couple of years made

me appreciate not only the years that we were successful early but even more so when we got back on top and won that other championship. I appreciated the second one a lot more than I did the first one because of those down years.

The league standings as a whole bore little resemblance to previous years, and not just because MLS had moved from two divisions to three and added a column for ties with the elimination of the shootout. United's longtime East rival, Columbus, fell to last place in the Central Division. The two last-place teams of 1999, Kansas City and the MetroStars, won the West and East, with Chicago taking the Central.

The MetroStars had one of the world's most recognizable players in Lothar Matthäus, though it often seemed he only played when convenient. Aside from international duty in the Euro 2000 tournament and the occasional injuries that a player in his upper 30s might pick up, Matthäus missed time in unusual ways. The team was surprised to learn from the press that their highly paid marquee player was in St. Tropez while they expected him to be rehabbing an injury.

But Mark Semioli says Matthäus's heart was in the right place, and that he was a good teammate and gracious host when he took the team to Germany for a tour:

> Lothar was a good addition. We got along really well. He was injured for a good portion of his time here. I have mixed emotions about him—I feel he like wasn't able to give 100 percent when he was here because of the injuries that he had. Down the stretch, when we needed him, he played exceptionally well. . . .
>
> You'd have to talk to the people that employed him to see if they got their money's worth. I know the MetroStars name got some press and good amount of press in Germany. Our games were shown there. Was that worth the million-dollar or 2 million-dollar investment in him? Possibly. . . .
>
> Of course, we want him to act professionally, but the league needs to meet those same requirements of professionalism. I think there were times when it wasn't as professional as it needed to be. I think you can see the changes in the way the league is run now. I put it down as learning

from your mistakes, that type of thing. I don't think [the St. Tropez trip] was Lothar's most shining moment. It was a little disappointing to see. But ultimately, we had enough problems going on with the MetroStars. One of the last ones we had to worry about was Lothar Matthäus.

While Matthäus had questionable impact in his 16 games—a listing of international impact players at the All-Star broadcast didn't mention his name—the MetroStars got a big lift with the acquisition of Clint Mathis, who had been put into a dispersal draft so Los Angeles could make cap room for Mexican striker Luis Hernandez. The unconventionally skilled player, reuniting with former Galaxy coach Octavio Zambrano, scored 13 goals with the Metros—16 on the season. Together with Colombian newcomers Adolfo Valencia and Alex Comas, each of whom chipped in more than 10 goals, the MetroStars finally had a dynamic offense.

Kansas City still didn't have that explosive offense, though Preki was still a midfield force, but coach Bob Gansler had the luxury of a stable, suffocating defense. Tony Meola, no longer quite as bitter about being traded away from his New Jersey roots, led the league with an 0.92 goals-against average, set the league's shutout record by the midway point of the season, and was the first goalkeeper to take MLS MVP honors. Peter Vermes, once a national-team forward, won the league's Defender of the Year honors while shepherding youngsters Nick Garcia and Brandon Prideaux at the back. Matt McKeon was an ornery defensive midfielder every bit as competitive as fiery Scot Mo Johnston, who still threw himself into the attack. Chris Henderson gave the Wizards another attacking option in midfield. Danish newcomer Miklos Molnar provided the few goals the Wizards would need, finishing with 12 in 17 games despite missing time along with Matthäus to play in Euro 2000.

Los Angeles, with Hartman once again in dominant form, chased the Wizards in the West but couldn't come up with many goals despite the May acquisition of Hernandez. The Mexican striker, long a target of U.S. fans' derision, scored 4 goals in 16 games, not that far off Cobi Jones's team-leading seven. Mauricio Cienfuegos's assist total dropped from 17 to 7 even as he led the team in minutes played.

Still, the Galaxy were easily the best team in California. Up the coast in San Jose, the revival of the "Earthquakes" moniker didn't help the team at the gate—attendance dropped from 14,959 to 12,460—and coach Lothar Osiander could do little in his first full year in charge. At 7-17-8, the Quakes posted the league's worst record and missed the playoffs for the fourth straight year. San Jose fans couldn't have imagined what was to come.

Tampa Bay had the league's dominant player in Senegalese forward Mamadou Diallo, who blistered defenses for 26 goals, only 9 fewer than the whole San Jose team and just one short of the league record Roy Lassiter had set with the Mutiny in 1996. With such a powerful target up front, Carlos Valderrama ran away with the league's assist record, finishing with 26. Yet the Mutiny didn't have much of a defense—only Scott Garlick's 184 saves, also a league record, kept Tampa Bay from conceding the most goals in the league.

Diallo also claimed MVP honors in an All-Star Game that took lax defending and easygoing fun to a new high. The retired Lalas clowned with broadcast partner Rob Stone on the sideline, while Garber cheerfully reported that the league had a commitment for a stadium in Los Angeles and progress in New York.

The Central teams were split between East and West—Columbus and Tampa Bay to the East, Chicago and Dallas to the West—and Fire mainstays Ante Razov and Peter Nowak staked the West to a 4-3 halftime lead. The East responded with six unanswered goals in the second half, with Valderrama assisting on four and Diallo scoring twice. Tony Meola spent the last few minutes racing around up front as a forward in Razov's jersey, perhaps trying to keep up with Zach Thornton, the hulking keeper who had won the skills competition's "power shot" event.

The 9-4 final would stand up as the highest-scoring All-Star Game in league history, unlikely to be topped after a format change a few years later. If not for the multiple saves of Garlick, possibly a better MVP choice than Diallo given the easy path to the West's goal, the score could've been even higher.

But later in the season, Diallo would find himself involved in the most controversial play the league had seen so far. As MetroStars goalkeeper Mike Ammann raced out to collect a ball, the big forward neither held up his run nor found a good path to jump to safety. Diallo planted himself firmly into Ammann.

The *St. Petersburg Times* said Diallo leapt to get out of the way as Ammann dove feetfirst, but that the striker's right cleat bruised Ammann's jaw. The more dangerous injury: Diallo's left leg struck Ammann hard, leaving the goalkeeper with three broken ribs and a pinhole puncture in his abdomen.[9]

MetroStars fans didn't see an attempt to leap out of the way. They were outraged, and general manager Nick Sakiewicz pressed for disciplinary action, telling the Associated Press that Diallo should be "in jail, not on a soccer field."[10]

But the league didn't suspend Diallo, with VP Ivan Gazidis explaining, "We unanimously concluded that there was no measure of intent to hurt Mike Ammann. We also determined there was no disregard for Ammann's safety." MetroStars defender Mike Petke, though, was fined $250 after lifting his jersey in a goal celebration to reveal a T-shirt reading "Aug. 16, Crime of the Century" on the front and the more ominous "Revenge is coming" on the back.

The New York soccer media corps—easily the largest in the country—kicked around the issue for weeks. One national columnist—yours truly, writing weekly for USATODAY.com that year—dared to go against the conventional wisdom that Diallo intentionally injured Ammann, ensuring a steady stream of angry e-mails.

Intentional or merely reckless, Diallo's impact left Ammann seriously injured. The fifth-year player, himself an All-Star in 2000, would make a courageous return for the MetroStars' playoff run but would not regain his form. He played one more year with D.C. United and ended his career at age 30, young for a talented goalkeeper.

Aside from that incident, MLS's off-field news was good. Several counts of the player lawsuit were dismissed in April, though they'd be appealed years later. Ironically, given the lawsuit's contention that two first-division leagues would've been better for players, MLS briefly threatened to issue a competing proposal for a first-division women's league but settled its arguments quickly, reaching a cooperation agreement with the Women's United Soccer Association (WUSA) in May. The leagues would work together on marketing, scheduling, and stadium development, a rare agreement in U.S. soccer's fractious history.

U.S. teams had mixed fortunes in international play. Under Bruce Arena's leadership, the U.S. struggled through its first group phase of World Cup qualifying, flirting with a devastating early exit. Better news came in the Olympics in Sydney, where a gaggle of current or former MLS players contributed to a strong fourth-place run, narrowly missing a medal. Pete Vagenas was an unlikely scoring leader, netting in a 1-1 tie against eventual champion Cameroon and putting home a late penalty kick in the quarterfinals against Japan to force a penalty-kick shootout that the USA won. Jeff Agoos served as one of the three allotted players over age 23, along with former MLS players Brad Friedel and Frankie Hejduk. Josh Wolff, Dan Califf, and Chris Albright scored goals, along with a future MLS star, Landon Donovan.

The Olympics unfortunately coincided with the end of the MLS regular season and the start of the playoffs. Colorado had two highlights in the season: a bicycle-kick goal (later named Goal of the Year) from Marcelo Balboa eerily mirroring his near-miss in the 1994 World Cup, and an overtime goal against Los Angeles to swipe the last spot in the bracket. Left out was Miami, which had taken dysfunction to new heights earlier in the season when Francis Okaroh publicly accused his teammates of tanking a game to get coach Ivo Wortmann fired. (He was.)

Without the shootout to break ties, MLS tweaked the playoff format from the simple best-of-three to a "first-to-five-points" system. A win (three points) and tie (one) over two games wouldn't be enough. Most series would end up needing three games.

Colorado did indeed force a third game in the first round against Kansas City, which fell into a goal-scoring rut at a bad time. After a 1-0 win at home and a scoreless tie in Colorado, the Wizards came home and awakened for a 3-2 win before an anemic crowd of 4,156, winning the series seven points to one.

Chicago also needed three games to knock out pesky New England, which had reached the playoffs for only the second time with new coach Fernando Clavijo coaxing 15 goals out of Wolde Harris. The Fire and Revolution traded 2-1 home wins before Chicago trounced New England 6-0 in Game 3, also before a weak crowd of 5,972.

Los Angeles and the MetroStars had no such worries. The Galaxy held Diallo in check for a 1-0 win at Tampa Bay, then rolled past the Mutiny 5-2 at home. The MetroStars won a playoff series for the first time, getting an overtime goal at home and winning 2-1 in Dallas.

The MetroStars made the semifinals interesting, bouncing back from a 3-0 loss in Chicago to win 2-0 at home. The Fire held on in Game 3, winning 3-2.

Kansas City and Los Angeles tested the limits of the first-to-five format. The Wizards' offensive slumber returned in a 0-0 Game 1. In L.A., the Galaxy took the series lead with an overtime goal in a 2-1 win. Back in Kansas City, the Wizards prolonged the action with a 1-0 win on a Molnar penalty kick.

With both teams stuck at four points, MLS saw its first "series tiebreaker"— essentially a sudden-death overtime for the series as a whole rather than one game. It didn't last long, with Mo Johnston battling to get the ball to Molnar for the winner in the sixth minute.

For the second straight year, the league's top two teams had emerged as the finalists. Yet Chicago was a prohibitive favorite. The Fire had the experience of the 1998 championship and would win their second U.S. Open Cup in 2000. Hristo Stoitchkov, a Bulgarian hero of the 1994 World Cup whose signing would've made more international headlines had Matthäus not upstaged him, was Matthäus's polar opposite—a passionate player who fought and scrapped his way through MLS games just as he had for Bulgaria and giant European clubs. Ante Razov was second in the league with 18 goals, playmaker Peter Nowak had 14 assists, and goalkeeper Zach Thornton was still in top form behind an imposing defense.

But in Washington's RFK Stadium, once again hosting the final and turning out a strong crowd of 39,159 on a sunny mid-October day, the Wizards surprised Chicago early. Chris Klein swiped the ball in his own half and raced down the right sideline before sliding a cross in front of the goal for the dangerous Molnar, who outfought the Fire defense for a scrappy goal in the 11th minute.

Chicago would dominate the rest of the way but would not find a way past Tony Meola and the woodwork. The Fire had a 22-6 edge in shots, 10-3 in shots on goal. The Wizards were forced into 26 fouls. Meola, though, stopped all 10 shots and left the Fire frustrated. Chicago pressed furiously in the last 10 minutes, forcing Meola into an astounding diving save in the 81st minute, but the 1-0 score held up. Kansas City, a last-place team the year before, lifted the trophy. Lamar Hunt, unusually missing a game between his Kansas City Chiefs and their NFL rival Oakland Raiders, celebrated with his team.

Some pundits fretted that a defensive team had won a trophy that had been reserved for swashbuckling teams like D.C. United and Chicago. But MLS, in Garber's first full season in charge, had little reason to complain. After five seasons, the league seemed settled.

But the off-season would bring a few ominous signs. MLS would head into 2001 with an important victory, but it was a fight the league would much rather have avoided.

5

The Lawsuit

MLS was always an odd target for an antitrust suit. Soccer is a global game, and the best Americans were finding suitable employment overseas. Some embarked on a year-round cycle between the A-League and the various indoor leagues that later consolidated under the MISL umbrella.

Besides, courts have rarely been sympathetic to underdog sports leagues challenging the big dogs with antitrust arguments. The USFL took on the NFL in the 1980s and left court as a punchline, with an award of $1 that was tripled to $3 under antitrust law. Less publicized was the NFL's payment of several million for the fledgling league's attorney fees, but that wasn't enough to keep the USFL in business. (That check, at least, was deposited—the $3.76 check for the monetary award plus interest remained in a desk as of 2006, the *Arizona Republic* found.[1])

The first major dispute between MLS and the players was resolved in favor of the players' way: Paul Caligiuri won an arbitration case that forced the league to move him to Los Angeles in 1997. The antitrust arguments filed the same year seemed far more difficult to win.

The landscape also had changed in the three years since the players filed. In 1997, MLS was looking to improve from a whirlwind debut season. In 2000, the league was treading water, not sailing to an inevitable brighter future. MLS execs could argue that losing the lawsuit would be the league's death knell, and few could doubt them. What did the players hope to gain by suing their own league out of existence?

Sunil Gulati had moved on from his deputy commissioner post and was working for the Kraft family managing the Earthquakes and Revolution. But he would endure more than a week on the witness stand:

> I think certainly that notion [that the league could crumble with a loss in court] was there. Partly because I think a number of the investors in the league fully believed that we needed something different to get the league off the ground and stabilized, and that was the notion behind the single-entity structure. If, in its infancy, you weren't going to have that model, the league didn't make economic sense.

The league in its early years was making huge investments. The investors were making investments far greater than they had anticipated.

Alan Rothenberg shared Gulati's concern over those investments:

> I think that we've all been concerned about the state of the league probably until the last couple of years. I think had we lost it, it might've been disastrous. I think the lawsuit had our hands partially tied and a lot of people distracted and a lot of money spent on legal fees. It would've been nicer if we hadn't had a lawsuit or if we had won on a summary motion at the very beginning and had it put to rest.

Perhaps the players seemed petty in such a counterproductive suit. But Mark Semioli, one of the named plaintiffs, felt the players' challenge had a positive goal:

> I don't think it was a concern among the players that were named in the lawsuit. We had all spoken with our lawyers. The idea was to win a verdict and then use that leverage, that hammer that we didn't have, to create a system that would be mutually amenable to all the parties. One of the biggest bargaining chips would have been the damages. We'll give up a certain percentage of damages if we can have this or that, those types of things.
>
> The entire time, we had no leverage with MLS. That was something that the players had experienced from day 1. The majority of players had signed contracts with a league they weren't even chosen to be in yet.

This would've finally given the players some leverage to create a new way that MLS could run. We weren't looking to change the world, we were looking to create a more fair and honest system. So no, I had no worries about bankrupting the league.

The league's image, though, would take a few hits. Players accused the league of taking retribution against some of the agitators. For several years, for example, the Wikipedia entry for Rhett Harty, one of the players who brought the suit, claimed that he had been blacklisted from MLS for his role in the suit—a debatable but damaging accusation.

Semioli isn't sure that the case led to direct retribution against him:

I can't draw a connection. No way I can draw a connection that it was retribution. It just seemed from that point forward, things didn't go as well in my career. I got injured a little bit, but I had a couple of strong years. I don't know. It wasn't just happening to people who had their names on the lawsuit, but it was happening to other players.

From the witness stand, several players painted an ugly picture of one-sided negotiations and insulting offers from the league office—particularly from Gulati, the league's primary personnel man in the early years.

Some of the officials who had drawn players' ire were long gone by the time the case reached court, Semioli says:

I can tell you at the beginning of MLS . . . some of the people who worked in administration were also new to running the league. A lot of the people who were involved in MLS were involved with running the World Cup. Running a World Cup is one thing—running a league in the long term is altogether different.

Don Garber is a tremendous leader and ambassador for that league. He brought a sense of professionalism that was not there at the beginning. He brought it to the Major League Soccer offices, and I think it's trickled down to the way the teams are run, the way they're marketed, the TV contracts and the way things are done. I wonder if Don Garber was sitting across the table during that time, things may have not played out the way they did. Because a lot of people who were involved with

MLS at the time were also in charge of the national team, they were soccer federation guys, they had a lot of different interests on the table and MLS was only one of them. Too many hats on not enough people. Don Garber—his job is he's commissioner of MLS. His goal is to make MLS a top-notch league or whatever their mission statement is, that's his focus.

Then there were the numbers—if the $3 award was the lingering image of the USFL case, the lingering image of the MLS suit was the $250 million the league claimed to have lost over the years. Players would dispute that figure, but journalists pounced on it, some even extrapolating in future years that the league must still be losing money at that rate. Plenty of teams and leagues in professional sports turn over empty pockets at the negotiating table, but MLS and its dwindling band of investors seemed to be flushing money down the drain.

"It was a difficult experience," Gulati says. "The whole lawsuit was a difficult time for the league and relationships and all those things. In some ways, it was an intellectual exercise, because the basic premise of the case from the MLS side were legal issues and economic issues that I had a lot of interest in. The emotional side of the whole lawsuit—you're talking about people you know—was very difficult."

Logan says the league and the players had some "back-channel" talks in the early years of the suit, but nothing came of it. The important verdicts in the case would be issued in 2000. But no one really won.

THE PLAINTIFFS

Eight players brought the suit:

Semioli, a defender who started his MLS career with Los Angeles but is best remembered for his time with the MetroStars. He lost his full-time starting role in 2000 and left the league after the 2001 season. He had a unique perspective on the suit, having already started law school to prepare for his post-MLS career. Before MLS, he had played in the APSL and USISL, winning the 1994 U.S. Open Cup with San Francisco's Greek Americans.

Iain Fraser, a Scottish-born defender who had gone to Hartwick College and stuck around in the United States to play indoor soccer. He was one of the lost generation of players who had hit their 30s by the time MLS started, and he lasted just one season with New England, starting 23 games. In court, he would claim the league gave him a lowball offer in 1997, possibly in retribution for his role in the suit. He returned to the indoor game.

Steve Trittschuh, a 1990 World Cup defender who had knocked around in the APSL, Czechoslovakia, and Holland before Colorado drafted him in the third round of the inaugural draft. MLS had revitalized his career, giving him another shot at the national team while he started consistently for the Rapids. He moved on to Tampa Bay in 1999 and kept playing through 2001, leaving MLS at age 36.

Sean Bowers, another indoor veteran and four-year starting defender for Kansas City who left the league in 1999, claiming the league had offered a severely reduced salary that was far less than he could make in the indoor game. Bowers said in an interview for this book that he wound up backing into the suit, replacing Mike Sorber as the player rep from the Wizards.

Harty, an imposing defender with the MetroStars who started 57 games in two years but was pushed out in 1998. He had played some indoor and USISL soccer, though an injury kept him off the 1992 Olympic team. After his MLS career, he traveled through India and Tibet for six months before taking a job preparing pacemakers and defibrillators at an Oregon hospital, according to a bio prepared by Olympic sponsor Monster.com.

David Vaudreuil, a defender who had the longest career of any of the plaintiffs, remaining in the league as a productive player through 2002. He was a part-time starter on D.C. United's 1996 and 1997 championship teams before moving through Miami, Colorado, and Chicago.

Mark Dodd, the highest-profile player in the suit, an accomplished goal-keeper for Dallas who had been an A-League stalwart with the Colorado Foxes before MLS debuted. After three strong years, he lost his starting job in 1999, returning to share time in the playoffs but not playing again after that. Ironically, Dodd and original co-plaintiff Tim Martin had played for the national team in a game boycotted by most national-team players, a 1996 drubbing in Peru, which some players resented.

Mark Dougherty, a goalkeeper who started with Tampa Bay for two seasons and was Columbus's starter by the time the suit went to court. He would see limited action in 2001 before leaving the league.

Tim Martin and Paul Caligiuri had been initially listed as plaintiffs but were removed from the case in September 1997. Caligiuri told Michael Lewis in 1999: "It wasn't me spearheading the lawsuit. A lot of players felt that this can't go on. I wish someone would step in and would find a solution."[2]

All of the players had some professional experience before joining MLS. Semioli, Dougherty, and Harty had played with the San Francisco Bay Blackhawks in the APSL and the USISL. While the league's biggest names weren't involved, all of the players had been solid starters at some point. Harty, Dougherty, Dodd, and Bowers had been their respective teams' nominees for Defender of the Year honors at least once. Dodd was the league's Goalkeeper of the Year in 1996 and a finalist the next two years.

Several players would argue they deserved higher salaries, and some left the league after getting offers that didn't match their previous pay or an offer from elsewhere. Whether the players were losing popularity contests or simply being pushed out of their spots as the league's talent pool grew younger and better is hard to say.

And as that talent pool evolved, fewer players understood exactly what was going on with the court proceedings in their name. Many younger players weren't told much about the suit, and it wasn't really their first priority to pry.

Ben Olsen, who went on to become a leader in the players union years later, was among those who concede they knew little at the time: "It was limited information, but at the same time, I was a 20-year-old kid coming into the league. I was not concerned with that stuff. I didn't understand the league then; I didn't really understand business, rights, unions, or any of that stuff. I was really naïve in that stuff early. I didn't know about it, didn't really even care to know about it."

Jimmy Conrad, later a leader of the players union that emerged after the suit, recalls, "When I came into the league in '99, that was kind of the big white elephant in the room, something nobody really wanted to talk about it. And the people that did, they acted like they didn't know the whole story. For a young player, there was a lot of gray area about what was going on and what we were supposed to do."

The suit was technically five counts, but two wouldn't be seriously argued. From the appeal verdict issued in 2002: "Count II, a challenge to FIFA's transfer fee policies, and a state law contract claim were severed and stayed pending final resolution of this appeal."

That left three substantial arguments:

- Count I: Violations of Sherman Act section 1, by agreeing not to compete for player services. This is a typical argument in many sports—essentially, it's an argument for free agency—but it was thorny territory for the players. Much of the suit depended on challenging the league's single-entity structure. This count was in some ways a contrary argument, that the teams were separate entities colluding to keep down salaries.
- Count III: Violations of Sherman Act section 2, by attempting to monopolize the Division I market by preventing any other Division I entity from being sanctioned. The appeals verdict restated the claims "that MLS monopolized the market for Division I professional soccer in the U.S.; that it attempted to monopolize that market; and that it conspired with the USSF to monopolize the same market."
- Count IV: Violations of Clayton Act section 7, specifically that the sheer weight of money and assets the MLS investor/operators poured into the league diminished competition.[3]

Semioli explains that the tactics were driven by a larger desire to protest an unfair system:

Generally speaking, it was more than just the single-entity structure. Players were disappointed about things that they felt were very unfair. Some things came directly from having a single-entity structure, some things were placed on players without their say.

Many players signed a multiyear contract, but it was really a year-by-year because every year MLS can end that contract. So it's not really a multiyear contract. They had the right of refusal, the right to void a contract before a certain date. So in fact, it offered no security to any player. That's just one example of many where players felt they were being aggrieved.

Whether that comes from a single-entity structure or not, I don't think is really the point. However, that would not be as egregious if you knew if the L.A. Galaxy didn't want you, that you could always talk to the MetroStars, or you could always talk to the Kansas City Wizards and say, "Look, they just cut my contract, but can I sign with you?"

The issue then became if MLS cut your contract and said, we'll re-sign you, but we'll re-sign you at a lower number. You had no way to renegotiate. . . . So while single-entity was part of the issue, many of the egregious terms that were in a basic player contract were also at issue. So I don't think it was just one thing.

In order to get those changes made in court, players—but really the attorneys—found a legal strategy that would put enough pressure on MLS to attack the system.

You have to also recognize that the idea was put out to openly change the system in court. However, there were many problems informally behind the scenes and also made by our side . . . to still work within their system and also maintain the single-entity structure. They were not amenable to any of those changes.

But by the time the players had their day in court, only one count was left standing.

MLS 2, PLAYERS 0

On April 19, 2000, U.S. district judge George O'Toole Jr. kicked the guts out of the suit, granting summary judgment for the league on Counts I and IV. His opinion effectively crushed the argument against the single-entity structure.

"MLS is what it is," O'Toole said. "As a single entity, it cannot conspire or combine with its investors . . . and its investors do not combine or conspire with each other in pursuing the economic interests of the entity."[4]

That argument more or less took out Count I. Count IV would fare worse, with O'Toole's arguments crippling the players' case. First of all, O'Toole argued, this wasn't a case of a juggernaut expanding and driving out existing businesses with unfair pricing and labor practices. This was an attempt to create something out of nothing:

There can be no [section] 7 liability because the formation of MLS did not involve the acquisition or merger of existing business enterprises, but rather the formation of an entirely new entity which itself represented the creation of an entirely new market. The relevant test under [section] 7 looks to whether competition in existing markets has been reduced. . . . Competition that does not exist cannot be decreased. The creation of MLS did not reduce the competition in the existing market because when the company was formed there was no market for Division I professional soccer in the United States.[5]

And no one could guarantee that any viable competitors could have sprung forth:

The plaintiffs further argue that, even though no one was playing Division I soccer in the United States at the time MLS was created, the market nevertheless existed because the World Cup promoters had promised FIFA that a premier soccer league would be established in the United States. As a result of the promise, they say, it was inevitable that there would be such a league. The operator-investors in MLS, therefore, would likely have been competitors in a traditional soccer sports league. The formation of MLS thwarted that prospective competition, violating [section] 7. . . . More fundamentally, the flaw in the plaintiffs' existence-by-inevitability argument is that the inevitability of a professional soccer league is not the same as the inevitability of multiple competitors. Granting that there would inevitably be a league, it was not inevitable that the league would be formed and would operate the same way as previous sports leagues.[6]

Mark Abbott, who had a big hand in drawing up the plans now under fire in court, saw it in simpler terms: "The basic theory is that what's prohibited under the antitrust laws is agreements in restraint of trade. By definition, it requires two parties. . . . The single-entity theory is that there's only one actor. So I can decide anything I want by myself as long as I'm not in a combination or conspiracy or agreement with somebody else. And the court agreed with that, saying the league is free to set the player wages any way it sees fit."

Jeffrey Kessler, the players' lead attorney, pledged to appeal the summary judgment. But for the moment, O'Toole's ruling left only Count III, the argument that MLS was an illegal monopoly.

The players tried to expand that argument in June. From the appeal verdict:

Subsequently, at a June 2000 status conference on the remaining section 2 claims, players indicated (apparently for the first time) that they intended to introduce evidence that MLS prohibited all competition for players among the MLS operators/investors as part of their section 2 claim as well. The court, however, prohibited players from introducing evidence on the operation of MLS—except to the extent it provided the jury with useful background information—finding this version of players' monopoly conduct argument precluded by its earlier section 1 summary judgment decision.[7]

By the time the trial opened in September, the players were arguing with one hand tied behind their backs.

THE TRIAL

Kessler had experience taking on sports leagues. He had done so earlier in the year on behalf of NFL coach Bill Belichick, whose unexpected spurning of the New York Jets' head coaching job in favor of the New England Patriots vacancy had wound up in court. In that case, Kessler was indirectly helping Patriots owner Robert Kraft. Here, he was directly opposing Kraft along with the other MLS investors.

The lawyer's opening argument: MLS and U.S. Soccer, all doing the bidding of the Hydra that is Alan Rothenberg, conspired to subdue the A-League/APSL and force down player salaries.

Kessler said salaries were being set by the league, not by competitive forces, and that MLS players were getting a smaller share of revenues than their counterparts in other leagues—28 percent compared to 42.7 in England's Premier League, 55 percent in the NBA, 57 percent in the NHL and Major League Baseball, and 59 percent in the NFL.

He segued into his assault on Rothenberg, painting him as a sinister force who had unjustly denied the APSL's bid for Division I status. Kessler said the APSL asked for Division I status as early as 1991, when Rothenberg was U.S. Soccer president, but was named a Division II league instead. Then an MLS precursor was founded in June 1993 as a subsidiary of the 1994 World Cup Organizing Committee, all under Rothenberg. Then came the December 1993 vote: 18 votes for MLS, 5 for the APSL, none for the renegade League One America plan. Kessler cast more shadow on the proceedings, saying the ballots were destroyed.

Kessler may have had a compelling target in Rothenberg, though league officials argued that Rothenberg had been adequately recused from the decision on which league to support. Less convincing was his argument that the APSL was a viable competitor for Division I status. He said Rothenberg and company pushed to have the Division I vote early, well before MLS would be ready to launch, because they wanted to make sure the APSL didn't grow stronger with each passing year. Kessler said Rothenberg invited the APSL teams to join him, like some sort of Emperor Palpatine enticing Luke Skywalker, but the owners resisted the Dark Side of single entity.[8]

The APSL likely wasn't as strong as Kessler argued. Even without MLS as competition, the league never did much at the gate. Historian David Litterer's figures show the occasional team averaging more than 5,000 fans per game along with some low-profile cable presence, but nothing more substantial until the Rochester Rhinos pushed near five figures in 1996, ironically MLS's first year. Several teams had a couple of good years followed by a quick decline into oblivion, leaving the small league to shuffle schedules with as few as five teams. Only after the APSL changed its name to the A-League and merged with the USISL's top division in 1997 did it manage a substantial number of teams, many of them healthy.

Veteran national-team defender and U.S. Soccer board member Desmond Armstrong, who cast a ballot for MLS in the Division I vote, said his decision was strictly on merit. "I don't have any love lost for the federation," Armstrong told the *Chicago Tribune*'s Philip Hersh in a 1993 story that raised several of the conflict-of-interest issues the players would raise in court. "It wasn't a matter of playing favorites, but of getting the best proposal out there so we can have jobs. I voted for Alan's plan because it had all the t's crossed and i's dotted."[9]

MLS lead lawyer Michael Cardozo was ready to strike back at the APSL in his opening arguments, saying the rival plan would have paid players half of the money MLS offered, with a third of the players living on $15,000 a year. And even then, the teams weren't viable—a majority of them had folded since the bid for Division I status.

Cardozo also sought to keep the jury focused on the text of Count III: "This case is about one question and one question only: was it improper for the United States Soccer Federation to designate Major League Soccer as the only Division I major league soccer league in this country for two years?" That's how other countries' leagues and other U.S. sports operate, Cardozo said.

Rothenberg and U.S. Soccer had to act in 1993, Cardozo said, because FIFA, the international governing body, had prodded him with a reminder that one condition of the World Cup being awarded to the United States was the formation of a Division I league. Hersh wrote in 1993: "The conflict-of-interest problems inherent in the decision-making process have overshadowed the fact that Rothenberg's plan was, for better or worse, seen as the most likely to succeed. . . . FIFA officials asked that a preliminary league plan be available for their review at meetings leading up to next Sunday's World Cup draw in Las Vegas."

And a Division I league wasn't easy to run, Cardozo said. "MLS is still a very, very fragile start-up company. It is fighting to gain fans and gain advertisers, and so far it hasn't succeeded. It hopes it will. It succeeded in doing one thing. It has succeeded in improving the prospects of the very people who have brought this lawsuit, the soccer players."[10]

In the midst of that came the startling admission: The league had lost $250 million. And the franchise value had dwindled, from the $25 million initial investment for each team to a recent offer of less than $10 million.

Besides, MLS wasn't a monopoly, Cardozo said. Players who weren't making much in MLS but could be stars in the A-League or indoor soccer were free to take more money there. Overseas competition also had forced MLS to renegotiate nearly one-third of its contracts in the past 12 months.

The last point would be one of the most contentious as the players took the stand. Dodd would try to state England's restrictive work permit rules, which kept several worthy American players out of the 92 professional English teams, while MLS lawyers objected. Gulati would counter in his time on the stand, running through an MLS media guide and naming players who had spent time overseas. Mark Dodd's point about England was valid, as unjustly denied players such as Brad Friedel could attest, but Gulati was able to at least nullify the point if not refute it entirely.

Gulati didn't think his testimony on the international market was a major turning point in the case but says it was "a very powerful tool. Michael Cardozo . . . would name a player and I was standing up and in one set of exercises, I would literally place a flag or a checkmark on a big board where a player came from or went to. . . . Since the trial in the end hinged on the definition of the labor market, that was a very important exercise."

The players left themselves open for withering cross-examination when making another point about Europe. Dodd was the first of several to claim that England's Premier League and First Division were both Division I leagues. Anyone who follows soccer, much less a U.S. Soccer or MLS lawyer, can easily refute that argument by pointing out that teams are relegated from the Premier League to the lower division. Perhaps both leagues had good players and good teams, but that argument could be made about MLS and the A-League, particularly with the A-League's Rochester Raging Rhinos holding the Open Cup trophy.

In cross-examination, Kessler grilled Gulati on England's leagues to such an extent that MLS lawyers cried foul. "They questioned me very aggressively on what, as it turned out, was completely misinformation and ended up, in front of the jury, having to apologize to me for having no basis for what he was saying," Gulati says. "That was pretty important."

Errors aside, the players had a difficult case to make under the constraints of arguing Count III only. Rather than arguing the merits of single entity—the part of the case that would work its way into many a law school syllabus—the plaintiffs were forced to spend hours asking tedious questions to establish conflicts of interest in Rothenberg and Gulati's roles with MLS, U.S. Soccer, and the World Cup committee. Gulati, who spent several days on the witness stand, wound up with the chore of explaining the composition of the various boards and committees that served as checks on Rothenberg's power. Ultimately, Gulati explained, the people who voted to award Division I status to MLS and not to the APSL were not beholden to Rothenberg. Gulati noted that he himself had been on the losing side of multiple U.S. Soccer elections.

Nor could many people with knowledge of soccer politics believe that the players involved in the decision would vote for Rothenberg out of fear for their paychecks. In fact, Desmond Armstrong was cut from the 1994 World Cup squad even though he went public with his vote in favor of MLS. Peter Vermes, who was eligible to vote, also didn't make the 1994 roster.

Regardless of any Rothenberg conspiracy, the players' argument hinged on a practical question: would players be better off if U.S. Soccer had established two Division I leagues? Rothenberg's answer from the stand: "If there were two competing leagues, the quality of play would have been so pathetic, it would have been gone overnight. There weren't enough players to go around." Columnist Paul Gardner put it bluntly: "Anyone who knows anything about the history of the APSL knows that it has never had anything approaching financial stability. Yet the players' case depended heavily on making out that the APSL had a bunch of seriously rich owners. The jury obviously did not buy that. Nor did it buy the even more ridiculous claim that the U.S. soccer market would support two Division I pro leagues."[11]

Fellow *Soccer America* columnist Ridge Mahoney agreed: "That the APSL, which consisted of seven teams at the time, could have some day attained the status of a full-fledged professional league if not for the U.S. Soccer decree is far-fetched, if not ludicrous. . . . According to an APSL business plan presented by the players' attorneys, the highest-paid APSL player earned $125,000, the lowest-paid players received $3,000, and the league intended to spend zero money on transfers."[12]

Semioli, who had a good experience in the APSL, didn't rule out the league's chances of putting forth a viable Division I product: "But who's to say if you let the A-League do it, they couldn't have done the same thing?"

The players called sports economist Andrew Zimbalist to show how Division I competition could have driven up salaries. Harty's 1996 salary, to give one example, would've been $115,275 instead of $41,356. Gardner was unimpressed: "For an entire session, this totally fictitious exercise dragged on, as the good Professor Zimbalist revealed charts and calculations to 'prove' what must have happened had a whole series of improbable conditions existed. They never did exist."[13]

John Kerr Sr. insisted to *Soccer America* that American leagues set a precedent for competition:

> The American Football League, the World Hockey League, the USFL, all of these other leagues came into business, but they didn't have to ask the USSF [U.S. Soccer Federation] for Division I status. They put money together and decided to go into competition. Then the consumers decided if they'll support one league or the other. There's no governing body from anywhere that can decide if another professional football league can exist, or another baseball league or basketball league.[14]

True, but the USFL had forced salaries to rise in a sport that was solidly established as a cash cow. Could anyone make the same argument for competing soccer leagues? And the APSL had several years to establish itself in the soccer marketplace before the Division I argument boiled over. Dodd painted a nice picture of his life in the APSL before MLS debuted and seemed eager to speculate on other players' salaries and situations (despite many objections) under direct examination, but he suddenly clammed up when he was asked whether he ate up most of the APSL Colorado Foxes' player budget.

In fact, the system of a Division I MLS and Division II A-League, along with the indoor game, seemed to suit the top-tier Division II players quite well. Gulati mentions three players—Henry Gutierrez, Scott Schweitzer, and Hector Marinaro—who turned down MLS deals to play in the A-League and/ or indoor. Bowers, who, according to his testimony, earned no more than a peak annual salary of $73,387 in MLS, found Kansas City unwilling to keep him past 1999. MLS offered him $48,000 to stay in the player pool, but he took an $80,000 offer from the Detroit Rockers, slightly outbidding the Baltimore Blast.[15]

The very best U.S. players could opt to collect millions in Europe or a high salary in MLS. The next tier of players would be well compensated in MLS. Beyond that, players had a choice—relative stardom and the top of the lower leagues' pay scale, or a bench spot and slightly lower pay in MLS. Some players, such as Bowers, might simply be better suited to the indoor game, whether they'd like to embrace that talent or not.

International leagues were also a viable option. Yes, work-permit rules were an obstacle in some countries. But Gulati's testimony helped. Since the lawsuit, MLS has faced far greater competition from overseas—Scandinavian leagues in particular seem inclined to raid MLS and poach fringe national-team players who can't quite command top dollar in the United States.

Besides, the single-entity structure had shown some flexibility. Ivan Gazidis, who later took over as deputy commissioner, explains the evolution since that frenetic first year:

> During the next two to three years under Sunil, that system was a work in progress, and it evolved from year to year and month to month as we gained experience about how this unique salary cap in an international market could work. After Sunil left, my first priority was really to try and provide more order to that system.
>
> So over the next number of years, we developed a more and more orderly system, less and less league decisions that were happening as a

result of league discretion. Instead what we have worked to create is a framework within which our teams can operate that is relatively understandable.

At the end of the day, the league is still creating that framework, the decisions are still made collectively by the owners, through the league, but teams have more flexibility as to how they want to make up their own roster, as to how they want to use these procedures to best serve their team. The league has less and less instances where it acts as a one-off basis. I don't want to say it never happens, but it's less and less over time.

THE VERDICT

Immediately after the close of testimony, the court dismissed MLS investor/operators as defendants, leaving only MLS and U.S. Soccer.

On December 11, the jury returned the verdict. MLS and U.S. Soccer won. The jury had been given a list of questions to answer but found it only needed to address the first two to find that MLS was not a monopoly. Mahoney's summary for *Soccer America*: "Once the jurors decided both a global market existed and other domestic entities could compete with MLS for players, the players' case collapsed. No further deliberations were necessary since the jurors had determined the monopoly alleged by the players did not exist."[16]

Logan, who still retained an ownership interest in the league, agreed: "At the end of the day, we were able to conclusively prove that the market was the world instead of the United States."

Semioli was disappointed that the jury saw it that way:

A big reason why the case was lost was on the market. The market was a strong argument for MLS. In order to have a monopolization claim, you have to identify the market. And if you can claim it's not just American soccer but it's a global market, then you have a chance.

So if you can't play in America, go play in Europe. I don't think they understood that there are obstacles to playing in Europe. It wasn't like I could go to Europe and play in the English first division. I have to get a work permit. So it's not realistic to me that England is part of my market. I could be very good, they could want me, but if I haven't played for my national team, that's not going to happen.

I think the jury just saw it as, "Look, go play somewhere else." After months and months of trial, maybe they got lost in minutiae as well. Perhaps they had the right to.

One mildly embarrassing aftershock of the case: Mahoney reported that the eight plaintiffs would've received $1.5 million if they'd won, which was news to some players.[17] Semioli, though, says the money wouldn't have gone into players' pockets:

> We had all spoken about using our damages to fund the players associa-
> tion and go forward. So it wasn't a money thing for me at all. If I wanted
> money, I wouldn't have played soccer in America. If I wanted money, I
> wouldn't be a teacher. I think all the people that put their name on that
> suit . . . it wasn't about the money. It was about the fairness of the system
> that wasn't treating good people in a fair and honest way. That's what it
> was about for me.

Semioli also says the damages would've given players some bargaining power. The plaintiffs could have offered to give back some money in exchange for a few changes to the system.

Kessler immediately pledged an appeal, despite the pleadings of pundits such as Gardner.

Count III, contested at trial, would be appealed with several allegations of procedural mistakes in court. The players also would appeal the summary judgment on Counts I and IV.

Meanwhile, some players had more questions than answers. Conrad was skeptical of the NFLPA's role: "Nobody knew what was going on. The NFLPA got involved. It's just hard to know what their motives were. This is just a young player's outside perspective: why is the NFLPA getting involved at all? It almost felt like they held us back more than they helped us. . . . There was that cynicism from me and some of the younger guys."

The veterans weren't necessarily happy with the NFLPA, either, wondering if they were motivated by a single-entity challenge rather than any benevolence toward soccer players. "I think they were," Agoos says. "If you asked them, they would say no, but I think they saw [single entity] as a threat to their league. If they had a single entity, it would destroy the players' rights and freedoms, and that's what they're all about. I really didn't understand the setup. I didn't understand why we were being fronted by them, why they were representing us, and in the end, I think it was a bad decision on the players to have to go forward with that."

And Logan certainly thought so: "I don't think they were as worried about what was going [on] in soccer and they were significantly more worried that someday the NFL or their successors might try the same thing if we were successful."

And was there a league-wide vote on the appeal? "Not that I recall," Conrad says. He continues:

> I don't remember ever being sat down and saying, hey this is the story, this is what we want to do, let's vote. I don't remember that happening at all. There was, at that point, a new wave of players coming in that just didn't understand what was going on. Due to the lack of knowledge, we were saying, well screw it, then. There was nobody coming up and saying, hey, we're doing this because. Not that I remember.
>
> When you're breaking into the league, you're just happy to be here. You're not really thinking long-term and that your decisions now are going to affect the future generations and how the sport is received in this country. That's a lot of responsibility on the young player, something we're still trying to talk to our younger players about.
>
> I don't really know for sure who knew what. There was a lot of pessimism about the situation, and I think everybody just wanted it to be over and then we could form a union and go.

Logan recalls, "That probably was done at the highest level . . . I think labor guys made that decision. There was probably very little from the standpoint of player involvement."

Semioli says the plaintiffs frequently had conference calls, and other players were usually invited:

> I would update the players on what's going on with the lawsuit from time to time whether it was formally or informally. I probably told the team what went down and I said these are the options, we're going to

have a conference call. Most of the players said, "You're a good representative, whatever you think is best." . . .

Most players said, "OK, if you're going to be on the call, just report
back and let me know what's going on."

Besides, the decision to appeal came during the off-season, when
players weren't in regular contact.

The appeal added 16 months to the legal wrangling. On March 20, 2002,
the First Circuit Court of Appeals gave a lengthy opinion that would give legal
scholars plenty to discuss for years to come. But the result was the same.

Count I, the direct challenge to single entity that O'Toole had rejected
with little fuss, gave the court an opportunity to expound upon the innovative
business idea, drawing comparisons to the landmark case *Copperweld Corp. v.
Independence Tube Corp.* The judges seemed unsure that MLS was a true single
entity, calling it a "hybrid" at one stage of the argument. Yet the judges virtually
conceded that this was of more interest for future cases than for this one and
concluded "that the single-entity problem need not be answered definitively
in this case."[18]

As for this case, the court found that MLS's structure hardly depressed
salaries:

> MLS and its investors did not compete previously; the arrangement was
> formed as a risky venture against a background of prior failure . . . and
> the outcome has been to add new opportunities for players—a Divi-
> sion I soccer league in the United States—and to raise salaries for soccer
> players here above existing levels. The possibility that a less integrated
> and restrictive salary regime might make some individual salaries even
> higher is hardly conclusive. Without the restrictions, MLS might not ex-
> ist or, if it did, might have larger initial losses and a shorter life. This
> would hardly enhance competition.[19]

On Count IV, the court once again added a few wrinkles for legal scholars
to digest. But when it came to soccer, the court was unmoved:

> The evidence indicates that the APSL was not as well financed or well
> managed as MLS (hence the USSF's decision to certify MLS and not the

APSL), thus increasing the risk that the new Division I league would fail in the long run. In addition, elevating the APSL to Division I status would not necessarily increase competition significantly, since the APSL, an existing minor league, may have already been in the relevant market.[20]

Garth Lagerwey, who went to law school at Georgetown after his playing career and practiced at Latham & Watkins before moving into Real Salt Lake management, believes the appellate opinion backed the players' belief that the single-entity arguments were the strong point of the suit:

> We tried to argue the single entity as being an illegal enterprise and a sham, and that was the count that was dismissed in summary judgment. We always felt that was the stronger legal claim. It's a case that's now studied in the law-school textbooks. At the end of the day, what it represented ultimately was that the judicial system was going to choose not to interfere in imposing legal judgments onto labor processes. They wanted to try to push everybody towards collective bargaining. And so as a result, we really didn't get a ruling on the merits of that claim. That's the way the judge came out. The appeals court basically found compelling reasons why we should've had the ability to argue the merits but ultimately decided not to overturn it. They left that summary judgment be and that was it. That's how the legal system works sometimes. You have claims that are better or stronger than others, and sometimes you take a crack at 'em. Sometimes you don't.
>
> Was it wise to go forward with the monopoly count argument and spend all the money even when you thought you were probably going to lose? I'll leave that to the professional, established litigators. Suffice to say it didn't work.

On Count III, which had been disputed for three months in the trial, the court spent much of its opinion sifting through the players' accusations of courtroom errors. Among them was that O'Toole should have allowed into evidence some correspondence between Clark Hunt, Lamar Hunt's son and business partner, and MLS executive Mark Abbott. Hunt had asked Abbott to trim the team salary budget by $70,000, suggesting that the cuts could come at the expense of the bottom 12 players on the roster "whose only alternative is to play in one of the other U.S. professional leagues or one of the lower division foreign leagues." The court ruled that other evidence made the letter redundant.

The players also argued that an A-League team co-owner, Seattle's Neil Farnsworth, should not have been allowed to testify that his team was competing with MLS for the services of two players because he declined to give their names. The court disagreed, saying other witnesses established that players were moving between leagues.

Where the players saw monopoly, the court saw competition: "The exclusivity agreement sought by MLS might be unlawful if it threatened adverse competitive effects but not otherwise; and this in turn required proof that someone who was the only purchaser of Division I soccer player services in the United States would control prices in an economic market."[21]

That's the verdict on legal grounds. On practical grounds, MLS had the persuasive argument that two competing leagues would've met the same fate as the NASL teams competing with the Cosmos—oblivion. Given the history of soccer in this country, prospective MLS investors couldn't be blamed for seeking some assurance that costs would be kept reasonable.

Perhaps emboldened by the theoretical legal hair-splitting in the opinion, the players pressed on to the U.S. Supreme Court. On October 7, 2002, the country's top judges declined to take up the case. A lawsuit that had hung over six of MLS's seven seasons was finally over.

THE AFTERMATH

The league won, but it suffered a few bruises along the way. The players were able to make MLS look heavy-handed at the very least, limiting their commercial opportunities and forcing them to deal with Gulati in New York rather than a locally based general manager. Perhaps the players' case wasn't strong enough for court, but the public had the right to ask if they deserved free agency.

While the players may have had legitimate grievances that they would address down the road in collective bargaining, the lawsuit cost them dearly. MLS said it had spent millions in legal fees, and that left the league in little mood to splash cash around. Richard Motzkin, from his unique perspective as a former U.S. Soccer general counsel turned player-agent, told Mahoney that "the lawsuit is part of the reason the league is looking very seriously at expenses across the board. This year, in particular, players are going to feel the brunt of it because there's a sufficient degree of frustration by the owners with the players for pursuing a lawsuit they don't believe makes a lot of sense."[22]

Players interviewed for this book still see some validity to the arguments even if they're unsure about the way the case was handled. Jimmy Conrad says:

> I think you can appreciate the merits of their argument. I think it probably would've been—always in hindsight—better to maybe wait and see how things played out before they started getting into it. Maybe if we had set up a players union then, we probably would've been a lot farther along from a player's perspective in terms of having a voice in the decisions the league makes. Clearly in hindsight, it doesn't look like a great decision. But at the time, you can understand why they were doing that and what they were fighting for. It's unfortunate it got dragged out as long as it did.

Alexi Lalas, now a veteran manager as well as a Hall of Fame player, also thinks labor progress was ultimately inhibited:

> The lawsuit itself I don't think was a mistake. I think "mistake" is too harsh a word. . . . It was a situation where we ended wasting a lot of time and more importantly wasting a lot of money. When we're going into our second [collective bargaining agreement] in the next couple of years, we should in reality be going into our third or fourth, had we had our ducks in order early on in the league's existence. But, live and learn. The day-to-day dealings as a player weren't dramatically affected by the lawsuit. It hung over everything with the understanding that this whole single-entity concept was ultimately what was at stake. We as players just recognized that it was part of what our representation was doing. We all testified at a certain point, guys said different things. It was difficult to a certain extent because we were in U.S. court dealing with an international game, and dealing with a game that in the United States was still very new.

The nuances, the understanding of how the game of soccer works, and the perspective on the international game was probably sometimes either lost or exaggerated.

Agoos recalls, "With the benefit of hindsight, I think it was the wrong thing to do. We lost any benefit of leverage we had as a players union at that point, we lost the lawsuit, I think it set the players back a number of years, nothing really got done for eight years, maybe? I think it would've worked better had we tried to negotiate rather than going straight to the lawsuit."

Semioli, who had voted for collective bargaining before putting his name on the suit, says he thought one advantage of suing was that it would go faster. But the legal system did no favors for any party:

I thought "Sue, do a little discovery, get a court date, bam, it's gone. See what happens. A year, maybe two years. Win, lose." Unfortunately—and these are things that you can't control—a judge that wanted no part of it, a judge who spent a long time in deciding matters that could've been handled quickly . . . a lot of things that you wouldn't think could've gone wrong went wrong.

All the legalese . . . a lot of that started rearing its ugly head after the judge would not move on the case. You can't choose your judge; you roll the dice. Unfortunately, it took way longer than we all expected. It was very frustrating to all the players including myself. It did no great things to my career. . . . Some things we probably could've done better. . . . I think we all regretted that it took that long.

Motzkin, though he says the single-entity structure is challenging for agents like him, is more direct in second-guessing the suit:

I'll tell you it was a mistake. I don't think the approach initially taken with the NFL Players Association was the right approach. Certainly history more than reinforces that point. Everyone has their own opinion about what happened in that situation. I'm not sure whether the motivation of the NFLPA was to operate in the best interest of soccer players or whether the motivation was to try to fight against the single-entity structure and challenge that it was an illegal organizational structure. What certainly did turn out was that on both accounts they were off.

For the players, there weren't a million people out there raising their hands and saying, "Hey, let us help you out." The fact that someone was approaching them and expressing that interest was something that was certainly enticing to a lot of players. If somebody had looked at it solely from what was the best interest for soccer players, the approach they took would've been far different than the one the NFLPA took.

If the NFLPA was out to discredit the single-entity approach, it failed miserably. Other U.S. leagues now use similar systems.

"The single entity revolutionized professional sports," Lagerwey says. "Mark Abbott's a genius. . . . [Abbott, Gazidis, and Rothenberg] thought of how to legally proof it so it was going to withstand scrutiny. My hat's off to them that they were able to do it. You have to look back now as a fan of the league and say perhaps there's some merit to the system. It's not for me to say how it works and whether it works well, but it stood up. Clearly the thought those guys put into it was valid and was found valid in a court of law."

Says Rothenberg:

I kick myself for not getting intellectual property protection so I could've gotten some royalties from all that. In all seriousness, I take some pride, but I must say that it should've been pretty obvious. Once we did it and once we passed the antitrust test in the courts, others would follow suit.

Logan says a minor hockey league had made a successful run with single entity but hadn't been challenged because "there weren't enough bucks to argue about." The unofficial interested party was the NBA and its women's league: "I had a conversation with [NBA commissioner] David Stern when we first got served. He said now you've arrived. You've got your first antitrust case—you're in the big time. There was no doubt that there was going to be a test case like this."

What's interesting is that the WNBA was a single entity in its inception— it isn't today. But they came after we did. So as a result, they were very, very interested in what was going on for us and followed the pleadings very, very carefully. We, I think, gave them an opportunity to participate with us in defending, but they said, no we'll just watch. Which was a good business decision.

The league won, but the headlines of $250 million losses were larger than those vindicating the arcane details of single entity. The players lost a case and left a transcript of embarrassing comments in their wake, though it didn't keep Trittschuh and Dougherty from taking coaching jobs with MLS and U.S. national teams down the road. All the players had accomplished was to put MLS officials in the awkward position of admitting in court that soccer is a tough sell in the United States, which isn't what they would want to tell investors.

Even the soccer leagues and organizers who weren't part of the suit came out sullied. MLS lawyers had been forced to portray the APSL as a bumbling league that couldn't possibly have pulled off a Division I effort. And the indoor leagues couldn't have been happy to see Sean Bowers, a marquee player by the standards of the fading sport, proclaim in court that he always considered himself an outdoor player.

Semioli does see a small silver lining from the years of legal wrangling:

All the information that did come out sure helped people negotiate that collective bargaining agreement down the road. I feel bad for the players that played during that time and weren't able to get some of the benefits that the collective bargaining agreement has now. . . .

I learned a lot more about the league I had never known from the time I was playing. There's a lot out there that really complicated the issue from both sides. It's not as simple as it looks. It's not just angry players or unfair management. It's a lot more complicated than that.

But he doesn't describe it as a positive experience by any means: "It was a tremendous burden for me and it was hard to focus on other things at the time. People would ask every day, 'What's going on with the trial?' It became, rather than being 'Mark, the soccer player,' I was 'one of the guys that's suing MLS.' . . . It was a somewhat time-consuming process, and it definitely took a psychological toll and a physical toll, a little bit, on me."

As it had done so many times in the past, U.S. soccer had split itself apart to the sport's detriment. The difference this time was that the leagues stayed in business.

6

The Low Point

The lawsuit victory gave MLS a momentum boost, though the appeal would hang over the league for another full season. At the very least, the jury had handed pro soccer a stay of execution.

In 2001, MLS lost one owner-investor and gained another one. Silicon Valley Sports & Entertainment, owner of the San Jose Sharks hockey team, took over operating rights of the Earthquakes from the Kraft family, which concentrated its efforts on New England. SVS&E had an option to buy the Earthquakes, just as Kraft had declined. Philip Anschutz took on a similar deal with D.C. United, where Washington Soccer L.P. had kept the team on the market for two years and finally given control to the league. Anschutz and Lamar Hunt's family now controlled half the league.

D.C. United also took the first step toward a traditional European club system, starting a youth team and entering competition in the Super Y-League, a recent project of the USL (United Soccer Leagues). The USL had dropped a couple of letters from "USISL" and had built a neat pyramid of semipro and amateur levels underneath the A-League. Chicago, New England, and the MetroStars followed suit. The MetroStars already had an informal reserve team playing locally.

The baby steps behind the scenes were important, but they weren't anything that would put the league in the spotlight. The Los Angeles Galaxy, though, gave MLS a chance to leap onto the international stage. FIFA was attempting to broaden the annual club championship, a single game between the South American champion and European champion, into a small-scale

World Cup for clubs. The World Club Championship would include the CONCACAF (Confederation of North, Central American, and Caribbean Association Football) champion. In the MLS preseason, the Galaxy beat Honduran club Real España on penalty kicks, went to another penalty shootout to get past D.C. United, and then took the CONCACAF title with a 3-2 win over a second Honduran club, Olimpia. Perhaps the Galaxy were lucky to have avoided the Mexican clubs in the draw, but that didn't matter—Los Angeles would appear in the World Club Championship draw along with the champions of Europe, South America, and elsewhere. D.C. United had won the CONCACAF title in 1998 and beaten Brazil's Vasco da Gama to lift the Interamerican Cup, but the press hardly noticed. The FIFA event would surely get much more attention.

A year after landing Lothar Matthäus and Hristo Stoitchkov, MLS didn't do much business in the European market. John Spencer, a target forward from Scotland, had a much lower profile than the past year's signings but did quite well on the field, scoring 14 goals for Colorado.

For a change, the newsworthy player joining the league was American. Landon Donovan, a California prodigy who had won the Golden Ball as the most valuable player in the 1999 Under-17 World Championships, was rescued from the drudgery of reserve games with Germany's Bayer Leverkusen and assigned to San Jose. Donovan recalls:

> At that age, not having been around a pro game at all, I didn't know what to expect. Kids now kind of know the game, when they play in college they watch MLS and they know what it's about. I was in Germany training and playing in the lower divisions, but I didn't know what to expect.
>
> I remember the first practice very vividly. I was excited to be in a place where I felt like I was wanted. And I think there was some genuine excitement about me being there from the team. I just felt like it was nice to be somewhere where I kind of fit in.
>
> I was ecstatic just to be playing. I came from Germany where everything in my mind at that time was so bad and so grim. The reality is it wasn't so bad, but in my mind, it was. I was just happy to be playing and getting a chance to play.

Donovan had a reluctant teammate in Jeff Agoos, the latest casualty of D.C. United's annual salary purge. The defender initially told San Jose coach Frank Yallop he didn't want to report to the Earthquakes. He changed his mind before too much time had elapsed, but it's a long story Agoos tells, starting with a national-team post-game interview in which he got a surprising question:

As I was coming out of the gate where the media is, a couple of people asked me, "What do you think about the trade?" I said, "I'm not sure what you're talking about." I thought they were referring to someone else in the league. They said, "How do you feel about going to San Jose?" I said, "I'm not sure what you're talking about." So obviously I had some red flags pop up.

I got on the team bus, called my agent at the time, and said, "What's going on?" He said, "I don't know, I'll find out." He made a couple of calls and said there may be a trade. I said, "Tell them I don't want to do it."

A couple of minutes later at the hotel, [coach] Thomas Rongen and [general manager] Kevin Payne show up and tell me we've made a trade. At the time, San Jose was the worst team in the league for a number of years. I asked them had the deal been done, and they said, "Yeah, it's done." So there was nothing I could say at that point. I was obviously very upset.

Frank and Dom [Kinnear] came in, and I listened to what they had to say, and I told Frank straight out, I'm not coming to San Jose, I'm not gonna go there, I've got a lot of things tied up in D.C., I've got a history there, and if I have to, I just won't play any more. We had a 5- or 10-minute conversation, and when I told him that, I saw his eyes pop open because he traded quite a lot to get me.

I guess I can look back on it now and always be thankful for him taking that chance on me. As we moved further on, it took a couple of days for everything to settle in. I spoke to my agent, spoke to my family, spoke to my brother. My brother basically told me you never know what's gonna happen, it could be a good thing. . . . He was the coach at Cal [University of California] at that time, so he was a little closer to the situation. Also because he was at Cal, he was close, so I thought why not. Over the next couple of weeks, we got to a point where I said, "All right, Frank, I'm gonna come. I'm gonna give it a shot."

I think I came in late due to national-team commitments. The first practice that I was there, it was basically a completely different team. There were just a couple of people that were holdovers. . . . I knew there was something different. It was a good group of guys. Ronnie Ekelund had just come in. I thought there was something special that could be done.

As things started moving along, we got to our first game. We were going to play L.A., who over time had been the best team in the league. I remember the first half of that game, and I think we completely destroyed L.A. in the first 45 minutes and were up 3-0, and I said I can't believe how well this is going. I couldn't imagine it being this good. L.A. came back in the second half and got closer but we eventually won it.

I give a lot of credit to Frank and to Dom because they put a lot of faith in me. They trusted me, and they made me the focal point of the team. They made me the captain. Looking back, it was probably one of the best things that could've happened to me.

To everyone's surprise and Yallop's delight, Agoos's career got a second wind in San Jose. He not only won MLS Defender of the Year honors but also became the first defender (excluding goalkeeper Tony Meola, the 2000 MVP) to finish in the final three in MVP balloting.

The Earthquakes improved dramatically, with Donovan joining Ronald Cerritos and Manny Lagos in a balanced attack while Agoos and goalkeeper Joe Cannon conceded barely more than a goal per game. But the league's most impressive team was built in Miami.

Ray Hudson was one of those old English-bred NASL players who liked the United States so much he decided not to leave. He took an assortment of odd jobs in Florida and joined the Fusion as a community outreach manager and TV analyst, where he unleashed a steady stream of passion and wit on the team's broadcasts to earn a cult following among the locals and some MLS Shootout subscribers. Early in the 2000 season, with the Fusion struggling at 1-3-4, Hudson got the call to jump from the broadcast booth to the sideline to replace Ivo Wortmann.

With Hudson in charge for his first full season, the Fusion had a potent mix of nastiness and skill, able to move the ball around the field like the Harlem Globetrotters of soccer while disrupting intrusions into their half of the field like a pack of wild dogs. Englishman Ian Bishop was a rough customer in midfield but also one of the top assist men in the league with 13. Ivan McKinley, acquired in 2000 in a deal with New England for the peripatetic Eric Wynalda, would leave MLS sharing the career record for yellow cards with 56 in 174 games and sole possession of the red-card record (seven), yet he could easily cope with the ball at his feet. Carlos Llamosa, another player who couldn't fit into D.C. United's budget, and Pablo Mastroeni would end the season as finalists for Defender of the Year honors, while second-year goalkeeper Nick Rimando matured into a solid starter.

The shrewd dealing of general manager Doug Hamilton also put two of the league's all-time best in midfield—Preki and Chris Henderson. While Henderson and Jim Rooney put up solid numbers as the fourth or fifth attacking options on a loaded team, Preki chipped in 14 assists, dismissing any idea that he was washed up at age 38. Preki and Bishop were third and fourth in the league's assist totals behind Columbus's John Wilmar Perez and yet another Fusion player—Diego Serna, who joined the exclusive 15-15 club with exactly 15 goals and 15 assists.

And while Serna was the second-leading goal scorer in the league, he wasn't even No. 1 on his team. That honor went to Honduran newcomer Alex Pineda Chacon, who led the league with 19 goals. He also took MVP honors ahead of fellow finalists Serna and Agoos.

While Miami ran away in the East, Chicago kept its stranglehold on the Central. The Fire dealt for Wynalda and were rewarded when the one-time dominant force on the national team regained his form after years of injury problems. Zach Thornton posted nine shutouts for the league's stingiest defense.

Out West, Los Angeles nipped ahead of surging San Jose. Once again, the Galaxy survived without an elite scorer but managed a healthy offense and got another good year from the defense and goalkeeper Kevin Hartman.

The defense included a player coming out of retirement. Alexi Lalas decided his broadcasting and music career could wait, signing with the Galaxy as an inaptly named "discovery player"—the term MLS uses for a player signed outside the draft and lacking the marquee status of the elite players, allocated through a different process—after enjoying a sabbatical of sorts. Lalas says:

> I also was able to look at [the game] much more from a fan perspective and travel around to these different places that I had only come to once a year or twice a year as a member of the opposing team and be in an environment that didn't involve me running around or that competitive part of it and to enjoy the game. I started to see some of the generation that had grown up watching MLS and started to meet these folks, whether it was in the parking lot before the game or out in the street or actually in the stadium. We recognized that we had developed, even at that point, a real family and a growing family of MLS people. It was fun to get into that. But it was also fun to not have to think about soccer 24 hours a day.

So what brought Lalas back?

> I started thinking about soccer 24 hours a day again. I think from a personal perspective, I did what I needed to do in terms of getting away from the game. I got that part of my life in order. If I'm honest with myself, I became a much better person for spending that time away. I got a little bit more mature in the way I behaved and the way that I approached life. I got the itch back and wanted to play. I was still 30 years old. And I was living in Southern California, and I called up Sigi and said, "Look, I'm hanging around, I'd love to come out and train." They were in the midst of their training, and he invited me out. I started training and doing what I was doing.
>
> After a couple of trainings—I was just doing it for fun, I wanted to run around for a little bit—he pulled me aside and said, listen, if you're thinking about coming back, we'd love to have you here. We would love to give you the opportunity. I sat down and said, "You know what, I want to play again. I want to do this." To be given the opportunity to do it in L.A., where I was looking at as my home, was great.
>
> That was at the point where we still had "replacement allocations" and all that. In Kansas City, I had left, and they had gotten Miklos

Molnar with their replacement allocation and gone on to win the championship. I was still in theory a Kansas City player, but then, it ended up being that L.A. "discovered" me, so Sigi was able to get my rights, and I started the second chapter of my MLS career and what proved to be a much more successful chapter of my MLS career.

SHARING THE STAGE

While an appeals court considered the lawsuit complaining that MLS and U.S. Soccer conspired to allow only one Division I soccer league, a second Division I soccer league started play, this one legitimately claiming many of the best players in the world. One catch: it was a women's league.

The WUSA (Women's United Soccer Association) and MLS had more of an arm-twister handshake than a shotgun wedding. No one involved with MLS could've been happy to hear, over and over again, that soccer-playing women had succeeded where men had failed. Yes, the Women's World Cup had been a stunning success, but the crowds had been even bigger when the men's tournament came to the United States in 1994. Common sense, especially among those who had seen devastating in-fighting in the past, dictated some sort of cooperation between the leagues.

The women's league debuted in Washington much as MLS had debuted in San Jose, with pregame festivities doused in history, a large and enthusiastic crowd (34,148), and ragged play between two teams that didn't know each other that well.

A few weeks later, RFK Stadium again drew a substantial crowd for a novel experiment: a doubleheader featuring the WUSA's Washington Freedom and MLS's D.C. United. The experiment worked. United and the Freedom didn't draw from the same fan base, but the supporters had enough of an overlap to coexist for a festive day with a crowd of 36,528, greater than the WUSA's debut. The Freedom game started with the typical WUSA crowd of families, then grew as more and more United diehards made their way into the stadium. The noise level grew, too. Freedom goalkeeper Siri Mullinix, an NCAA champion with North Carolina and the USA's keeper in the 2000 Olympics, was overwhelmed by the singing and drums as United fans mixed their European and Latin-American influences with the screaming youngsters on hand to see Mia Hamm, the only American soccer figure of the time whose fame truly transcended her sport. Helped in part by the double-headers, D.C. United led the league in attendance despite a last-place finish.

The league's newest star, Landon Donovan, took to the spotlight in the All-Star Game, scoring four goals in a 6-6 tie and shedding his shirt to reveal a sports bra in the style of Brandi Chastain.

But the summer of 2001 would close on a somber note, for MLS and all Americans.

THE INTERRUPTED SEASON

FIFA was responsible for the first hitch in MLS's summer plans, canceling the World Club Championship in May. The European powers, who had little to gain from the tournament other than the potential for an embarrassing loss to an unknown team, were never really on board, and the tournament wouldn't survive the collapse of FIFA marketing partner ISL. Los Angeles, due to play Spanish giant Real Madrid along with Ghana's Hearts of Oak and Japan's Jubilo Iwata, was left with a gaping hole in its July/August schedule. MLS lost the opportunity for international exposure, not to mention a likely seven-figure payday.

That loss paled in comparison, of course, to what happened on September 11. With the country reeling and the economy bruised, the fortunes of a soccer league seemed a low priority.

Indeed, few American athletes played their sports in the next few days. But some soccer players would be exceptions, and not just those plying their trade in Europe.

Eddie Johnson and Santino Quaranta, along with several players soon to make their way to MLS, were already in Trinidad and Tobago for the Under-17 World Cup. Undoubtedly unnerved and grief-stricken by events back home, the team played on but finished far worse than expected, surely far worse than they would have if their hearts had been in the games.

Kansas City was already in Peru and played the day after the attacks, losing 2-1 to Sporting Cristal in the Copa Merconorte, a pan-American tournament MLS teams had entered for the first time. The Wizards then spent three bewildering days waiting for a flight home while coach Bob Gansler tried to keep the team in shape.

The Wizards finished third in their group, managing only a win and draw against Barcelona—the Ecuadorian version, not the Spanish giant. They protested in vain when a neutral officiating crew failed to turn up for a game with Mexico's Santos club, forcing a local crew into action. The MetroStars got two forfeit victories when Guadalajara—the popular Mexican club commonly known as Chivas—got cold feet about traveling to the United States in the wake of the attacks, but two losses to Colombia's Millonarios and a split with Venezuela's Deportivo ItalChacao kept them from the next stage.

CONCACAF also started up another tournament, an odd contrivance called the Giants Cup. D.C. United and Columbus were selected to go against popular teams from Central America and the Caribbean. In the spring, Columbus lost a difficult two-leg quarterfinal against Costa Rican power Saprissa, while United duly dispatched Jamaica's Arnett Gardens. In August, United beat Guatemalan club Comunicaciones 2-1 in the semifinal but came up short 2-0 against Club America, one of Mexico's marquee clubs. United may have been in last place in the MLS East, but it continued to post respectable performances overseas. The Giants Cup, though, would not continue.

Back in the United States, the NFL and Major League Baseball scrambled to rearrange their seasons. MLS, which had only a handful of games left before the playoffs, looked at the standings and found something fortunate—eight teams had already clinched playoff berths, with only a couple of seeds left to be determined. Four teams had one game remaining; the other eight had two. MLS canceled the games and used an average of points per game to set the final standings.

The only team that suffered from the cancellation was San Jose, which was only two points behind Los Angeles in the West. At 45 points (13-7-6), they lost a tiebreaker with Columbus and wound up with the fifth seed. The Crew, riding another big season from Jeff Cunningham and the 15-assist performance of John Wilmar Perez, took the fourth seed and home-field advantage in the playoffs against the Earthquakes.

The MetroStars were only three points behind the Crew and Earthquakes and would've had an outside shot at taking home field. But they lacked a reliable goal scorer. Young goalkeeper Tim Howard, who had served an apprenticeship behind Tony Meola and Mike Ammann since signing with MLS as a teenager, led the league in saves.

Several points behind the MetroStars, Dallas and Kansas City had been battling for the meaningless distinction between the seventh and eighth seeds. Dallas, behind the triple threat of Jason Kreis, Ariel Graziani, and playmaker

Oscar Pareja, finished one point behind Kansas City but had played one fewer game, edging the Wizards on points per game. The Wizards made the playoffs despite an atrocious goal difference—33 scored, 53 conceded.

The other four teams were never factors. New England, led in scoring by Marco Antonio Cate, finished 7-14-6 for 27 points. One point back, with one fewer game played, was fallen power D.C. United, which had 14 goals from Abdul Thompson Conteh along with slightly quieter seasons from holdovers Jaime Moreno and Marco Etcheverry. Colorado got 14 goals from prized newcomer Spencer but managed only five wins.

Tampa Bay was simply atrocious. The Mutiny's 14 points set a record low, though the 1999 MetroStars played five more games and managed only 15 total. The defense conceded 68 goals, while Mamadou Diallo's output dropped from 26 goals in 2000 to 9 this season.

Miami and Chicago, the two 1998 expansion teams, finished with 53 points each. The Fusion, which had played one fewer game, claimed the top seed and the Supporters Shield, a trophy given to the top regular-season club.

Perhaps the layoff took the teams out of their rhythm, or perhaps MLS had settled into some sort of parity. Whatever the reason, the playoffs didn't follow expectations. San Jose and Columbus, tied in the regular season, played the most lopsided series, with the Earthquakes winning 3-1 in Columbus before 20,883 shocked fans and clinching the series 3-0 at home. Chicago and Dallas, two years removed from a memorable and brutal playoff match-up, were less competitive this time around. Dallas forced a third game with a 1-1 draw in Game 2, surviving a near-miss in overtime, but managed more cards than shots in a 2-0 loss in Chicago. The Fire took the series seven points to one.

Kansas City put up more of a fight, handing Miami a shocking 3-0 loss to even the series at three points each as Pablo Mastroeni and Diego Serna were sent off. The Wizards took a brief 1-0 lead in Game 3 in Miami, but former Kansas City players Preki and Chris Henderson responded to take a 2-1 win. The Associated Press picked up a typically colorful Hudson quote: "It's like the last days of Pompeii" in the Fusion locker room,

The MetroStars put a scare into third-seeded Los Angeles, taking the lead in Game 1 on a Rodrigo Faria goal before Paul Caligiuri equalized. The Galaxy took a 1-0 lead in New Jersey but lost defender Greg Vanney to a second yellow card, opening the floodgates for four MetroStars goals. Under the first-to-five format, the Galaxy needed an outright win at home just to force a series tiebreaker, just as Kansas City had done to them the year before. They did so with a struggle, twice giving up a one-goal lead and seeing Dan Califf sent off en route to a 3-2 win. Mauricio Cienfuegos settled matters with a deflected free kick in the series tiebreaker.

Between rounds, MLS took another short break, this time to let the national teams convene for World Cup qualifying. On October 7, Bruce Arena's U.S. team clinched its fourth straight appearance on the world's biggest stage, a massive relief and a cause for celebration in any country. The game, a 2-1 victory over Jamaica won when Joe-Max Moore scored his second goal in the 80th minute, coincided with the U.S. invasion of Afghanistan. While Arena's team learned the news before kickoff, ABC dumped its broadcast of the game and was unable to find space on one of ESPN's networks. Soccer fans flocked to the Web to catch the score from the U.S. game and two unlikely results— Costa Rica tying Mexico, and last-place Trinidad and Tobago stunning Honduras, which had beaten the USA 3-2 in RFK Stadium a month earlier. Stern John, who had moved from Columbus to start a long career in England, did the honors for Trinidad and Tobago.

The USA barely squeezed into the World Cup with one game to spare, but plenty of teams also left it late. Mexico didn't clinch its berth until beating Honduras in the finale a month later, and mighty Brazil only won 9 of 18 qualifying games. David Beckham added to his legacy, capping an inspirational effort with a late free-kick goal to tie Greece and book England's place in the World Cup.

Back in MLS, both semifinals hung in the balance until overtime of Game 3. Miami took a 1-0 win in Game 1, then suffered a 4-0 loss in a testy game in San Jose that saw three players sent off. The teams were scoreless through 90 minutes in Miami, but the game was settled in overtime on a San Jose corner kick headed home by Troy Dayak, the big Earthquakes defender who had missed two years with a neck injury and claimed the league's comeback Player of the Year award.

Los Angeles and Chicago topped that series with more overtime drama. Game 1 was a 1-1 tie, with Wynalda and Luis Hernandez trading goals. Game 2, played at Cal State Fullerton's Titan Stadium because the Rose Bowl was unavailable, saw the Galaxy take control when Olympic scoring hero Peter Vagenas scored the game's lone goal in overtime. The Fire, playing without injured playmaker Peter Nowak, needed a win in Game 3 and took an early lead on a goal from teen star DaMarcus Beasley. Califf scored just before halftime. In overtime, with the Fire scrambling for the goal they needed to extend the series, Cienfuegos once again decided the series with a 35-yard blast.

The two top regular-season teams, Miami and Chicago, were out, much to the disappointment of Fire fans who had already booked travel plans to Columbus for MLS Cup. The stands at cozy Crew Stadium would end up with a few empty spaces for an all-California matchup taking place while many travelers were still jittery about stepping onto an airplane.

The no-shows missed a lively final. Greg Vanney put a long through-ball into Hernandez's stride to stake the Galaxy to a 1-0 lead in the 21st minute. But once again, Los Angeles couldn't hold a lead in the final. Landon Donovan, disappointing no one in his first MLS season, whipped in an equalizer late in the first half for his fifth goal in six playoff games. A scoreless second half sent the game to overtime and set the stage for an unlikely hero— Dwayne De Rosario, a dreadlocked Canadian who had spent 2000 with the A-League's Richmond Kickers, placed a shot just past the outstretched hand of the despairing Kevin Hartman.

San Jose, so long an afterthought by the end of each MLS season, had completed a "worst-to-first" transformation. Under Frank Yallop's guidance, Ronnie Ekelund and Richard Mulrooney formed a fluid midfield combination free of the rigid divide between attacking midfielder and defensive midfielder that too many MLS teams employed. Donovan grew better and better as the season wore on. Agoos anchored a defense that gave up very little in the postseason, with Joe Cannon stopping almost everything that slipped through.

For all of Agoos's reluctance to join the Earthquakes, he had become the first MLS player with four championships. Yallop was able to laugh at Agoos's adaptation, saying the defender had contributed "right from day 1 . . . well, from day 1 he didn't want to come . . . but from day 7, I think it was." Agoos continued, "I think it was just a different circumstance. In D.C. there were so many good players, so many big names there, that it was hard to find your way. When I went to San Jose, Frank and Dom put a lot of responsibility on me, being the captain. That was something I always wanted to be. [In D.C.,] I never had the privilege to do that."

And in the Bay Area, fans enjoyed a unique "double"—the CyberRays won the WUSA final on penalty kicks before 21,078 in Foxborough.

Everyone was able to smile on a sunny day in Columbus, but MLS executives flew back to bitter reality in the front office. The league was in trouble.

CONTRACTION PAINS

Four MLS teams had struggled at the gate in 2001. San Jose had a championship but fewer than 10,000 fans per game at Spartan Stadium in the first year under Silicon Valley Sports & Entertainment. Tampa Bay and Kansas City were under 11,000. Miami wasn't much better at 11,177. Dallas was one tier higher at 12,574, and all other teams were above 15,000.

The MetroStars were second in attendance at 20,806. Yet something wasn't right in the Meadowlands.

Stuart Subotnick and John Kluge, the Metromedia tycoons who had operated the MetroStars, had seemed committed to MLS. As recently as 2000, commissioner Don Garber had told *Sports Ilustrated*'s Grant Wahl that the MetroStars owners would soon have a second team in the New York area.

In November, Subotnick and Kluge were all the way out of the league. Anschutz Entertainment Group once again took operating rights, bringing their portfolio to five teams.

The rumor mill kicked into gear, and MLS fans watched nervously. Would their teams survive? Would the league survive?

In December, the league took the unusual step of announcing that its investors were committed through 2006, perhaps the only thing it could do to assure fans and sponsors to keep the faith.

Robert Wagman of *SoccerTimes* reported in late December that the owner/investors had split into two factions. Anschutz and Hunt wanted to invest more resources for the long term; Kraft, Subotnick, and Horowitz wanted to keep spending down. The Florida teams were clearly on the chopping block. Another proposed move to shut down the Burn but move the Wizards franchise to Dallas was shot down by Hunt, Wagman reported, even though the rent at Kansas City's Arrowhead Stadium upset other owners. Colorado had a stadium issue—Invesco Field was replacing Mile High Stadium, and Anschutz had not yet managed to make a good deal on the rent.

Another tidbit of good news emerged January 2, when Garber announced an innovative TV deal tying MLS's broadcast rights to those of the 2002 and 2006 World Cups, along with the rights for the 2003 Women's World Cup. ESPN and ABC would once again be the broadcasters, keeping

MLS on major networks at least through 2006. The league would also have ample opportunity to promote itself on World Cup broadcasts. Between that announcement and the investors' commitment, MLS fans could feel confident that the league wasn't going to disappear.

But it would get smaller. Six days later, the hammer fell. The two Florida teams were contracted.

Fort Worth Star-Telegram writer Tobias Xavier Lopez explained the decision: Miami had the "lowest corporate sponsorship revenue and fewest season tickets."[1] Tampa Bay never attracted an investor-operator. The Glazer family, which owned the NFL's Tampa Bay Buccaneers and shared a stadium with the Mutiny, declined to get involved, instead saving their money for a massive purchase a couple of years later—England's Manchester United, perhaps the biggest club in the world depending on who's counting the money and fans.

"We got very close with the Glazers, actually to the contract phase, and ultimately, they didn't close," Garber says. "When they passed on it, we had no other prospects in Tampa, and I knew we were going to have to fold or move that team."

Logan recalls that Glazer's sons grew up as soccer fans in Rochester, New York. But even apart from the ownership issue, the former commissioner—who later lived not far from Tampa—thinks the league ultimately misunderstood Tampa Bay's health as a soccer market:

Tampa was a market we should never have gone into. . . . Tampa was a market that people went into because there was a real false reading over what the Tampa market had been during the NASL. Their attendance numbers were to a large degree overmystified in the NASL days. The reality was that on good seasons they were only drawing 12 to 13,000 paid. . . .

Tampa is a very difficult sports town. Look at what's happening with the [NHL] Lightning and the [baseball] Rays. It's a football town, and on top of everything else, it's a city whose economy is not predicated upon large corporate interests. It's a hodgepodge of financial institutions and medical business and kind of geared toward real estate and toward tourism. It's real difficult to get a clawhold there. What sponsorship there is there goes almost 100 percent toward football.

The Fusion and Mutiny players were uprooted in a dispersal draft three days later. Pablo Mastroeni, not surprisingly, was the first pick, landing with Colorado. Mamadou Diallo went second to New England, followed by a run on the Fusion's loaded roster. Preki was one of the last players selected, heading back to Kansas City after one year in exile. Much of Tampa Bay's roster wasn't selected at all, though several players would win jobs in preseason.

MLS was afloat but listing heavily. With Subotnick, Kluge, and Miami's Ken Horowitz out of the picture, the league was down to four owner-investors. Robert Kraft kept one team, New England, in the same stadium as his NFL Patriots. Silicon Valley Sports & Entertainment hung around for a second season in San Jose and agreed to buy into the league but would partner with Anschutz, who now controlled five and a half teams. Lamar Hunt and family would take over Dallas, adding the Burn alongside Columbus and Kansas City. Players and executives around the league would laud Anschutz and Hunt's loyalty, but the reliance on two investors clearly was far from ideal.

Still, selling the league-owned teams was a sign of progress. "It wasn't like we had a business plan that indicated we would have league-owned teams," Logan says. "It was that we only had scoured up seven investors by the time the first season rolled around. We thought it was important to have 10 teams for competition purposes. We became the managers of last resort. . . . The second issue was that the better markets were taken by investor-operators. It wasn't like we had New York or Chicago or L.A. sitting out there waiting to be sold."

The restructured league had a bit of mystery to it in that a man who said virtually nothing in public controlled so many teams. Philip Anschutz had made "an extraordinary exercise of faith," in Logan's words, but few knew his motives. Fans chatting nervously on the Internet were grateful that one of the world's richest men had such an interest in the game, but no one understood why he would make such a commitment.

Rothenberg sheds some light on Anschutz's motivation:

The closest I can come to [explaining it]: He's a smart businessman and thought there was a significant upside to doing this, No. 1. No. 2, he actually enjoyed the sport.

Two stories stick out in my mind. One, about the time the Home Depot Center was being opened, only half-jokingly, he said to me, "Alan, you know those free tickets you got me to the 1994 World Cup final? They've so far cost me $250 million." So partly he got hooked by what he saw at the World Cup.

But the other, and this is really interesting, at the time that there was an attempt to get an NFL expansion team to Los Angeles that ultimately went to Houston, it coincided with when he bought the Galaxy for what from a soccer standpoint was a huge sum of money. And people had solicited him to become involved in the NFL expansion move, and he had not. I said to him, "Phil, just curious—an NFL team, you could almost guarantee your investment. How come you're gung-ho spending this money on the Galaxy but don't want to go ahead with an NFL team?" His response: "In the NFL, I'm just another rich guy. In soccer, I think I can make a difference." And so I think it's a combination of he got hooked on the sport, he's a smart businessman, and he really had a desire to do something that had lasting value and created a legacy.

No one was thrilled by the decision to let two teams go. The Fusion, for all its attendance issues, had put one of the league's all-time best teams on the field—D.C. United pounced quickly to snap up coach Ray Hudson. The Mutiny had just finished an awful season, but failing in one of the NASL's better markets surely stung. No one could ask any more of Anschutz and Hunt, whose efforts resembled mass philanthropy at this point, but why couldn't the league attract investors such as the Glazer family, whose purchase of Manchester United a couple of years later dwarfed the amount of money the Mutiny needed?

Along with Anschutz, Hunt, Kraft, and the league office, players kept the faith. Ben Olsen remembers:

I always had faith in the league. I think I'm a bad one to ask on that because I've always been at D.C. United, and we've always been such a healthy franchise in all aspects of it. I'm very spoiled to be a part of this team. The winning tradition is there, the trophies are there. . . .

I always kind of knew there were healthy teams and teams that weren't so healthy. I think there are enough places in this country that they'll figure out the right places to put the teams and have a successful league.

This was MLS's darkest winter. But the spring would bring new hope.

7

Building Back

Philip Anschutz and Lamar Hunt hadn't been shy about investing in MLS. Anschutz, the reclusive megamogul, was supporting more than half the league's teams. Hunt, the outgoing Texan, had built the first stadium specifically designed for MLS and also had a share of multiple teams.

In 2002, both men would make bolder investments in the game. Their timing would be perfect, thanks to a couple of big games halfway around the world.

In February, MLS celebrated its second groundbreaking. The Galaxy's new home would be far removed from the simple but effective stadium in Columbus. On the campus of Cal State Dominguez Hills in Carson, California, Anschutz and other investors would put the glittering 27,000-seat soccer stadium at the hub of one of the country's most diverse sports complexes, featuring an 8,000-seat tennis facility, a cycling velodrome, a 10,000-seat track and field stadium, and countless training fields in several sports. Home Depot, then a sponsor of many of the Olympic athletes who would compete and train here, bought the naming rights over the summer.

One day later, MLS and Hunt got bad news in Texas, where the city of McKinney abruptly withdrew a pledge of $30 million toward a $51 million soccer complex that would've housed the Dallas Burn. Hunt Sports Group, which would eventually take over the team, would put its money into the stadium as well. Just as he did in Columbus, Hunt would need patience to get through the political process.

Much better news came March 20, three days before the season was due to start, with the First Circuit Court of Appeals ruling in favor of the league on the player lawsuit. The players would attempt to press on, but for all intents and purposes, the suit was dead. The U.S. Supreme Court made it official in October, just before MLS Cup, refusing to hear the case.

Less tangible than stadiums or court victories was the formation of a new company, announced just before the Florida teams were contracted.

Few observers knew what to make of the press releases on the complex partnership between Anschutz Entertainment Group (AEG), Hunt Sports Group, and Dentsu, with Don Garber at the helm. But everyone knows the World Cup, and the company cleverly packaged World Cup broadcasting rights and MLS rights, essentially tying MLS telecasts to those of the world's biggest single-sport event. Anschutz had bought the World Cup rights for $40 million, according to the *Denver Business Journal*.

Soccer United Marketing (SUM), the name given to the new company in March, would launch with vague language about "one-stop shopping for the sport's diverse community" (Garber in a press release), "continued integration and strategic management" (Hunt Sports President John Wagner, same press release), and "we intend this portfolio to include other soccer-related programming and marketing rights" (AEG President Tim Leiweke, same press release).

Beneath the *Dilbert*-style language, SUM was an audacious effort to stop the in-fighting that had always plagued soccer in the States. The soccer audience had always been a pie split too many ways, with a patchwork system of leagues competing with sporadic exhibitions and TV broadcasts—Fox Sports World and Setanta were already carrying several European leagues to a growing number of cable and satellite subscribers, and GolTV would join them in 2003. No one could put all of those deals under one roof, but SUM started by uniting the country's two most important soccer entities—its professional league and the World Cup viewing audience—and expanded to make deals with Mexican teams and others who occasionally toured in the States. The new company gave MLS a chance to collaborate with its would-be competitors, a shrewd idea that would pay off in years to come.

Putting everything together was always part of the plan but couldn't be implemented when MLS was launched, Alan Rothenberg says:

The aggregating of the rights was a difficulty because the first piece of the puzzle had to be the U.S. national team. There, there was so much controversy with the dual roles that I was playing, I was worried that if I put that in, there would be political negative reaction, number one, and on the other hand, we were bringing in some investors, some owners who really didn't understand the soccer lay of the land and would not understand the necessity of putting up a guarantee to the U.S. Soccer Federation in order to buy their marketing rights, so we dropped that out of the plan. But no one ever abandoned it, and once again, to his great credit, Philip Anschutz a couple of years later . . . basically they were bidding for the World Cup rights and thought that was the right way to go, and ultimately that's how Soccer United Marketing was formed.

Don Garber had arrived at the same conclusion soon after his arrival:

I always found it odd that the U.S. Soccer Federation was represented by IMG, that IMG represented U.S. soccer rights, not the federation itself. We found ourselves bumping into each other at the sponsorship level and the television level. Here we were, an emerging sport that had limited commercial interest to start, and yet you had two competing interests in the marketplace. And they were competing commercially yet they were also strategically connected with players and the overall development of the sport, particularly as it related to players being called up to the national team.

At a meeting Garber says is "probably the most important meeting in the history of the league," the board agreed it was time to fold teams without owners and make another investment—tens of millions of dollars to buy the World Cup rights and launch SUM around that. Garber explains:

Without it, Major League Soccer wouldn't be in existence today. Not necessarily because of the company itself but because of how the company is an outgrowth of the strategy that we settled upon . . . our future success will be about growing the sport of soccer overall, not specifically about just focusing in on the league. And if we can get soccer itself to be more commercially viable, then Major League Soccer, a growing professional league, will benefit by that.

We sat in a board meeting at Phil Anschutz's ranch and talked about how we could create this company—and this point, it was unnamed. The core, first property would be the 2002 and 2006 World Cup rights. In many ways, the strategy was a big part of forming the company, but it also was opportunistic in that the World Cup rights for '02 and '06 had yet to be purchased by ABC or anybody else, and FIFA was concerned that the World Cup wouldn't be on English-language television in the United States. And Alan Rothenberg had brought that to our attention. We very quickly went out and met with [German media company] Kirch, which owned the rights, to see if there was some sort of deal where the league could actually purchase the rights and resell it as part of an integrated package with Major League Soccer's broadcast rights.

MLS already was showing signs of stanching the red ink. Before the season, Garber claimed that Columbus, happily taking the revenue from its prized stadium, was making money.

"I think the league has been on an upward trend since then," Garber says.

PLAYERS ON THE MOVE

Contraction had squeezed the rosters, leaving fewer opportunities for players. A couple of European players packed up and went home, but the most surprising move came from one of the league's first American stars. Pity the 2002 draft class, which had a couple of second-round gems but saw only a handful of players make an impact.

Eric Wynalda, fresh from a rebirth in Chicago, headed to Los Angeles but wasn't able to get a deal he liked.[1] Instead, he signed with the A-League's Charleston Battery. MLS's old legal foe turned ersatz minor league, now firmly entrenched in the USL, had often picked off some of the marginal talent on MLS rosters, but a player of Wynalda's experience and recent success had never dropped from MLS to the lower divisions.

Wynalda's pro career, though, would end abruptly. He tore his right ACL in a preseason exhibition against New England and wound up spending the summer arguing with New York Cosmos legend Giorgio Chinaglia, who tended to romanticize the NASL days, on World Cup broadcasts. He didn't play professionally again, embarking instead on a broadcasting career in which he gained a reputation as a brutally candid lightning rod for controversy with plenty of fans and detractors alike.

The 10 remaining MLS teams made plenty of other changes in the post-contraction era. D.C. United, the three-time champion that had fallen on hard times, seemed to be remaking itself in the Miami Fusion's image. Coach Ray Hudson moved north with goalkeeper Nick Rimando, enforcer Ivan McKinley, and Lazo Alavanja. Honduran defender Milton Reyes also signed on, along with former Kansas City defender Brandon Prideaux and prodigal son Richie Williams, back from the MetroStars. The team had the Fusion's nastiness and the skill as well, with Marco Etcheverry and Jaime Moreno tutoring youngsters Bobby Convey and Santino Quaranta.

New England also had a heavy infusion from the Florida teams, with Mamadou Diallo, Steve Ralston, and reigning MVP Alex Pineda Chacon sure to invigorate the offense, while Jim Rooney and Carlos Llamosa played key roles. From the draft, the Revs added talented forward Taylor Twellman. Like Landon Donovan, Twellman hadn't found a happy home in Germany.

The MetroStars tossed out Adolfo Valencia and brought in temperamental but talented forward Diego Serna. Marcelo Balboa and Joseph Addo seemed set to solidify the defense in front of Tim Howard. If Tab Ramos and Clint Mathis could stay healthy, anything seemed possible.

The two teams moving from the defunct Central to the East made less of a splash. In addition to Wynalda, Chicago let Diego Gutierrez go, while forward-heavy Columbus shored up their defense.

In the West, the big deal was a Dallas–San Jose trade, with Ariel Graziani heading west and Ronald Cerritos joining the Burn. Dallas went for defense in the draft.

Colorado signed Nigerian star Daniel Amokachi, only to find that he wasn't in shape to play. But the Rapids made the biggest splash in the dispersal draft, picking up Pablo Mastroeni, Kyle Beckerman, and Chris Henderson, and traded Balboa for Mark Chung, a potent winger to complement Henderson.

Preki went back to Kansas City after his one year in Miami, setting aside any bitterness over his post-championship exile.

The Galaxy picked up Chris Albright in a trade with D.C. United and replaced Mexican striker Luis Hernandez with fiery Guatemalan Carlos Ruiz, best known to U.S. fans for charging into Kasey Keller and then scoring a few minutes later in a heated World Cup qualifier.

The makeovers didn't stop when the season kicked off. After a 2-4-1 start, New England fired coach Fernando Clavijo and promoted assistant Steve Nicol for his second interim stint in charge, one that would last much longer than his first. A day later, the Revs pulled the trigger on a massive deal—Diallo, longtime Rev Ted Chronopoulos and Andy Williams to the MetroStars for the disgruntled Serna, Brian Kamler, and Daniel Hernandez.

Yes, that would be the same Mamadou Diallo who had been Public Enemy #1 in Giants Stadium since the incident that mangled goalkeeper Mike Ammann and left Mike Petke swearing revenge. In a swift bit of irony, Diallo slid into goalkeeper Adin Brown in his first appearance against his short-term New England teammates, picking up a red card. But Diallo did his part to ingratiate himself to MetroStars fans—in one July game, he scored twice and lifted his jersey to reveal a T-shirt reading, "NY Believe In Me."

While the games went on in MLS, the soccer audience's attention turned to South Korea and Japan, where several players would earn the league much better publicity than any violent penalty-box collision ever would.

THE CUP OVERFLOWS

Bruce Arena announced the USA's World Cup roster on April 22. Players based in Europe would play big roles. Kasey Keller and Brad Friedel were competing for the starting goalkeeper spot. Claudio Reyna, an Arena player at Virginia who had the most successful European career of any U.S. field player, was the leader in midfield along with unusually healthy John O'Brien, who had spurned Duke University to sign with Dutch power Ajax as a teenager. Earnie Stewart, who grew up in Holland but had American citizenship, was still a vital player eight years after his goal in World Cup 1994. David Regis, who gained his citizenship just before the 1998 Cup, had proved his loyalty and usefulness in qualifying. An Arena player from D.C. United, Tony Sanneh, was playing in Germany and had impressive performances at right back leading up to the Cup. Frankie Hejduk's credible 1998 performance had helped him move from MLS to Germany. Joe-Max Moore and Eddie Lewis had made the leap to England, joining journeyman defender Gregg Berhalter.

Yet MLS players had a strong presence as well. Brian McBride, the only American to score in the 1998 debacle, was back up front. Eddie Pope was the undisputed anchor of the back line. DaMarcus Beasley earned his spot in the nick of time alongside former youth national teammate Landon Donovan. Pablo Mastroeni, an N.C. State alumnus but a native of Argentina, got his citizenship papers in order and joined the team despite missing all the qualifiers. Josh Wolff's clutch goals in qualifying nailed down his spot. Jeff Agoos, denied a roster spot in 1994 and kicked out of a starting role to make way for Regis in 1998, finally got his shot, as did Carlos Llamosa. Cobi Jones made his third World Cup roster to lend veteran leadership. Tony Meola, the starting keeper in 1994, gave Arena an experienced backup for Keller and Friedel.

The last spot on the roster was cursed. An ill-timed knee injury robbed Chicago midfield anchor Chris Armas of his opportunity. Greg Vanney, now playing in France, took the spot but was injured four days later. German-based defender Steve Cherundolo made it to South Korea with the team, only to be injured himself.

The poster boy of the team was Clint Mathis, the phenomenal talent who seemed to be coming into his prime and was attracting interest from top European clubs such as Bayern Munich. He was on the cover of *Sports Illustrated* and featured at length in *USA Today*.

The publicity raised some questions on Mathis, though. He came across as a night-crawling party animal, perhaps not as focused on soccer as critics would like. *USA Today*'s Kelly Whiteside gave a glimpse of his townhouse: "There's Bud and Bud Light on tap, but the liquor shelves are empty because the surround-sound system rattled the bottles off the ledge."[2]

Mathis struggled with knee and hamstring issues and wound up playing less than expected, but he came through when needed—as did virtually everyone on the team.

On June 5, the USA opened without Mathis and the ailing Reyna against heavily favored Portugal, featuring Luis Figo and the rest of a golden generation of players. The Americans needed less than five minutes to equal their goal total from 1998. A corner kick bounced in the Portuguese box, and O'Brien alertly fired through a mob of people into the net. 1-0 USA.

The Portuguese defense, stunned to see the unheralded Americans pressing the attack, gave up an own goal. Jorge Costa was the unlucky name on the scoresheet, redirecting a cross from Donovan, who donned a sheepish, slightly bewildered look as he accepted congratulations. 2-0.

Then Sanneh found space on the right, looked up, and saw McBride, his old teammate with the USISL's Milwaukee Rampage. Sanneh's cross sailed over the defense, and McBride threw his body parallel to the ground to get his head on it. 3-0 in the 36th minute, and even those who thought ESPN announcer Jack Edwards was prone to hyperbole had to admit people were gasping worldwide.

Portugal roared back with a goal before halftime and cut the lead to one on a spectacular own goal from the unfortunate Agoos. But Friedel, who would play too well to let 1998 starter Keller see the field, allowed no more. With a 3-2 final, the Americans had a stunning win.

Next up was host South Korea, not the most talented team but a ferocious opponent before its fanatical home support. In a cauldron of noise, Arena decided to give the mohawked Mathis a start. With two deceptively simple touches, Mathis rewarded Arena's faith, settling a cross and slipping a shot into the net.

South Korea answered, celebrating its goal by mimicking a skating motion, a belated protest of a controversial decision to disqualify South Korean short-track skater Dong-sung Kim in the 2002 Olympics and give American star Apolo Anton Ohno the gold. Once again, Friedel limited the damage, stopping a penalty kick—a controversial foul called against the truly luckless Agoos—along the way to preserve a 1-1 tie.

With four points through two games and a mediocre Polish team up next, the USA seemed all but certain to advance. Then disaster struck. As the Americans had stunned Portugal in the opening minutes with a scrambled goal, Poland got on the board first with a shot from naturalized player Emmanuel Olisadebe. Donovan scored the apparent equalizer, but a ludicrous decision from referee Lu Jun—one of many controversial decisions in the World Cup—nullified the goal. Donovan had barely finished pleading his case when Poland made it two.

The USA went on to miss chance after chance, falling behind 3-0 and needing another Friedel penalty-kick save to stop a fourth. Donovan scored a meaningless goal late for a 3-1 final. But fortune would smile on the Americans once again.

Portugal had handily beaten Poland. With a draw against South Korea and a USA loss, Portugal would advance along with the hosts. Instead, Portugal self-destructed with two red cards. When Ji-sung Park scored the game's first goal against the short-handed Portuguese in the 70th minute, TV viewers across the United States found themselves flipping rapidly between the two ESPN networks, holding their breath and hoping South Korea's late goal would stand. While the USA played out the loss, news began to filter out. The unfair result against Poland wouldn't matter. The USA had advanced to the round of 16. And the opponent would be a familiar foe—Mexico.

For decades, Mexico had delighted in beating its massive and occasionally overbearing northern neighbor on the soccer field. In the 1990s, the USA started to fight back, usually winning if the game wasn't in Mexico City. The Americans gave Mexico a fit in World Cup qualifying this time around, setting their home game in frigid Columbus and winning 2-0. Now the regional rivals would face off on a neutral field, miles from home, with much more than mere bragging rights or a CONCACAF Gold Cup on the line.

The U.S. roster was thinning, forcing Arena to keep juggling. Agoos, victimized too many times, suffered a calf injury and would join Cherundolo in missing the rest of the Cup. Hejduk had two yellow cards and was unavailable. Beasley also was banged up and wouldn't play against Mexico.

Even with the depletion, the lineup came as a shock. Arena switched to a 3-5-2, with Berhalter getting his first playing time on a three-man backline with Sanneh and Pope. Mastroeni returned to give the USA more defensive midfield bite. Lewis and Wolff, who had barely played to that point, got their first starts, with Stewart and Mathis on the bench.

On the fly, Arena had all but reinvented his team as a counterattacking squad bent on frustrating Mexico with a bunch of players thrown into the fire. After millions of Americans arose at 2:30 a.m. Eastern time to watch, Arena soon looked like a genius on the scale of chess legend Bobby Fischer.

Wolff, who had scored first in that Columbus win, got into the act first, taking an incisive cross from Reyna and playing it to McBride. The big Crew forward, already the first American to score in two World Cups, scored his second of this tournament. 1-0 USA in the eighth minute.

Mexico had the bulk of possession, but Berhalter, Mastroeni, and company held up the attack. Friedel came up big as needed.

The USA finally got a break with the officiating as well. Referee Vitor Melo Pereira, hailing from first-round victim Portugal, didn't notice John

O'Brien's handball in his own box early in the second half, denying Mexico a penalty kick that could've tied the game.

Ten minutes later, Lewis raced down the left on the counterattack. He looked up and saw former San Jose teammate Donovan. His cross was perfect, and Donovan headed it cleanly to claim his first World Cup goal at last.

Mexico managed little in response. The frustration showed on the face of Luis Hernandez, taunted by "L.A. reject" chants from the American fans. It boiled over when Cobi Jones, sent into the game to help the USA keep possession and kill the clock, took a brutal head butt from Rafael Marquez. The Mexican captain earned a red card.

Final score: 2-0, same as the Columbus game. "Dos a cero" would be a popular taunt from U.S. fans for years to come.

The Americans had reached the World Cup quarterfinals for the first time since the tournament's low-key debut in 1930, when the team reached the semis. Not since 1930 had an American team won two games at a World Cup. President Bush called the team. Several players appeared on ABC's *Good Morning America.*

With the bandwagon in top gear, the USA faced a powerful German team that had demolished the woeful Americans four years earlier. This time, they wouldn't embarrass themselves. But they would run into the only goalkeeper in the tournament to have a better Cup than Friedel.

Oliver Kahn particularly frustrated Donovan, saving two excellent first-half chances. "His hand came out of nowhere," said the young American star of one Kahn save. Lewis also had a good chance stopped in spectacular fashion.

Against the run of play, Germany took the lead late in the first half. Michael Ballack rose between Sanneh and Berhalter on a free kick to win the header and place it past Friedel.

Aside from a post-rattling shot from Miroslav Klose a few minutes later, the USA dominated the rest of the way. This time, a missed handball went against them—Berhalter's shot off a corner kick clearly hit Torsten Frings's arm on the goal line, but no call was made. Kahn made one mistake, racing out of his box in a bit of confusion and letting the ball fall awkwardly to Reyna at midfield, only to be relieved when the American captain's long half-volley went just wide.

A semifinal bid and rematch against South Korea simply weren't to be.

Late in the game, Sanneh rose for a header and just missed the post. That was it. Donovan was credited with three shots on goal, one more than the German team, but Kahn and a bit of luck kept Germany going.

The Americans had lost in noble fashion, defeated but not in the least disgraced. Several team members made an appearance with David Letterman, who encouraged Mathis to boot a ball across Broadway.

Then everyone went back to work.

AFTER THE CUP

MLS often had bad luck with the weather at its marquee events, and the 2002 All-Star Game August 3 gave league execs a massive headache. With a storm plowing through RFK Stadium, Don Garber and staff had to juggle a narrow broadcasting window with the demands of a sponsor-driven halftime show. The game was truncated to accommodate the performance by Latin recording star Paulina Rubio, unknown to most English-speaking MLS fans but clearly a sex symbol with few peers among Spanish speakers.

Garber had experience with Super Bowl halftime shows from his NFL days, and he knew he had a dilemma:

> We had sponsor commitments, we had broadcast commitments, we had a commitment to Paulina, we had a commitment to many fans who had come to watch her perform. I remember getting called down by Ivan [Gazidis] to the officiating room and sitting down with [supervisor of officials] Joe Machnik, sitting down with people from ABC, the representative of Pepsi was there. We all kind of turned to each other and ultimately to me to make a decision. I made the decision I thought was in the best interest of the league. Not an easy decision to make but probably one that I would make again next time around.

Rubio's erotic exhortations awakened a crowd that had sat through a scoreless first half between a loosely defined U.S. national team, with former internationals such as Juergen Sommer, Alexi Lalas, Mike Burns, and Preki filling the shoes of the Europe-based players, and an MLS All-Star team. Donovan scored first for the nationals, but MVP Marco Etcheverry delighted his home fans in guiding the "MLS" comeback. Etcheverry scored the second goal, Jason Kreis notched a goal and an assist, and the MLS Stars won 3-2.

The format would change again the next year, with All-Stars pulled from the entire league facing visiting clubs from Europe or Mexico.

"All-Star games are an interesting sort of animal for sports leagues," Garber says. "The hard-core fan doesn't believe in them and thinks they're all just an exhibition showcase. . . . It's a way to celebrate the game. It's not necessarily entirely about the game. It's about the experience."

The playoff race would be chaotic, especially in the East. Defying preseason predictions, all five teams struggled. Under the new MLS system, the playoffs would omit the worst two teams regardless of conference, leaving all but one team unsure of its postseason plans until the last week.

In Columbus, Jeff Cunningham's 16-goal season had kept the Crew competitive in McBride's absence, and the Crew clinched a playoff berth with a game to spare, beating Chicago 2-0. The Fire returned the favor the next week at its raucous temporary venue, Naperville's 15,000-seat Cardinal Stadium, winning 2-1 on goals by Peter Nowak and runaway scoring leader Ante Razov. The Fire had struggled while Wolff and Beasley were at the World Cup and stumbled to a four-game losing streak late in the season but got the clutch win in the end.

The Revolution, still unsure of a playoff spot entering the last week, clinched the East title with a win over the MetroStars, beating the Crew on a tiebreaker. New England's 12-14-2 record wasn't impressive for a conference champion, but the playoff berth was a just reward for the turnaround under Nicol. The Revs won five of their last six games, with Twellman surging to the points-system scoring title with 23 goals and 6 assists.

The MetroStars, who played that finale in New England without suspended stars Mathis and Tim Howard, missed out by losing seven of their last nine. The stretch included back-to-back losses to rival D.C. United, which plummeted after the World Cup and surged too late.

The West was clearer. Carlos Ruiz, unencumbered by World Cup duty, scored 24 goals to lead Los Angeles to a 16-9-3 record, best in the league. The Galaxy clinched the division and MLS's Supporters' Shield with back-to-back 1-0 wins over San Jose, both on late Ruiz goals, in the last two games.

The Earthquakes finished six points back after a curious late skid. Ariel Graziani picked up the slack during Donovan's absence and finished with 14 goals, while Joe Cannon had 8 shutouts.

Dallas got 14 goals from Jason Kreis and challenged the top two for the

overall lead before a late three-game skid. Colorado endured a four-game los-
ing streak during the World Cup but was otherwise steady, with Mark Chung,
Chris Henderson, and Chris Carrieri scoring 11 goals each to compensate for
John Spencer's injury problems.

The West's last-place team eked into the playoffs in the last week. Kansas
City shipped Roy Lassiter back to D.C. United, where he was held scoreless,
and had no one with more than seven goals—Chris Klein shared the honors
with the ageless Preki.

THE PLAYOFFS

Dallas, the only team besides Los Angeles to reach the playoffs all seven seasons, went out in the first round for the fifth time. The Burn took Game 1 at
home 4-2, then lost 1-0 in Colorado. At home, a 1-1 tie sent the series to a
tiebreaker, which ended quickly when Colorado's Mark Chung scored on a
first-minute header.

Columbus made surprisingly quick work of San Jose with two 2-1 wins,
getting a goal and an assist from midsummer acquisition Freddy Garcia in
the away leg and getting a late winner from McBride at home.

The division winners needed three games each but won the decisive
games with ease. New England, playing before its second straight home playoff crowd under 7,000, knocked out Chicago with a 2-0 win. Los Angeles, by
far the best-attended venue, beat Kansas City 5-2 behind two goals each from
Ruiz and Cobi Jones.

Columbus and New England played a strange semifinal, with no home
team winning a game. After a scoreless tie in Game 1, Jay Heaps scored a
third-minute goal that stood up for a 1-0 Revs road win. New England took
a 2-0 lead at home in Game 3, but the Crew answered twice in the last 10
minutes to make it interesting. The 2-2 final sent the Revs through with five
points.

No such excitement in the other semifinal, where Los Angeles beat Colorado 4-0 before 24,742 at home and got a Ruiz goal to win Game 2, 1-0.

MLS was guaranteed a first-time champion. Los Angeles had been frustrated in the final three times. New England had never been close.

The timing was perfect for the Revolution. MLS Cup was set for Gillette
Stadium in Foxborough. The weather cooperated, and 61,316 fans turned up
for the final October 20.

What they saw wasn't good. Neither team managed much offensively, particularly the Revolution. The home team wasn't credited with a shot on goal until Alex Pineda Chacon, the former MVP now reduced to sub duty, put one on frame near the end of regulation.

The Revs wouldn't force another save out of Kevin Hartman in overtime, either. At the other end, Carlos Ruiz kept pressing. And pressing. And finally, he beat Adin Brown with a deft touch off Tyrone Marshall's cross, giving the Galaxy a golden-goal winner in the 113th minute. At last, Los Angeles had its championship.

Ruiz deserved no less after his dazzling season. He took MVP honors for his regular-season heroics, including the goals to clinch the West and Supporters' Shield, and his MLS Cup goal was his eighth in the postseason.

Off the field, the season had been quiet for MLS since the appeals court ruling in the player lawsuit. A deal with Spanish-language Radio Unica, announced in August, was the only bit of news to emerge.

Yet for all the progress MLS had made after bottoming out in late 2001, the league still had no more investors. In December, AEG bought out Silicon Valley Sports & Entertainment in San Jose, officially giving Anschutz 6 of the league's 10 teams. Hunt had three more, while Kraft held on in New England.

The faces would continue to change. The fiery Diallo was sold to a Saudi Arabian club after the season. Carlos Valderrama, Tab Ramos, Peter Nowak, Marcelo Balboa, and John Harkes had played their last games.

But MLS would find ways to build on its World Cup momentum in 2003, taking more steps to ensure that the league could outlive the relatively short careers of any soccer player.

8

More Groundwork

In 2003, MLS stepped into its eighth season in the mood to make a deal.

Three World Cup players signed up. Joe-Max Moore returned to the Revolution. Frankie Hejduk came back from Germany and signed up with Columbus. Earnie Stewart, who had overcome his discomfort flying to play so many vital games for the U.S. national team, committed to air travel with his club as well, joining D.C. United.

The A-League launched another raid on MLS talent, this time from Virginia Beach, whose Mariners signed Dante Washington and the fading Roy Lassiter.

The big deals were on the small screen, where ESPN and ABC would no longer have a monopoly on MLS broadcasts. In a four-day span in April, MLS announced a four-year deal for regular-season and playoff games on Fox Sports World, Fox Sports en Español and overseas affiliates, then a three-year deal with Mark Cuban's high-definition channel HDNet. With ESPN no longer airing a highlight show, Fox Sports World jumped into the void with *MLS Wrap*, co-hosted by veteran commentator Sean Wheelock and the recently retired John Harkes.

In the midst of the TV expansion came another stadium deal. Lamar Hunt finally got a deal done for the Dallas Burn, which would play at the centerpiece of a sprawling soccer complex in Frisco, Texas. MLS stadiums now had three models to follow—the stand-alone stadium Hunt had built in Columbus, the multisport complex that the Galaxy would call home, and a collection of fields ideal for youth tournaments that happened to have an

MLS-worthy stadium at its core. The Frisco model would end up inspiring others to follow.

Just after the season kicked off, the league had one more important deal. With the lawsuit officially dead, MLS players were able to organize as a union. The MLS Players Union, only one letter away from MLSPA but not driven by the forces behind the lawsuit, petitioned for recognition. The league quickly granted it.

The league wasn't quite finished with off-field news—in early May, MLS launched an "Iraqi Aid" campaign to donate soccer gear—but the centerpiece of the season would be the stadium already under construction.

BRIGHT LIGHTS IN L.A.

The Home Depot Center in Carson, California, was one of the most ambitious multisport complexes ever built in the United States. Many colleges have a midsized stadium, practice fields, a track, and some tennis courts. Not many have a legitimate tennis stadium and a track and field venue capable of hosting international meets. Even fewer have a velodrome for track cycling. Little wonder Olympic athletes were thrilled to see the facility built.

The Galaxy, though, would be even more excited. The stadium gave MLS all the things it sought in building its own venues—for example, revenue control, a wider field, and freedom from confusing American football lines in the fall. But it was more than that. The stadium was a combination of latter-day American features such as luxury boxes and traditional European design. Galaxy adviser and German soccer legend Jurgen Klinsmann urged the team to put a roof over the stands to enhance the atmosphere, trapping noise and giving a cozier feel. Klinsmann's argument carried the day.

The bad news for the Galaxy: like Columbus in 1999, they would have to start the year with a long road trip while their stadium was completed. Unlike Columbus in 1999, the defending champions had a horrid start—four ties, four losses.

No one expected that sort of struggle. Nearly everyone from the championship team of a year before had returned, joined by South Korean defender Hong Myung Bo and former MLS MVP Alex Pineda Chacon. Carlos Ruiz was still scoring goals; Kevin Hartman was still stopping them. But the Galaxy would struggle all season to get back to form.

The Home Depot Center helped shake Los Angeles out of the early-season slump, with a sellout crowd of 27,000 on hand and Pelé trotting out for pre-game ceremonies. Hartman was a spectator most of the way through a 2-0 Galaxy win over Colorado. Meanwhile, an upstart competitor boasting traditional soccer powers threatened to steal the spotlight.

ChampionsWorld, a company including former MLS executive Charlie Stillitano and New York Cosmos great Giorgio Chinaglia, booked several European teams for a series of exhibitions in U.S. cities over the summer. That wasn't unusual in U.S. soccer history—European teams had toured America off and on since at least 1905, when an English all-star team called the Pilgrims visited. MLS teams had faced plenty of pedigreed European teams, including Fiorentina, Galatasaray, Benfica, Ajax, Bayer Leverkusen, and Bayern Munich.

For this tour, MLS teams were not invited. The invited teams would play each other. Manchester United would open in Seattle, still without an MLS team, against Celtic. The Scottish power would then skip over to Cleveland to face Argentina's Boca Juniors. Barcelona and Juventus, each of whom would later face Manchester United, would start against each other in Foxborough. Milan also would come over from Italy to face Barcelona in Washington.

The true insult on the itinerary was Manchester United's venture to the L.A. Coliseum to face Mexico's Club America. In a USATODAY.com column, your author wrote that this matchup was the equivalent of the Galaxy going to Manchester to play Scotland's Aberdeen. A few playful insults were tossed about as the column wondered if Manchester United had perhaps ducked a matchup with the Galaxy. Manchester United fans responded en masse, claiming a matchup with an MLS team would be an utter waste of time. The argument that Bayern Munich hadn't taken the same attitude didn't appease the angry e-mailers.

Publicly, MLS took no offense, taking the "rising tide lifts all boats" approach. But the touring teams posed a PR nightmare for the league. Critics could easily ask why 60,000 fans were showing up to see foreign teams in a country whose domestic league struggled to draw 15,000 consistently. And Chinaglia, given the color commentator slot on Fox Sports World broadcasts, wasn't shy about telling viewers that they were watching a brand of soccer they didn't usually see in this country.

Sports Illustrated's Grant Wahl called out Chinaglia in his review of the 2003 season:

The insufferable former New York Cosmos great has resurfaced as a broadcaster and senior vice president of ChampionsWorld, the company that organized Manchester United's summer exhibition tour of America. Never mind the conflict of Chinaglia's singing ChampionsWorld's praises on TV without mentioning his financial interest, or the fact that he's a third-rate commentator lacking the most basic of insights. What's most galling is his blatantly revisionist history of the NASL—he'd have us believe that every team played to sold-out stadiums—and willful denigration of MLS (whose players, he told *Sports Illustrated* in 1998, "couldn't shine our shoes"). Memo to Giorgio: MLS provided the bulk of the attack that led the U.S. to a better World Cup finish than your Italy had in 2002. And just because you can make money on one-off exhibition tours doesn't mean you know jack about running a viable league—and actually growing the sport—in America.[1]

As Wahl noted here, any comparison between a few exhibitions and an actual league was unfair. Americans generally turn out for big events, one of many reasons why World Cups and Olympic Games fare so well here. The first ChampionsWorld tour was successful, particularly when Manchester United was involved. Future tours wouldn't go as well, as fans recognized that the European clubs were treating the games as the preseason exhibitions they were. In the long run, they couldn't replace the drama of a league season.

The gap was bridged over the summer by a fluke of timing. Tim Howard, the promising young MetroStars goalkeeper, signed with Manchester United. While some journalists scoffed at the notion of the internationally inexperienced goalkeeper competing for the starting job, Howard adjusted quickly in preseason games, starting with a sparkling debut in a 4-1 win against Juventus at Giants Stadium. By the start of the season, Howard had beaten out erratic Fabien Barthez, the starter for France's 1998 World Cup triumph and 2002 debacle.

MLS took its own international approach in revamping the All-Star Game into a matchup of league stars against a visiting international team. This year, MLS stars would not be split into East and West or some other contrivance to show off in an easygoing affair in which the result hardly mattered.

The first team lined up was Mexican giant Guadalajara, popularly known as Chivas. The league showed off its shiny new stadium near L.A., even though the area's thousands of Chivas fans would certainly turn up. The stadium sold out for the August 3 showdown.

After a scoreless first half, the local stars took over. Mauricio Cienfuegos had an assist on Ante Razov's opening goal. After Jair Garcia's equalizer, Carlos Ruiz answered quickly to stake the MLS team to a 2-1 lead. Galaxy keeper Kevin Hartman had nine saves to preserve the lead, while Chicago's DaMarcus Beasley put it out of reach with a late goal.

While the league took pride in Howard's accomplishments and the All-Star Game, another international move was announced with a touch of sadness. Brian McBride, the face of Columbus soccer since the Crew's debut, left for England's Fulham. The announcement was headline news in Columbus, with the media reporting his departure as if a longtime NFL coach were stepping down.

No one could begrudge the ever-loyal McBride's interest in capitalizing after a couple of successful short-term stints in England, but his transfer fell after a disappointing season in Columbus. The Crew, the defending Open Cup champion and some pundits' pick to win the East, hit a seven-game winless skid in the summer. McBride had 12 goals but couldn't carry the load. Edson Buddle had 10, but Jeff Cunningham's production slipped. Columbus made a late run but couldn't snare the last playoff spot in the resurgent East.

That last spot went to D.C. United, back in the playoffs after a three-year absence. With longtime bulwarks Eddie Pope and Jaime Moreno gone to the MetroStars, Ray Hudson still hadn't managed to rebuild the once-dominant club. Aging playmaker Marco Etcheverry and tough midfielder Dema Kovalenko shared the team lead with six goals. Hristo Stoitchkov, who had announced his presence by breaking an American University freshman's leg with a horrific tackle in a preseason scrimmage, scored five and brought his singular passion to each game. Blossoming defender Ryan Nelsen and goalkeeper Nick Rimando kept the club in most games despite their shocking tendency to lose games (five) in the short overtime session.

One of those losses forced the league to reexamine its substitution rules. In one of the few remaining exceptions to international practice, MLS allowed teams a fourth substitution as long as one of those subs was a goalkeeper. Bob Bradley, who moved from Chicago to the MetroStars, used this rule as a loophole to bring youngster Eddie Gaven onto the field against

United. Gaven served briefly as goalkeeper before handing the gloves back to Howard, then ran forward to score the winning goal—his first—a few minutes later. "I hate this rule," said ESPN's Rob Stone on the broadcast. Bradley was unapologetic for violating the spirit but not the letter of the rule, which was changed to the international standard after the season.

Bradley had gone to great lengths to transform the MetroStars. *Soccer America*'s Will Kuhns counted 73 players who took part in some part of the team's preseason camp, though few had significant MLS experience. For all the turmoil, the team started brightly, with a five-game winning streak in the spring giving them a cushion against the summer doldrums. Honduran Amado Guevara proved to be a capable playmaker, though former United player Mark Lisi surprisingly led the team with 11 assists. Clint Mathis carried the scoring load with nine.

Howard's departure left a void in net, but the MetroStars found a capable replacement. Jonny Walker was, to that point, an American goalkeeper whose career had existed mostly in rumor among U.S. soccer fans. He had worked his way to Chile, rich in history but not closely followed by the international media. Through a few Internet sources and magazines, U.S. fans were aware that he had played in the Copa Libertadores, a big tournament but not one easily found on American airwaves. His Universidad Catolica side had posted a stunning result, winning 3-1 over Brazil's Flamengo in the famed Maracanã stadium. With Walker coming home and fitting in nicely, Bradley got the MetroStars back in the playoffs.

New England, in its first full season under Steve Nicol, stayed the course and took second in the East with minimal fuss. The preseason disappointment was Peter Nowak's decision to retire rather than accept a trade from Chicago. Taylor Twellman tied Ruiz for league lead in goals (15) despite a late injury. Shalrie Joseph emerged as a powerful central midfielder, Adin Brown held off former Galaxy keeper Matt Reis as the starter, and Jose Carlos Cancela arrived during the season as a potent playmaker. The Revolution finished on a five-game winning streak.

The East's top seed and Supporters' Shield winner was a minor surprise. Chicago lost Bradley, Josh Wolff, Stoitchkov, Nowak, and Kovalenko, but new coach Dave Sarachan kept the pieces together. Damani Ralph gave Ante Razov a solid running mate up front, and the Fire scattered losses through a

15-7-8 season, concluding with a meaningless 6-2 loss to Columbus with a third-stringer playing in goal. Chicago dominated the postseason awards—Sarachan was Coach of the Year, Ralph was top rookie, Carlos Bocanegra was top defender, and Chris Armas took the comeback award. The Fire also took the Open Cup with a 1-0 win over the MetroStars.

The major honors to elude the Fire went to the top teams out West. The league's top goalkeeper was Pat Onstad, a 35-year-old Canadian international who had spent several years in the A-League. He replaced Joe Cannon, the previous Goalkeeper of the Year, in San Jose and posted a 1.04 goals-against average. With Landon Donovan in his usual form, the Earthquakes raced away with the conference lead and finished 14-7-9, though a four-game winless skid at the end would give them reason to worry heading into the playoffs.

The MVP and scoring champion was a stunner—40-year-old Preki, the league's first two-time winner. The league would claim him as the oldest MVP of any league in American professional sports history. Kansas City desperately needed his 12 goals and 17 assists—Wolff battled injuries and managed only two goals, while the defense leaked goals. A nine-game winless skid late in the season didn't help, though the Wizards rebounded to win four straight and claim second in the West.

Third place went to the Colorado Rapids, who shook off the Grimandi shenanigans and got consistent scoring from John Spencer and Mark Chung. Scott Garlick held the starting goalkeeper spot despite lashing out with biting humor when the team signed Cannon upon his return from France. "I don't care whether they bring in Joe Cannon or Joe Bazooka or Jim Tommygun," he told the *Denver Post*'s Allison Ann Otto. Cannon's response: "I don't care if it's Scott Garlick, Scott Salt, or Scott Pepper. I'm very confident in my abilities. I can compete for the job anywhere and may the best man win."[2]

Los Angeles finished 9-3-3 in the Home Depot Center, 0-9-6 on the road. That record would've been a problem if not for Dallas's horror season on the overheated artificial turf at a high-school football stadium in Southlake, where the Burn averaged only 7,906 fans. Young goalkeeper D. J. Countess and fellow keeper Jeff Cassar were shelled, giving up 64 goals. Colin Clarke took over coaching duty from Mike Jeffries, and the Burn moved back to the Cotton Bowl for the 2004 season while construction raged on in Frisco.

NEW MONEY AT LAST

The Frisco stadium and the TV deals weren't the only good news for MLS on the business front. After seeing its list of owner-investors drop to three, the league finally lured someone new.

Selling the Colorado Rapids, his original team, might not have been Philip Anschutz's first choice. But Stanley Kroenke was an investor he wouldn't want to turn away. He was introduced as the Rapids' new man September 23, ending Anschutz's stint as a six-team owner-investor after less than a year.

Kroenke Sports Enterprises already owned the NBA's Denver Nuggets, the NHL's Colorado Avalanche, the National Lacrosse League's Colorado Mammoth, and a share of the Arena Football League's Colorado Crush. All four of those teams played in the Pepsi Center, which Kroenke's group happened to own and operate. His vision for the Rapids certainly would not include paying rent to share a stadium with the Denver Broncos, and he immediately turned his attention to the search for a suitable stadium site.

Kroenke also bought into Soccer United Marketing (SUM), again taking some of the burden off the broad shoulders of Anschutz and Hunt. He also had an eye toward broadcasting, forming the local Altitude network to air his teams' games. His soccer interest stretched across the Atlantic—in future years, he would buy a substantial share in English power Arsenal.

The importance of committed investors had been driven home a week earlier with some bad news elsewhere in American soccer.

THE WUSA FOLDS

In 1999, women's soccer had all the momentum in the world. Over the years, Mia Hamm and company had gradually won the hearts and minds of a generation, and that generation made plenty of noise as the USA won the World Cup at home.

In 2003, the World Cup was once again in the United States thanks to the SARS epidemic that forced its removal from China. Don Garber had flown to FIFA HQ in Switzerland to support the USA's emergency bid, and several MLS venues—including the two soccer-specific stadiums in Columbus and Los Angeles—would host games. But the atmosphere was in stark contrast to the celebration of four years before.

As the U.S. team prepared for its first game, the players got sobering news: after this tournament, you're unemployed.

The timing was shocking. The news was not. WUSA attendance hadn't been bad, though it had predictably dropped from the first-year boom. The quality of play was solid, with most notable internationals joining the deep U.S. talent pool. The keys were the lack of TV ratings and corporate sponsorship.

After the first year, the TV backers bailed, leaving the broadcasts stranded on the unknown PAX network, surrounded by programming that had absolutely nothing in common with sports, much less soccer, much less women's soccer. Worse still, the time slot was at 4 p.m. Eastern time on Saturdays, directly in conflict with MLS's Soccer Saturday broadcasts.

With the WUSA's demise, MLS no longer had to put up with any columnists' suggestion that the women's game was the dominant form of soccer in this country. But MLS wasn't about to gloat. A well-run women's game was a solid complement to an American pro men's league. And everyone could empathize with the difficulty of getting a soccer league to survive.

Adding to the deflation, the USA lost its World Cup title. The Americans dominated a tricky group, defeating eventual finalist Sweden 3-1 before shutting out Nigeria and North Korea. The reward was a difficult path to the final. Perennial rival Norway fell 1-0 in the quarterfinals, but an unimaginative attack caught up with the Americans against Germany. While Mia Hamm and company kept lobbing the ball into the German box, the experienced European side played for the counterattack, adding two late goals in a 3-0 win. The game may have been closer than the score would suggest, but Germany was no lucky winner. They went on to beat Sweden on a golden goal in the final, while the USA contented itself with third place by defeating pesky neighbor Canada 3-1.

CALIFORNIA MIRACLE

A couple of weeks after the women bowed out of the spotlight, the MLS playoffs kicked off with a new format. The first round would be a two-leg series decided by aggregate goals. The advantages: each team would still have a home playoff game, and the aggregate system was familiar to anyone who followed the international game. The disadvantage: home-field advantage would be minimized—instead of hosting two of a possible three games, the higher seed would only gain the upper hand if the series went to extra time.

The second round, also called the conference final, would be a single game at the higher seed's stadium. Home-field advantage would be crucial here, though a team could find itself out of the running with one ill-timed mistake.

Three of the higher seeds sailed through the first round with little trouble. Chicago swept aside D.C. United with two 2-0 wins. New England took a 2-0 win in Giants Stadium and finished off the MetroStars with a 1-1 tie at home, with Cancela assisting on all three goals. Kansas City reversed those scores, tying 1-1 in Colorado and knocking out the Rapids with a 2-0 home win.

The California matchup, conversely, showed just how thrilling the new format could be.

Los Angeles, drawing the largest crowd of the playoffs at 20,201, beat San Jose 2-0 in the first leg on second-half goals by Sasha Victorine and the ever-dangerous Ruiz. In San Jose, the Galaxy quickly doubled up, with Ruiz striking again and Peter Vagenas finding the net in the 13th minute. That made it 2-0 on the evening, 4-0 in the series. The path toward MLS Cup, also scheduled for the Galaxy's comfortable home, seemed clear—move on to Kansas City and get one more win. Teams just don't come back from a four-goal deficit.

No one watching on the MLS Shootout package or in person at Spartan Stadium on November 9 could've imagined what was about to transpire.

Jeff Agoos cut the deficit to three goals with a free kick in the 21st minute. Landon Donovan made it a respectable 2-2 on the night with a 35th-minute goal. But the hints of an astronomically improbable finish didn't really start until the 50th minute, when Jamil Walker, who hadn't started a game all season but was included in the first 11 for this encounter, made it 3-2 on the scoreboard, 3-4 in the series.

The inspired Earthquakes pressed but couldn't find a way through. The great comeback seemed doomed to fail. When defender Chris Roner stepped on the field in the 89th minute, the expectations of a miracle had faded.

Roner immediately got into the mix as Richard Mulrooney lobbed in a free kick. Somehow, he got his head to it and drilled it past the shocked Kevin Hartman—4-2 in the game, 4-4 in the series. Mulrooney had his third assist. The series was going to overtime.

Less than six minutes into the extra session, it was over. Donovan threaded a pass to Rodrigo Faria, the one-time Rookie of the Year with the Metro-Stars who had nearly given up the game after his father had died back in his Brazilian homeland. Faria went far post. Goal. He fell in tears to the field, mobbed by his teammates.

Five goals in less than 90 minutes. A 5-4 series between the teams with the league's best defenses. Unlikely heroes in Walker, Roner, and Faria. *Sports Illustrated*'s Grant Wahl didn't restrain his praise: "Let's call it what it was: the greatest game in MLS history."[3]

Donovan, not one to adhere blindly to sports clichés, says the Earthquakes had a funny feeling all along that anything was possible: "That was probably the most incredible night of soccer I've ever been a part of. There was some tangible feeling in the air like something special was going to happen. I don't know why, I don't know how. Even after they went up a couple of goals, there was this overriding belief that we could do it."

That belief persisted when the clock was running down and San Jose still needed another goal to force overtime. Donovan continues, "At that point, the tide had shifted so much, and we were just pouring on the pressure on them. We were all over them, we were all over their goal. There are some games you play in where you just go, 'Oh, I don't think we're going to win this game.' That day, you never got that feeling, and you just felt that, eventually, it was going to happen."

The Earthquakes weren't finished with postseason comebacks. In the single-game West final, Kansas City twice took a second-half lead, only to see San Jose conjure an equalizer. Donovan broke the 2-2 tie in the 117th minute, taking a feed from Ronnie Ekelund.

New England went into the East final without Twellman, Joe-Max Moore, and Joe Franchino. The Revs produced little offense but held the Fire scoreless through regulation. In extra time, Justin Mapp raced down the right and centered. Ralph couldn't finish, but the ball landed at the feet of Chris Armas. Chicago reached the final for the third time in six years.

The top seeds, each seeking a second title, advanced to the final at Home Depot Center on November 23.

This time, San Jose stormed out to the lead, getting a fifth-minute free kick from Ekelund and a Donovan goal in the 38th for a 2-0 halftime margin. DaMarcus Beasley cut the lead in half in the 49th, but Mulrooney answered before the Fire could settle back into action.

The Fire nearly made up the two-goal deficit in two minutes. As Evan Whitfield's cross floated toward the Earthquakes' goal, Game 3 San Jose hero Roner tried to head the ball to safety but put it in his own net. A minute later, Roner fouled Damani Ralph in the box, sending Ante Razov to the spot for the first penalty kick in MLS Cup history and a chance to tie.

Though the game would end as the highest-scoring final so far, a goal-keeper made the crucial play. Pat Onstad smothered Razov's penalty kick.

Razov would manage a couple more chances, but Donovan restored the two-goal lead, tapping into a wide-open net after 2001 final MVP Dwayne De Rosario slipped the ball past the defense.

Donovan took MVP honors, Agoos took his fifth MLS championship in eight years, and San Jose had its second title in three.

GROWING AGAIN

Two more original MLS stars, Marco Etcheverry and Mauricio Cienfuegos, would leave after the season, along with Hristo Stoitchkov.

Going forward, MLS had a few announcements at the end of the year. First came expansion, though the news wasn't quite clear-cut. A Cleveland group headed by Bert Wolstein had a letter of intent for a new team, though several hurdles remained before a second Ohio team took the field. Mexican giant Chivas would operate an MLS team, location to be determined.

The cooperation across the Rio Grande would extend to SUM, which took responsibility for the InterLiga, a tournament of Mexican clubs in the United States to determine who would advance to South America's prestigious Copa Libertadores.

The big news would bring more attention to MLS than it had seen since its debut season. A 14-year-old phenom was ready to turn pro.

9

In the Spotlight

Hard-core soccer fans had tracked Freddy Adu since his pre-teen years. He broke through the mainstream media as early as 2001, when stories surfaced of major European clubs offering his family deals that were difficult to refuse. Inter Milan admitted interest but denied the family's contention that they had offered $750,000.

"I get calls from people in England and Italy, and people back in my home country [Ghana] who said they would take care of Freddy if he leaves," Emelia Adu, Freddy's mother, told Amy Rosewater for a 2001 *USA Today* story. "People tell me they can take care of me. I just want him here with me."

Freddy had spent his early childhood in Ghana playing in pickup games. The Adu family won a green-card lottery in 1997 and relocated to Potomac, Maryland, a Washington suburb. A couple of years later, at age 10, Freddy traveled to Italy with a U.S. youth team for an Under-14 tournament and sparkled against Italian youth teams. Emelia turned away calls from professional teams and agents, but she agreed to let him move to the U.S. Under-17 residency program in Bradenton, Florida.

In August 2003, Adu had shown fans what all the fuss was about, giving an electrifying performance in the Under-17 world championships. He slashed through South Korea's defense with a darting run in which he shed several defenders with each touch before finishing one of his three goals in that game. He provided a late winner against Sierra Leone, but a loss to Spain left the USA facing a powerful Brazilian team in the quarterfinals, in which they lost 3-0.

The international market for players as young as Adu is murky, and FIFA has been tightening regulations over the years to prevent exploitation. But Adu had options.

Richard Motzkin represented Landon Donovan, who signed with Bayer Leverkusen at age 16. Now representing Adu, he knew the market:

The rules are in a constant state of flux about age requirements. That being said, there are always exceptions to every rule as well as there are different ways to look at it. Without naming names, there were multiple teams as well as MLS that were interested in Freddy. Freddy went to the U-17 tournament a complete free agent in Finland, and among other things scored three goals against South Korea, which only increased and piqued the interest of a lot of people overseas. His mom was prepared to move and be with him. There were very real options for Freddy overseas, and at least two different clubs had prepared a lengthy legal analysis and hired outside counsels to determine how they would sign him, what avenues they could take and how they would qualify him. There was very real and serious interest from multiple clubs, including two in particular at the time.

In the MLS office, Ivan Gazidis understood the challenge:

There are ways, first of all, on a practical level, that clubs push the envelope on the regulation. Even putting that aside, what was very possible is that you can sign a player to a contract. FIFA regulations don't say you can't pay somebody and have him contracted—what they say is you can't register him and have him play for you. So the scenario would have been someone who was interested in Freddy's rights would have signed him to a long-term contract and either loaned him out to a club for his development or just had him train in the U.S. national team program in Bradenton and visit the club on a regular basis . . . just not play. So there was competition for Freddy's signature, regardless of what the FIFA regulations were. . . .

Freddy Adu was obviously on everybody's radar from the age of 11 or 12. We had resisted signing him—what really prompted us to take the step to sign him was his decision to go professional, regardless of whether it was MLS or somebody else.

MLS signed Adu in November. D.C. United maneuvered—with some critics crying foul over perceived league interference—to trade with Dallas for the first draft pick and make it possible for Adu to live at home and commute to practice with his mother.

"I was very young and I didn't want to make the jump overseas," Adu said in our 2008 interview, by which time he was still only 18. "I wanted to be close to home and be allowed to grow up. Things that didn't really turn out the way I wanted as far as the growing up goes because it was a little tough. I just wanted be close to home, be comfortable, and have as normal a life as possible."

The ever-quotable Ray Hudson, who had seen Adu train with his D.C. United team, said "a blind man on a galloping horse" could see the youngster's talent, comparing him to a "Fabergé egg" that would need special treatment. But Hudson wouldn't be around to provide that guidance. United gambled by easing him aside in favor of Peter Nowak, an inexperienced coach just a couple of years removed from the Chicago Fire midfield.

Nowak was stuck with a thorny challenge. With a charismatic smile and precocious interview skills, Adu was a marketer's dream, charming magazine and TV interviewers on a media blitz after his signing. ("He had classes probably on how to talk to guys like you," says then-teammate Ben Olsen. "He's a bright kid; he knows what's going on.") Fans in each MLS city came out to see him play. The no-nonsense coach, though, would prefer to bring him along slowly rather than tossing a slightly framed 14-year-old prodigy into the lion's den against hard-nosed MLS defenders who would sooner serve hard time than let a high-paid high schooler strut past them without a sturdy challenge. Besides, Nowak had games to win.

No one really understood the ramifications of bringing such a young player into the pro game. Around the world, young players might begin to build a reputation at 14 or 15, then get occasional playing time at 16 or 17. In other North American sports, phenoms stay in the junior or high-school ranks until ready. Even so, most players need an adjustment period—Kobe Bryant wasn't a dominant NBA player in his rookie year, and baseball players signed from high school still spend time in the minor leagues. Hockey player Sidney Crosby, who spent his teen years battling other top prospects in juniors even though everyone knew he was a No. 1 draft pick in waiting, is a rare exception as a young standout rookie. And for every Crosby, there's a Damon Bailey, the middle-school basketball star who followed through on his commitment to Indiana but never played in the NBA.

Nowak was working in unfamiliar territory. But he seemed better prepared than the pundits, who took the extremes ranging from dismissing Adu as a gimmick to assuming he should step onto the national team any day now. The United coach would opt for a middle ground, giving Adu steady substitute appearances and occasional starts to develop him slowly while appeasing the crowds who turned out to see him.

His debut drew national attention even as MLS tried to keep expectations reasonable. "This is not the savior for soccer," said commissioner Don Garber as he dutifully addressed Adu questions before the game. "The sport doesn't need to be saved."

With 24,603 watching on April 3, 2004, at RFK Stadium, a packed press-box and a national TV audience, Adu made his debut. "I was very nervous," Adu says. "It was one thing training and whatnot, but there were so many people at the game, and I didn't know what to expect. I just wanted to get it over with. It took me a while before I got somewhat comfortable playing."

D.C. United didn't exactly build a team around the prodigy. They built one on top of him. To some extent, that was an accident. Jaime Moreno rejoined United to little fanfare after an injury-plagued year with the MetroStars, then suddenly found his 1990s form. Argentine playmaker Christian Gomez paid off far better than most foreign signings. Add Santino Quaranta to the mix, and it became hard to fit Adu on the field. Yet D.C. continued to get more offensive talent during the season, signing Lucio Filomeno.

Still, Adu didn't disappoint those who had reasonable expectations. He made plenty of mistakes, as any young player would, and he was easily muscled away from the ball by bigger guys. Yet he provided moments of greatness that gave a glimpse of his rare talent. He scored a spectacular goal against Los Angeles, fooling defenders with a couple of touches and finishing with power and accuracy.

Defenders didn't take it easy on him. Asked if he felt accepted around MLS, Adu says:

I did and I didn't. Obviously when a young kid comes in with all that media attention and all that money and whatnot, there are going to be other guys that are just not gonna take it the right way. If I'm 30 years old, been there done that, put in my time, and here comes this kid with all this media attention and all this money, obviously I'm not happy about it. But that's just the way it was—human nature. Everything that came with when I first came in the league . . . it just sort of happened that way, and I've gotta deal with it.

It got to a point where I was just sick and tired of getting pushed around a little bit by the older guys. You've gotta fight back sometimes.

Adu aside, MLS started the season with two more developments, good news for Chicago fans and traditionalists. The suburban village of Bridgeview agreed to chip in most of the money for a new Fire stadium, putting another MLS team on the road to its own venue. From the league office, the last vestiges of nontraditional rules were wiped away—no more overtime, no more fourth substitute for the goalkeeper. At year's end, the league even did away with the "scoring champion"—determined by a system of two points per goal, one point per assist—in favor of a more traditional "golden boot" given to the top goal-scorer, with assists used only as a tiebreaker. Fans who shunned the league because it didn't play the game the way it was played around the world were running out of excuses.

While Chicago built a new stadium, Dave Sarachan had new holes to fill in the Fire side that had won the Supporters' Shield and Open Cup. Fulham, which had already signed Columbus icon Brian McBride, added Carlos Bocanegra. Benfica, one of a couple of well-supported Portuguese clubs, snared Zach Thornton. European rumors continued to swirl around DaMarcus Beasley, never a statistical monster but always a pesky two-way presence on the wing.

The MetroStars, who had already lost Clint Mathis to Europe, picked Michael Bradley in the late rounds of the draft. The midfielder wasn't just another 16-year-old phenom in the youth national pipeline—he was coach Bob Bradley's son. An older addition was Sergio Galvan Rey, a 30-year-old Argentine forward, cleverly but rather optimistically known as the King of Goals.

Steve Nicol's Revolution made few moves outside the draft, where they picked up attacking player Clint Dempsey. Columbus picked up veteran defender Robin Fraser to anchor its rebuilding effort, while one-time MVP Alex Pineda Chacon was quietly let go to ply his trade in the A-League. McBride would be irreplaceable.

Out West, Los Angeles made the biggest noise in the off-season market, bringing one-time Manchester United prospect Jovan Kirovski back to the United States after a long tour of Europe. Austrian Andreas Herzog got a shot at filling Mauricio Cienfuegos's shoes in midfield, while Alexi Lalas retired for the second time.

But Lalas didn't return to his ESPN duties. Instead, he moved up the coast and into the front office as the president and general manager in San Jose, tackling the tricky task of solving the team's off-field problems while maintaining the core of a team that had won two MLS Cups in three years.

Lalas says it started when Galaxy coach Sigi Schmid told him he wouldn't be included in the team's plans in 2004:

> I'm a big boy. I wasn't happy with the decision but I respected that this was a different direction that they wanted to go. I walked out of the office and said, "What the hell am I going to do now?"
>
> Literally, one door closes and the other one opens. I got a call a week or so later from our ownership, with Tim Leiweke [president of Anschutz Entertainment Group, owner of the Quakes and Galaxy, among others]. . . . He invited me over to have a lunch, sat me down, and said, "We have this opportunity in San Jose. We know you don't have the traditional background in your education or experience, but we believe that you can do a job. Would you want to be the president and GM of the Earthquakes?" I took about two seconds and said, "Hell yeah." . . . It was an opportunity that doesn't come around all the time and a great way for me to kind of jump off.
>
> I could've hung around and bummed around the league or gone someplace else, but once again, I had an understanding that my career was certainly coming into the twilight, and I probably wasn't going to get this type of opportunity if I wanted to say I'm going to play this out as long as I can. So I packed up the car and drove up to San Jose.

While Lalas gladly posed for several features profiling his transformation from long-bearded guitar-strumming defender to responsible, clean-shaven (the long beard was long gone, occasionally but not usually replaced by a few days' growth) executive in a business suit, the Earthquakes changed little from their title team.

Colorado let Fraser go to Columbus and settled on Joe Cannon in goal, sending Scott Garlick to Dallas. The Burn shuffled the defense, landing Cory Gibbs on his return from Europe along with Steve Jolley, Carey Talley, and bruising defensive midfielder Simo Valakari. Kansas City just hoped to get another good year out of Preki and Tony Meola.

EXPANSION GOES WEST

The MLS expansion rumor mill had always been lively. Doug Logan had pledged a team to Seattle, though the league hadn't followed through. New York was due for a second team before Subotnick and Kluge backed out and sold their interest in the MetroStars and the league. Rochester, where the A-League Rhinos drew five-figure crowds and were working on a stadium, was often mentioned as a possibility for expansion or even relocation of a wayward franchise such as the Mutiny. Traditional soccer cities like St. Louis and Philadelphia were always in the running, as were old NASL markets such as Atlanta, Portland (Oregon), Minnesota, and Tulsa. Like the NASL, MLS would look north of the border to Toronto or Vancouver. Houston and Milwaukee were on the short list, San Antonio had a flurry of interest from local lawmakers, and a group of North Carolina businessmen sought to fill the Southern void with a team in Winston-Salem.

Cleveland had been penciled in as the next expansion site, but the death of Bert Wolstein, who had a letter of intent for the team, derailed the plans.

"I really hit it off with him, just loved the guy and thought he was really passionate about the sport," Garber says of Wolstein. "He came in and he basically said give me an option, I don't want to pay much of anything for it, but I'm going to build a stadium and put my family's name on it. I was able to convince the MLS board to go forward with it. But unfortunately, he passed away and that option expired."

Wolstein associate John McGill pledged to continue his efforts, but without public financing lined up, the effort was doomed.

One city not mentioned often was Salt Lake City, the Utah oasis that had successfully hosted the 2002 Winter Olympics. The city isn't one of the country's biggest, and the NBA's inaptly named Utah Jazz are the only major league team calling it home. The University of Utah's Rice-Eccles Stadium was designed to hold a wide field ready for international soccer, but the area had no top-flight soccer tradition and no other tangible signs of interest in the game. The 2004 MLS media guide listed 13 potential expansion sites, not including Salt Lake City.

On July 14 came the surprise announcement: Salt Lake City was getting an MLS team.

After the fact, the expansion news started to make sense. Utah had over-whelming interest in youth soccer. A couple of suburbs were interested in a stadium development. Most importantly, Salt Lake City had a new investor—Dave Checketts, a Utah native who had plenty of experience in New York sports business with the NBA Knicks and Madison Square Garden.

From the other edge of the Rockies came another piece of development news. Stan Kroenke hadn't needed much time to find a suitable stadium site for the Rapids. The team would build a complex of youth fields surrounding a stadium, similar to the Burn's Frisco development, in Denver suburb Commerce City, with the city and Kroenke sharing the financing.

With Colorado building and an expansion team juggling stadium prospects in Utah, the question remained of a venue for the other expansion team, the affiliate of Mexico's Chivas. They came up with an easy answer. The new team would share the Home Depot Center with the Galaxy. Los Angeles had supported the Galaxy so well that a second team didn't seem unreasonable, particularly in a region already obsessed with Mexican soccer. The Chivas brand name and colors, the theory went, would draw a new group of fans to the stadium and the league as a whole.

ChampionsWorld staged another series of exhibitions featuring some of the same European giants—Manchester United, Celtic, and Milan were back, along with Chelsea, Liverpool, Roma, Bayern Munich, Galatasaray, and Porto. But attendance dipped slightly, and the company would soon struggle with the enormous expense of hosting the games.

PARITY POWER

While MLS made progress off the field, teams were playing to stalemates on it. No player scored more than 12 goals. No team won more than half its games. No team lost more than half its games. The regular season mimicked the old *Simpsons* send-up: "Ties, ties, ties!"

Even the All-Star Game, a one-year reversion to the East-West format, was subdued in comparison to past free-for-alls. The teams combined for 14 shots on goal before a smallish crowd of 21,378 at Washington's RFK Stadium.

Adu, added to the roster as a commissioner's pick, joined the fray in the second half alongside United teammate and fellow No. 1 draft pick Alecko Eskandarian. But Amado Guevara, from the rival MetroStars, would claim MVP honors with two goals and an assist on Eskandarian's goal in the 3-2 East win.

Columbus's collection of role players took the Supporters' Shield with a 12-5-13 record, seven points ahead of D.C. United in the East. The Crew gave up barely a goal a game behind diminutive goalkeeper Jon Busch and the unflappable Fraser, Defender of the Year for the second time. Edson Buddle scored 10, while nontraditional playmaker Simon Elliott contributed 10 assists.

Kansas City won the West with defense and a 14-9-7 mark, just missing out on the Shield. Tony Meola snapped back into form, while Josh Wolff stayed healthy long enough to score 10 goals. Los Angeles was in first place late in the season, yet the team found the 9-6-7 record enough of a disappointment to fire coach Sigi Schmid and hire Steve Sampson, the former U.S. coach who had also spent time with Costa Rica's national team.

While the midtable teams—the Galaxy, Colorado, D.C. United, and the MetroStars—wound up separated by only two points at the end, the excitement down the stretch was at the bottom of the standings, where a few accomplished teams fell on hard times. San Jose and Dallas boasted the league's leading scorers, Brian Ching and Eddie Johnson, respectively, but found themselves dueling for the last spot in the West. One year after playing in the East final, New England and Chicago fought for the last East spot.

Coincidentally, all four teams were paired up on the final weekend. San Jose got the draw it needed in Dallas, taking a 2-1 lead and holding on for 30 minutes after the Burn tied it. Dallas, rebuilding from a horror season the year before, finished 10-14-6 and would have qualified if the West and East standings were mixed. The Burn improved on the field and at the gate, trickling back up over the 9,000 mark after the Southlake misery, but it wasn't enough to avoid another year without a playoff game.

New England needed all three points at home against Chicago. After a taut first half, the teams traded quick goals—Clint Dempsey for the Revolution, Nate Jaqua for the Fire. Steve Ralston scored a couple of minutes later to give the Revs a 2-1 lead, and the defense made it stand. Chicago fell from an MLS Cup berth to the worst record in the league.

The playoffs seemed wide open after such a tight season, and lower seeds Colorado, San Jose, and New England followed through by taking the lead in the home legs of each series. Only D.C. United, which had slowly strengthened over the season, avoided a stumble on the road with a 2-0 win against the MetroStars.

While United followed through with a 2-0 home win, the Wizards and Galaxy played catch-up. Spurred on by a crowd of 20,026, easily the best in the first round, Los Angeles got goals from Ruiz and Tyrone Marshall for a 2-1 series win. Kansas City, down 2-0 after the trip to San Jose, got a first-half goal from Khari Stephenson and an own goal from Brian Ching to level it, then won on a stoppage-time effort from Jack Jewsbury. Preserving the shutout was Bo Oshoniyi, the original Columbus keeper and longtime Wizards backup pressed into service late in the season by a Meola injury.

Disaster struck in Columbus, where intimidating New England goalkeeper Matt Reis stopped two penalty kicks. Taylor Twellman then staked the Revs to a late 1-0 lead. Edson Buddle scored in stoppage time, but it wasn't enough—New England knocked out the Supporters' Shield winners on 2-1 aggregate.

The Wizards, who had already beaten the Fire to take the Open Cup, earned their way to MLS Cup but wound up with the headache of a goalkeeper controversy. Oshoniyi once again came up with a shutout in a 2-0 win over Los Angeles, denying the Galaxy a chance to play for the title at home. But Meola was returning to health. Coach Bob Gansler was left facing a "Tony or Bo" question over the long nine days between the West final and MLS Cup.

United and the Revolution played a classic in the East. Alecko Eskandarian scored early for United; Taylor Twellman answered. Jaime Moreno fooled Reis in the 21st—with the Revs keeper playing for a cross, Moreno ripped a curling shot inside the near post. Steve Ralston tied with a penalty kick that bounced off the post but deflected off diving keeper Nick Rimando in the 44th. Earnie Stewart notched his second assist of the game as Christian Gomez gave United their third lead in the 67th; Pat Noonan headed home a third tying goal in the 85th.

After a scoreless overtime, the exhausted teams went to penalty kicks. Reis saved the first effort from United's Ben Olsen, but Ralston hit the woodwork. After Santino Quaranta put United ahead, Reis took a shot of his own and forcefully converted to tie it.

Freddy Adu stepped into a situation so fraught with pressure that veteran players' legs sometimes turn to jelly. The 15-year-old coolly finished. Twellman followed suit.

The fourth round finally gave United the advantage as Eskandarian scored and Rimando saved Jay Heaps's effort. But Moreno, clearly showing the effects of an intense 120 minutes, managed only a weak effort. Shalrie Joseph made it 3-3, forcing the tiebreaker to continue.

Between United's Brian Carroll and New England's Clint Dempsey, the Revs surely had the advantage in the sixth round. It didn't work out that way. Carroll converted his, Rimando made another save, and the crowd of 21,201 managed one last roar after a long evening.

It was a finale of sorts at RFK Stadium. After several years of keeping the multipurpose stadium reserved for soccer teams, United would begin sharing the creaking venue with the Washington Nationals, a relocated baseball team formerly known as the Montreal Expos. United's pristine pitch would be torn up to accommodate infield dirt and uneven patching around the pitcher's mound. Worse, the team's loyal fans were left scratching their heads as the same city government that dragged its feet over an inexpensive soccer-stadium contribution approved up to $611 million to put a baseball team where the sport had failed twice before.

Yet D.C. fans would end the season celebrating.

United fell behind early in the November 14 final at suburban L.A.'s Home Depot Center as Kansas City's Jose Burciaga, a left back with a cannon of a shot, drilled one into the net in the sixth minute. The anxiety wouldn't last long, and D.C. took control over a seven-minute span in the first half. Eskandarian scored in the 19th and 23rd minutes, and Alex Zotinca steered one into his own net in the 26th. The Wizards would respond with a Wolff penalty in the 58th minute, but Nick Rimando kept them at bay after that. With a 3-2 win, D.C. United had returned to the top of the league for the first time in five years.

Adu, the league's fresh new face, had helped United keep possession in the second half and merrily celebrated with his team. But the win meant even more to two men more than twice his age. Earnie Stewart, who spend so many years crisscrossing the Atlantic to play with class and flair for the national team, had sparkled down the stretch for his MLS team. Peter Nowak, the rookie coach, proved himself capable at managing his team and the media with a soft-spoken but firm determination. With the flair of Adu, MVP finalist Jaime Moreno and Christian Gomez supporting Eskandarian's nose for goal, the team had a style that seemed lacking through much of MLS that year.

"It was awesome," Adu says. "Being in an MLS Cup your first season and actually winning it was a great experience. I really enjoyed it. It sort of spoils you a little bit. You keep thinking maybe you're going to be there every year, but nahhhhh. It doesn't happen like that. Never got a chance to go back there after that. You just cherish moments like that. I'm glad I got a ring."

And Adu brought plenty of attention to United.

"That was interesting," Olsen says. "It certainly was a show. It was great on one side because it brought attention to our team. It brought attention to the sport. It was nice to have cameras all around, have this guy playing with you. It was nice to have us in the limelight for a little while. I think all the players really enjoyed it. It was never overwhelming. Everybody dealt with it the right way."

Yet United would be shut out in the postseason awards. New England's versatile, combative Dempsey took Rookie of the Year honors ahead of Adu. Greg Andrulis, who coaxed a first-place run out of the Crew without Brian McBride, was Coach of the Year ahead of Nowak. Colorado's Joe Cannon was Goalkeeper of the Year for the second time—and second team—in three years.

The league prepared once again to build back from 10 teams to 12. Chivas USA stocked much of its roster with unknown Mexican prospects, a decision that would haunt them. Real Salt Lake, perhaps too obviously borrowing its name from a European giant, landed perennial scoring threat Jason Kreis from Dallas, which also went European in changing its name from the Burn to FC Dallas.

Expansion wasn't the only sign of the league's improved fiscal health. MLS signed a massive sponsorship deal with Adidas—10 years, $150 million. The Project-40 program, previously funded by rival shoe company Nike, would be renamed Generation Adidas. Don Garber confirmed that the five-year pledge from league investors, issued in the dark days of contraction three years earlier, was now a moot point. Rosters expanded to 28, including 10 "developmental" slots that could include Generation Adidas players, and MLS planned to launch reserve-team competition in 2005.

A few days after the Adidas deal was announced, MLS and the players union signed a collective bargaining agreement through the 2009 season. Two years after shedding the albatross of the players' lawsuit, the league was guaranteed labor peace for the foreseeable future.

The league was stable, but two teams were not. In San Jose, Anschutz was scrambling to find a new owner or a new stadium, with not-so-subtle threats that the two-time champion Earthquakes would move. Lamar Hunt also insisted it was time to cut his holdings, putting the Kansas City Wizards for sale even though they shared space with his football team, the Chiefs. Two teams with significant hardware in the trophy case would enter the tenth MLS season in limbo.

2005: SEASON 10

The year in American soccer had a rocky start. U.S. players threatened to miss a World Cup qualifier against Trinidad and Tobago in a contract dispute with the U.S. Soccer Federation. Bruce Arena was forced to compile a team of USL and indoor players to avoid a forfeit that would all but shut down the national-team program. The regular players managed to work out a deal in time, and the only lasting impact on American soccer was the emergence of Clyde Simms, a midfielder from the USL's Richmond Kickers, who impressed scouts and wound up with D.C. United.

ChampionsWorld went bankrupt and would later sue the Federation along with MLS in an antitrust action "against the purported national governing body for soccer," according to the public biography of ChampionsWorld lawyer William Charron.[1] Anyone with the slightest inkling of soccer history, whether a Fed fan or not, would have to cringe at the word "purported."

San Jose started the season with a loss many had expected. Landon Donovan had only been in MLS all this time through the agreement of Bayer Leverkusen, the German club that signed him as a teenager and still technically had a share of his rights. MLS had managed to keep him for four years, but that was enough. Leverkusen, in the midst of a Champions League campaign while trying to stay near the top of the Bundesliga, called Donovan back to Germany.

It was an awkward reunion. Donovan had never made a secret of his disillusionment in Germany, playing reserve-team soccer on cold fields far from his California climate and close-knit family. His extended family was growing—Donovan was in a serious relationship with actress Bianca Kajlich, whom he would later marry. Donovan dutifully returned to Germany, but his heart was clearly in California.

Yet Donovan says it wasn't tough to go back. "I felt an obligation to go back there," Donovan says. "They had been great to me, and they gave me a chance to come here and do what I wanted to do, which was to play. I was under every impression that going back there, I was going to have a real chance to play."

Since his Under-17 exploits, Donovan had always faced immense expectations unlike any other U.S. player with the recent exception of Freddy Adu. Nothing he did was quite good enough. If he scored two goals in the World Cup—which he did—it should've been three or four. While he made his teams better by any objective standard, he was never even a finalist for league MVP and only once took team MVP honors with the Earthquakes. He was named to the league's Best XI only once, though he would end up named to the All-Time Best XI after 10 seasons of play.

American soccer fans also had long itched for a homegrown talent to shine under the bright lights in Europe. Brad Friedel and Kasey Keller had proud careers in goal, but Americans wanted to see a field player with even more success. Claudio Reyna had played well whenever healthy, but mostly as a leader of mildly accomplished teams or a role player on Scotland's Rangers side. After 10 or 15 years of slowly building toward international respectability, Americans wanted a star. For all the sniping and criticism directed his way, Donovan was clearly the best shot.

It didn't happen. Perhaps it was homesickness, perhaps it was a lack of chemistry, perhaps it was unsuitability for Leverkusen's style of play. Whatever the reason, Donovan didn't click with the German team. He worked his way into the starting lineup for a few games but got horrible reviews after a Champions League outing against Liverpool.

Even the best players sometimes have trouble fitting into a good team, as Ukraine's Andriy Shevchenko can attest after his experience at English Premier League giant Chelsea. Usually, these players spend an unhappy few months getting intermittent playing time before transferring somewhere else at the end of the season or the January transfer window. Donovan, though, had a parachute and was able to leap earlier.

The rumors flew in March, just a couple of months after Donovan's departure. He had been seen in California, some said. He was talking with MLS and his agent. The agents said the right things in public, that everything was fine and Donovan was excited about Leverkusen.

Privately, the dominoes were set in motion. The Galaxy sent Carlos Ruiz and his big salary to Dallas, opening some room under the cap. MLS worked out a way to pay Donovan far more than the supposed league maximum, just as they had for a select few marquee stars of the past. A compensation package was sent from Los Angeles to San Jose, two teams under the Anschutz umbrella. Donovan signed with the Galaxy.

Donovan explains how it happened:

> I was at a low spot and not happy about it at all. Initially, there was a feeling there was no chance it was going to happen. The more I thought about it and the more we spoke to MLS, we wanted to make it happen. Then I spoke to the Leverkusen people. I opened up with them and I was really honest with them, and I just told them this is not something that I want to be doing right now. To their full credit, they were very understanding. They came a long way from initially saying, "That's the way it goes. You'll be OK." They kind of put the business side to the side and saw me as a human being and said, "OK, if that's what you want to do, we'll make it happen." . . .
>
> I wanted to be home. Sometimes people say that's the way sports goes . . . but the more I thought about it, the more I thought it can happen, that can be possible. I don't need to be somewhere I'm not enjoying my life. Family was a big part of that and just wanting to be happy was a big part of that.

The Golden Boy of U.S. soccer had set himself up as a lightning rod of controversy. San Jose fans howled in protest at the machinations that saw their star player land with their haughty downstate rival. Many U.S. fans seethed that he lacked the mental toughness to compete at the club game's toughest level, griping that Donovan's development would be stunted in a league that demanded less of him than the Bundesliga and Champions League. "No Longer the Great U.S. Hope" read a headline on an *ESPNsoccernet* column by Jen Chang.

"It's a fair argument from a competitive standpoint," Donovan says. "Fortunately for me, I'm the one who lives my life. I'm the one who needs to live my life. I've said it a million times: it's very easy for someone sitting on their couch to say, yeah, you should go there and play there and take his family there. But it's not always the case when you're in that situation. I don't tell other people what they should do, and I expect the same in return."

Little wonder the 23-year-old was noticeably losing his hair. But he settled into L.A. life, moving in with Kajlich in a beautiful house featured on MTV's *Cribs*. Donovan recalls, "It's funny because I probably get that comment from people more than any other comment: 'Hey, you were on *Cribs*, right?' It's not, 'Hey, you're a soccer player.'"

Donovan joined a team in transition. Ruiz was out, along with solid core players Sasha Victorine, Dan Califf, and Alejandro Moreno. Andreas Herzog was also gone, as was South Korean defender Hong Myung Bo, who had soaked up plenty of international acclaim after the 2002 World Cup but never looked dominant at the back in MLS. Sampson restocked with a couple of players he knew from his days in Costa Rica, some draft picks, a couple of unknown Brazilians, and Guatemalan midfielder Guillermo "Pando" Ramirez. If not for Kevin Hartman in goal and Cobi Jones in midfield, the team would be virtually unrecognizable.

San Jose also was retooling. The offensive (Donovan) and defensive (Agoos) stars were gone, along with central midfield partners Ronnie Ekelund and Richard Mulrooney. The backline, which also lost Todd Dunivant and Ramiro Corrales, got reinforcements in Califf and Wade Barrett, returning to the fold from Norway. Brad Davis and Ricardo Clark floated into midfield, and Ronald Cerritos rejoined the Earthquakes after an unproductive time in D.C.

Dallas eagerly took Mulrooney and completed a transatlantic shuffle on defense, with Greg Vanney returning to MLS from France while Cory Gibbs went back overseas. The big change was up front, with Ruiz slated to replace Salt Lake-bound Kreis.

The merry-go-round of proven forwards also reached Colorado, where Jeff Cunningham arrived as a replacement for the retired John Spencer.

Of the two expansion teams, Real Salt Lake had a head start with proven MLS talent—Kreis, Eddie Pope, Clint Mathis, and Andy Williams seemed to be a solid nucleus if healthy. Chivas USA had a legit Mexican star in Ramon Ramirez, surrounded by a lot of question marks. Salt Lake did go young in the draft, taking 16-year-old Nik Besagno with the first overall pick, while Chivas took goalkeeper Brad Guzan.

With the expansion teams slotted in the West, MLS Cup finalist Kansas City moved to the East, adding Sasha Victorine but parting ways with Tony Meola to let Bo Oshoniyi start in goal. The champions, D.C. United, lost Bobby Convey and defensive anchor Ryan Nelsen to Europe and bid farewell to Earnie Stewart, who played a few more games in the Netherlands before moving into management.

Columbus, the Supporters' Shield holders, seemed set to compete with the 2004 finalists, replacing Cunningham with Ante Razov. Chicago, reeling from the European moves of DaMarcus Beasley, Damani Ralph, and Carlos Bocanegra along with Razov's departure, reloaded with Honduran players Samuel Caballero and Ivan Guerrero. Tony Sanneh, a late addition to the Crew the year before, moved to Chicago.

New England bade a sentimental farewell to Joe-Max Moore, but in typical Nicol fashion, the Revolution built through the draft—defender Michael Parkhurst was the first-rounder this time around. Nicol's team started with an 11-game unbeaten streak.

That left the MetroStars to make the year's high-profile acquisition—French midfielder Youri Djorkaeff, a starter for the 1998 World Cup champions. Agoos replaced former United teammate Pope at the back.

McBride and Bocanegra came back to the States with their English club, Fulham, for the All-Star Game in McBride's longtime Columbus home. The hometown appeal succeeded in bringing out an overflow crowd to see the MLS stars gain control, conveniently after the two Americans were substituted. Another ex-Crew man, Jeff Cunningham, scored two late goals to clinch a 4-1 win, but Taylor Twellman took MVP honors.

With ChampionsWorld no longer operating, MLS resumed its role as travel agent for European clubs. Two years after Manchester United fans scoffed at the idea of their team lowering itself to play an MLS team, Chelsea rallied past D.C. United 2-1, Milan beat Chicago 3-1, and Real Madrid beat the Galaxy 2-0. MLS teams would fare better the next year.

In general, MLS's international results weren't flattering in Year 10. A team of MLS stars traveled to Real Madrid's Bernabeu stadium in the midst of an exhausting stretch of league play and World Cup qualifiers, only to get lost in the glare and suffer a 5-0 rout. The league extended its long run of futility in the CONCACAF Champions Cup since the Galaxy's 2001 triumph, seeing Kansas City knocked out by Costa Rica's Saprissa in the quarterfinals and D.C. United embarrassed in the semifinals by Mexico's Pumas. United came close to putting Chile's Universidad Catolica out of the Copa Sudamericana, scoring twice in Chile for a 3-1 aggregate lead, but gave up three goals to bow out.

D.C. United, though, would claim a new trophy. Its deep bench came through in reserve-team play with an 8-4-0 record, and a couple of hundred hard-core fans gathered at the RFK practice field to watch United clinch and lift the Reserve Division trophy.

The expansion teams gave MLS two new entertaining rivalries. Real Salt Lake and Colorado fans followed the Chicago-Dallas Brimstone Cup model, instituting a Rocky Mountain Cup with a beautiful trophy made in Scotland and engraved with a relief of the mountains, punctuated with a mission statement pledging to "send annoying thoughts each other's way and then make up for such blasphemous mental burps with a round of drinks purchased by the losers at the nearest locally licensed or unlicensed establishment for such imbibing." The Galaxy and Chivas USA hyped their meetings as "superclassicos" and drew 88,816 fans to a doubleheader in L.A. Coliseum that also featured the original Chivas against Mexican rival Club America. Chivas USA president Antonio Cue lost a succession of amusing bets on the games and was forced to dye his hair green, wash Galaxy counterpart Doug Hamilton's car, take 50 kids to a Galaxy game, and donate to the Galaxy's charitable foundation.

Yet neither expansion team managed to get anywhere close to playoff contention. Chivas USA brought in reinforcements from Mexico in Francisco Palencia and Juan Pablo Garcia, but it was far too late. Real Salt Lake's mix of young and old turned into inexperience and injury. Both teams conceded more than two goals per game; neither scored more than one. Salt Lake took the honors between the two and avoided last place with a 5-22-5 record, edging Chivas's 4-22-6 mark. Both teams were successful at the gate, at least—the doubleheader with its Mexican parent pushed Chivas to a 17,080 average, while Salt Lake's fan base impressed fellow MLS faithful with an 18,037 average.

At the other end of the West table, San Jose ran away with the conference and the Supporters' Shield. Dwayne DeRosario, improving steadily each year after scoring the 2001 Cup–winner as a sub, led the offense, while Pat Onstad slammed the door for an 0.97 goals-against average. The Earthquakes finished 18-4-10, 18 points ahead of the West pack.

With San Jose far in front and the expansion teams far behind, the other three teams in the West had little to play for. Donovan racked up 12 goals and 10 assists in only 22 games for Los Angeles, but the Galaxy still wound up fourth at a middling 13-13-6 mark. Colorado, led by Cunningham's 12 goals, had an identical record. Dallas claimed second, three points ahead, despite missing Carlos Ruiz for almost half the season.

The East race was tighter, with New England claiming first behind Taylor Twellman's league-leading 17 goals and Clint Dempsey's offensive inspiration. D.C. United led the league in scoring as Jaime Moreno (16 goals), Christian Gomez (11), and part-time starter Freddy Adu combined to play stylish soccer. Still, even with Nick Rimando posting another good year in goal, United finished five points adrift of the Revs but ahead of Chicago, which welcomed back goalkeeper Zach Thornton to solidify the defense and take third.

Adu occasionally had fits over Peter Nowak's unwillingness to start him more often. New MetroStars general manager Alexi Lalas told the *New York Times* he would love for the prodigy "to get fed up with D.C." and move up the coast—a great comment for reporters but not so well received in various boardrooms and offices. D.C. executive Kevin Payne said in June:

There are some people around Freddy who don't understand sports at this level or soccer at this level. Unfortunately, some of them think they do. They've been doing some talking, and they need to stop. The worst thing anyone can do with Freddy is to be too impatient. He's still 15, he's got a lot to learn. He has a guy who's perfectly suited to teach him in Peter. . . . Peter talks all the time about how he thought he had all the answers all the while, then realized people older than him knew what they were talking about. . . . Sometimes he'll be learning on the field, and sometimes he'll be learning on the bench.[2]

The 15-year-old wasn't the only player with a chip on his shoulder. The race for the last spot between the MetroStars and disappointing Kansas City had a personal overtone to it as Tony Meola, fuming after the Wizards declined to keep him around, resurfaced midway through the season in his original home of Giants Stadium. The MetroStars, who had exiled previous goalkeeper Jonny Walker to Columbus, also had a potent offense with Amado Guevara notching 11 goals and 11 assists, while Djorkaeff proved to be one of the better high-profile signings with a solid 10-goal campaign and occasional glimpses of world-class play. The Wizards' hearts would be broken on the last weekend.

For Columbus, it was also a season of heartbreak. Unable to replace Cunningham's scoring and battered by injuries, the Crew simply sank. Halfway through the season, sitting with a 4-10-2 record, Columbus fired Greg Andrulis and gave longtime midfielder turned assistant coach Robert Warzycha the interim job. The Polish coach guided the Crew to respectability, winning 7 of his 16 games in charge, but the playoffs were long out of reach. The Crew sank from first in the East to last, leaving both of Lamar Hunt's East teams wondering how they failed to live up to expectations.

In the playoffs, very little went according to expectations.

The playoff-hardened Revolution defended their top seed, shrugging off a 1-0 loss in New Jersey to put three goals past Meola in Foxborough to win on 3-2 aggregate. They were the only higher seed to advance.

D.C. United seemed set to renew a budding postseason rivalry with the Revs, tying 0-0 in Chicago. But United simply imploded at home against the Fire. With Christian Gomez sent off for spraying C. J. Brown with spit, United suffered a 4-0 loss before a stunned crowd of 20,089.

In the West, new coach Fernando Clavijo imparted a bit of fighting spirit in the Rapids. They drew the first leg 2-0 in Colorado, traded goals for a 2-2 tie in Dallas, then beat the former Burn on penalty kicks.

The California rivalry, already in the record books for San José's stunning comeback against Los Angeles two years earlier, took another strange turn. Landon Donovan, one of the catalysts of that classic game, was in fine form against his former teammates. The Galaxy took the first leg 3-1. Donovan then ignored the heckling San Jose fans as Los Angeles knocked out the Supporters' Shield winner with a 1-1 tie in Spartan Stadium.

The Galaxy went on to Colorado and disposed of the Rapids 2-0. New England advanced with a typically efficient 1-0 decision over Chicago, with Matt Reis denying the Fire.

The final matchup wouldn't have seemed surprising before the season. New England had been strong in the postseason under Nicol, and Los Angeles had an intriguing collection of talent. Some fans, though, wondered how the Galaxy could look so average during the season and then win two playoff matchups with relative ease.

THE SHOWCASE

Leading into MLS Cup, the league unveiled its All-Time Best XI. Tony Meola was the goalkeeper, along with fellow U.S. World Cup veterans Marcelo Balboa, Jeff Agoos, and Eddie Pope on defense. The midfield had a more cosmopolitan mix—foreign playmakers Marco Etcheverry, Carlos Valderrama, and Peter Nowak joined young American Donovan and not-so-young American Preki. Brian McBride and Jaime Moreno took the forward spots.

That was the only major announcement leading up to MLS Cup. The big off-field news for the league was the September 28 groundbreaking on the Rapids complex in Commerce City. Early in the season, MLS had been on the verge of expanding to San Antonio, but a mayoral election brought to power Phil Hardberger, a man with absolutely no interest in the league.

American investors started bidding for Premier League clubs, led by the Glazer family, which bought Manchester United a couple of years after not making a deal in Tampa Bay.

Lalas had crept back into the spotlight over the summer, switching from management of one Anschutz team to another. He returned to New Jersey as president and general manager of the MetroStars, leaving behind a troubled MLS presence in San Jose.

The November 13 final itself was a showcase of the league's progress— three-month-old Pizza Hut Park in Frisco, Texas, new home of the team soon to be known as FC Dallas rather than the Dallas Burn, was the venue.

As they had in 2002, the Galaxy and Revolution produced a final that was far from a classic. Kevin Stott whistled 51 fouls. The game would have as many yellow cards as shots on goal—10 apiece. Most of those shots went to the Galaxy, but Matt Reis stood equal to the task. The Revolution didn't manage a shot on goal until the 62nd minute, when defender Jay Heaps burst through and shot. Taylor Twellman, one of the league's most consistent scorers, didn't get a single effort on frame.

The Galaxy had a couple of good chances late in regulation, but the game went scoreless into extra time. Overtime sessions often go one of two ways—two tired teams sit back in exhaustion and hope for a break, or two tired teams finally lose their grip on defense and allow the game to loosen up. This game had the latter. The Revolution finally got a second shot on goal, a good one from Jose Cancela, and the Galaxy kept pressing.

The game changed on the foot of the least likely hero. Guillermo "Pando" Ramirez had been a disappointing acquisition for the Galaxy. He set a record for shooting futility with 62 shots, 30 on goal, with only one goal—that on a penalty kick—to show for it. In the 107th minute, he made it two when Reis punched away a Donovan corner kick, and Ramirez drilled it into the net.

The "golden goal" rule was no longer in effect, so the teams played out the rest of extra time. But New England would come no closer, while the Galaxy's ever-dangerous counterattack almost doubled the lead. Los Angeles, which finished the regular season with the league's ninth-best record, lifted the Cup. With the lone regulation goal of his MLS career, Ramirez claimed MVP honors.

The Galaxy exposed a flaw in the playoff system. But the problem was not that an unworthy team won the title. The problem was that this talented team had no incentive to compete once it became obvious that expansion teams Chivas USA and Real Salt Lake had no hope of advancing to the playoffs. When it mattered—in the playoffs, in the U.S. Open Cup—the Galaxy showed up and won. For all the regular-season mediocrity, the Galaxy had become the third team to take the "double" of MLS Cup and U.S. Open Cup.

In the off-season, the league would have far more to worry about than a team that saved its best soccer for knockout tournaments.

10

Hardball

By 2006, with one decade in the books, MLS had achieved the stability so many other soccer leagues had failed to achieve. No other U.S. league had managed 10 years with such stability, and MLS had made steady progress with investment and stadium construction. The league was entrenched, in every sense of the word—stadiums, youth programs, business deals. Years 11 and 12 would see a rapid boom in investment.

Yet the power brokers were losing patience with some of the persistent problems. Lamar Hunt, who had two teams safely camped in their own stadiums in Columbus and Dallas, had served notice that he wasn't going to keep the Kansas City Wizards afloat in Arrowhead Stadium, the venue it shared with Hunt's Kansas City Chiefs. Anschutz Entertainment Group (AEG) had been a reluctant owner in San Jose for a couple of years, the latest in a succession of stopgap operators that had included the Krafts.

Sunil Gulati, who moved from the MLS office to Kraft Soccer, recalls the problems:

They got into that market because at one point Alan Rothenberg and some partners, including Dentsu, were going to be taking over the team from the league. That deal didn't come to fruition. The league had hoped it would come into private hands rather than league hands, and so the Krafts stepped in to operate that team. In the case of the Kraft family, it was a difficult venture because it was 3,000 miles away from their base. I think that is what made it particularly challenging. There's no question that if you can have local ownership that's got a vested interest and got contacts and so on the way the Kraft family does in Boston, that's a huge plus.

Alexi Lalas, who once ran the team on AEG's behalf, had a closer view but was equally doubtful of the team's prospects to stay:

We understood that the San Jose market was a dead man walking if we couldn't get a stadium deal done up there. I very quickly was educated into the reality of real estate of getting a stadium deal done. And it became apparent that it wasn't going to happen. I'm glad they went back there [a couple of years later]. In the two years I was there, I saw some great people and great support for their team and also a history that goes well beyond MLS.

It was disappointing to see them leave, but I was also privy to the economics and the realities of the situation.

This wasn't 2002. MLS wasn't in a defensive position, huddling together 10 teams for survival. In 2006, backed by a decade of stable existence and sound business interests, the league was in a position of strength at last, no longer willing to put up with situations that hurt the bottom line.

It was time to play hardball. No more "we hope we can work this out." No more "we're still searching for an owner and a stadium." No artificial deadlines and extensions.

On November 15, MLS gave San Jose a 30-day ultimatum to find local ownership. San Jose took it seriously. The grassroots Soccer Silicon Valley (SSV) group immediately asked Earthquakes fans to contact elected officials and attend a December 6 San Jose City Council meeting.

"Our presence alone will be a good indication of that but we also plan to make use of the Open Forum portion of the meeting, in which any citizen can address the council for two minutes," read a Soccer Silicon Valley statement issued the same day as the ultimatum. "They may tire of our message after the first couple hundred of us have spoken but we will talk all night if that's what it takes to make our point."

SSV is that rare activist group that combines pragmatism with its passion, and so the council members were released after roughly 20 people—the transcript isn't quite clear—had spoken. They raised economic arguments, with several speakers saying they drove from out of town to spend money in San Jose that otherwise would be spent elsewhere. They cited their kids' loyalties to the team, most poignantly in the story of a young boy who died suddenly a day after having a wonderful time at a Quakes game, leaving his family with a happy memory of his last hours.

The deadline did spur local politicians into action, and the city stepped up talks with Silicon Valley Sports & Entertainment, the Quakes' one-time co-operators.

But the council couldn't make a deal. Talks broke down December 13. The next day, SSV came to terms with the inevitable, saying they would petition—successfully, as it turned out—to reserve the name Earthquakes and the team's historical records for a future MLS expansion club.

The final news came December 15, 2005:

Dear Earthquakes Fans:
AEG, the investor-operator of the San Jose Earthquakes, announced Thursday that the city of Houston, Texas, will become the new home of the team. The move is effective immediately and all players and coaching staff currently under contract will transfer to Houston as part of the new organization.

So began a somber press release posted on the Web in place of the San Jose Earthquakes site. The letter painted a bleak picture of the Earthquakes' finances, saying AEG had invested more than $20 million with heavy losses since 2002.[1]

The league did its best not to burn any bridges in the Bay Area. "[T]he City of San Jose and Major League Soccer have signed a Letter of Intent which provides a wide variety of support elements to attract a local investor for an MLS expansion team," commissioner Don Garber said. "The Earthquakes name, colors, and competition records have been retained by MLS for this future expansion team." Maybe as soon as 2007, he said.

A *Mercury News* editorial spread the blame widely—AEG's marketing, Donovan's exit and subsequent return with the Galaxy, the San Jose government's lack of timely action. The editorial summarized what the *News* viewed as two frustrating years: "The Earthquakes' exit is a betrayal of fan loyalty and a black mark on Major League Soccer and on San Jose" and "the final act in a drawn-out drama of procrastination, phony deadlines, and false starts."[2] Yet the editorial board conceded that AEG had a bad deal at Spartan Stadium and not enough fans. A "letter of intent" to the city signed at the last minute to secure an expansion team was ridiculed as too exorbitant—the price given was $90 million for a stadium, plus operating expenses for four years (revised in a subsequent *Mercury News* article to $80 million total)—but the paper left little doubt that the fan base deserved better.

Assistant coach John Doyle, a Bay Area fixture who had played for the team when it debuted as the Clash in 1996, ripped city officials. "I do believe that San Jose has had 10 years to come up with a plan to keep the team here, but it never did," Doyle told the *Mercury News*.[3]

Columnist Ann Killion was characteristically blunt, calling the whole process "sickening" and "a pathetic joke." The city council didn't escape her wrath, but she saved most of her epithets for Garber, AEG, and MLS. Most of the complaints sound petty—not enough visits from Garber, not enough effort from AEG—but she raised one point that could still come back to haunt the league: Houston was no closer than San Jose in terms of building a stadium.[4] Garber says San Jose simply showed no signs of getting closer.

> Moving the Earthquakes was a tough decision. But at that time, we would not have been able to succeed in that market long-term with the same scenario going forward that we had in the market at that time, trying to begin the process to get Phil Anschutz down to only owning one team, moving towards in every market getting our teams to develop soccer-specific stadiums. In that market, we had no chance at that time of any of that happening.

Whether the hardball experiment worked is something the league wouldn't know unless it paid off somewhere else—in Salt Lake, Kansas City, or any other city that has trouble finding an owner or a stadium. Unfortunately for the league's image, one such city is Houston. And that wasn't the team's only problem.

With the "Earthquakes" name remaining in San Jose, the Houston MLS club needed a rebranding. The *Houston Chronicle* sponsored a "Name the Team" contest with 12 choices. The winner, announced January 25: Houston 1836.

Like Real Salt Lake and FC Dallas—and before that, D.C. United—the name sounded vaguely European, along the lines of German clubs 1860 Munich or Hannover 96. Rather than call it "2006" after the year the club was founded—or at least relocated—Houston opted to reach back to the day the city itself was founded.

Unfortunately, the historical name carried some historical baggage. The founding of the city of Houston roughly coincides with Sam Houston's defeat of the Mexican army and the secession of Texas from Mexico. Many Houston residents do not celebrate this occasion.

Dissent spread quickly, with the *New York Times* picking up the story just two days later:

> Many Latinos in Houston, though, greeted the unveiling of the team's name this week with a shudder. Eighteen thirty-six also happens to be the year that a group of English-speaking interlopers waged a war of secession that resulted in Mexico's loss of Texas, ushering in more than a century of violence and discrimination against Mexicans in the state. In fact, the team's owner, the Anschutz Entertainment Group of Los Angeles, appears to have upset some of the very soccer-crazy fans they were hoping to lure, after basing its venture in part on the crowds of Spanish-speaking fútbol aficionados who regularly fill stadiums here to attend the matches of visiting clubs from Mexico.[5]

The dissent, of course, was far from unanimous, with the usual disdainful "political correctness" accusations thrown into the mix. But Houston bowed to the pressure and came up with another vaguely European name—Houston Dynamo. A Lone Star Soccer Alliance team of the late '80s had been known as the Houston Dynamos, while the Carolina (formerly Greensboro) Dynamo had played USL ball for years. (The LSSA also had an FC Dallas for a couple of years.)

The Dynamo took up a temporary home at the University of Houston's Robertson Stadium, though not without some public sniping from AEG executive Tim Leiweke. His complaints over the university's handling of stadium negotiations amused *Mercury News* columnist John Ryan back in San Jose: "Ah, looks like the old AEG friends are up to their old tricks. If Leiweke ever realized that goodwill thing in the first place, would the team even be in Houston?"[6]

Back in San Jose, city officials withdrew the proposal of $80 million in public money, which hadn't been approved anyway and likely would never be granted. But over the summer, the situation improved. Lew Wolff, the owner of baseball's Oakland A's, bought an expansion option in the Bay Area in May, barely a week after the USL announced that Spanish club Alaves would operate an expansion team in the area.

The *Mercury News* editorial board quickly heaped praise on a proposal to build a stadium at the Santa Clara County fairgrounds:

> Things have changed since the city's clumsy proposal to keep the Quakes last winter. Developer Lew Wolff now has the rights from the professional soccer league to bring a team back to San Jose and says he would build a stadium, which would cost $60 million to $80 million, if the land is donated and if the city finances whatever road improvements are needed.
>
> That is a big improvement over the city's idea of financing a soccer stadium with public money—a burst of irrational exuberance to save the Quakes at the 11th hour. It would have been a non-starter at the polls, and voters have to approve any public spending on a stadium.
>
> Now another shift needs to happen: Forget the downtown site the city proposed. It could be great for a baseball park, but the county fairgrounds would be vastly superior for soccer.
>
> There's room for a state-of-the-art athletic complex with fields for a variety of sports, helping to meet a countywide shortage of playing fields. The combination of youth, amateur, and professional soccer would benefit every level of the sport.[7]

Killion and *San Francisco Chronicle* columnist Ray Ratto were less complimentary. Killion kept up the quips on Garber, saying "MLS" stood for "Making Little Stadiums."[8] Ratto called him "Ski Mask Donnie Garber . . . using soccer as bait for land and construction shakedowns."[9]

That specific stadium proposal wouldn't end up as the long-term solution, and the cynical columnists might never be won over. But the league had managed to keep a foothold in the Bay Area despite the painful stripping of a proud team.

By 2008, Houston had made progress, with popular boxer Oscar De La Hoya buying into the team and a stadium deal appearing close. In a 2008 interview, Garber stood by the decision, albeit with some regret:

> It wasn't the NFL, which can leave Cleveland one day and move into a brand-new stadium in Baltimore. It's taken us three years to get to where we want it to be. More importantly, we've gotten to the goal of having a very committed local owner.
>
> It was a very tough decision, painful for the fans. It's something that will always go down in my legacy as one of the black marks against my tenure. But I believe long-term it was absolutely the right thing to do.

Some Dynamo players and coaches, including Dominic Kinnear, didn't hide their reluctance to leave California. Yet the former Earthquakes kept the core of a two-time champion intact as they relocated and proved over the summer they would still contend while other cities took turns in the soccer-business spotlight. By summer's end, it would be the busiest year of expansion, ownership, and stadium battles in league history.

INVESTMENT BOOM

The good news for the league was that investors were popping up, including one that changed the face of a team.

Red Bull, the Austrian energy-drink company that had been spreading its wings in sports sponsorship, bought the MetroStars from Anschutz in March. The MetroStars name disappeared. From now on, the organization would be known as Red Bull New York, while the team would be the American-sounding New York Red Bulls. AEG would remain a co-investor in a long-promised stadium effort now focused on Harrison, New Jersey.

Red Bull had already rebranded a team in Austria, turning SV Wustenrot Salzburg into Red Bull Salzburg, which would coincidentally hire former MetroStar Lothar Matthäus on the coaching staff. The logo also was familiar to fans of Formula 1 racing and other international sports.

Yet this investment was curious to many. Inside soccer circles, few knew what to make of the new ownership. Outside soccer circles, MLS was appearing more foreign by the month. Team names were following the European or Latin American tradition rather than the dynamic 1970s and 1980s names at the league's inception. Jersey sponsorship, common around the world but only subtly present in U.S. team sports, would get a kick-start in MLS with the Red Bull logo staring down opposing teams.

Within a few weeks, Alexi Lalas jumped ship under tragic circumstances. Los Angeles president and general manager Doug Hamilton, so successful in molding the Miami Fusion, had died of a heart attack while flying home from a CONCACAF Champions Cup game in Costa Rica. The shocking loss of a seemingly healthy family man at age 43 clearly rattled the Galaxy. But the team needed a new man in charge, and with Red Bull inclined to start fresh, Lalas took the job in Los Angeles.

Lalas's move immediately kicked off the Steve Sampson firing watch among MLS pundits. In the ill-fated 1998 World Cup venture, Lalas was one of several veterans who lost playing time and openly criticized then-coach Sampson. Lalas insisted that the two had smoothed over their differences. But when the Galaxy started 2-8-1, Lalas wasted little time replacing Sampson with Frank Yallop, who had coached the Canadian national team since leading the Earthquakes to two titles.

Canada gave up a coach but got a team and stadium in Toronto. Facing an MLS-imposed deadline in late 2005, several Canadian governments agreed to chip in for a stadium. The breakdown: $27 million from the federal government, $9.8 million from Toronto, $8 million from Ontario. The rest would come from private contributions: a big check for naming rights and the balance from the new investors—Maple Leaf Sports and Entertainment Ltd., already the owner of the NHL's Maple Leafs and NBA's Raptors. Garber was happy to welcome MLSE to MLS.

The league held off on announcing details until a few weeks into the 2006 season, but construction was already well underway on its stadium, built to host its share of national-team games as well. Following the trend of European names, MLSE introduced the team as Toronto FC. MLS gave the new team a few special provisions on foreign players to allow it to sign several Canadian players, and the team prepared for a 2007 start. Toronto would claim a departing Red Bulls manager—Mo Johnston, the former Kansas City striker who had replaced Bob Bradley with the MetroStars, would be the team's first coach. Bank of Montreal (BMO) would claim the naming rights in a deal the *Toronto Star* pegged at $27 million over 10 years.

Meanwhile, Kansas City was the next team in danger of moving, still for sale almost two years after Lamar Hunt put them on the market. Garber tossed out the possibility of a move to suburban Philadelphia, where Rowan University was pitching a stadium to share with an MLS team in Glassboro, New Jersey.

Wizards fans would prove luckier than Earthquakes fans. In August, a group of local investors formed a group called OnGoal LLC and immediately took over operation of the team. The lead investors were Neal Patterson and Cliff Illig, the chairman/CEO and vice chairman, respectively, of medical software company Cerner. Robb Heineman would take the most public role as the Wizards president, joining fans for tailgating and interacting on popular message-board site BigSoccer in the style of Peter Wilt, the popular longtime Chicago executive.

As Hunt himself faced in Columbus and Dallas, a couple of setbacks in finding a stadium site would test the new owners' enthusiasm. But they were determined to stick it out, taking care to calm any nerves among fans.

The relief spread far beyond Kansas City. In late 2002, MLS was down to three investment groups—Anschutz's AEG, Hunt Sports Group, and Robert Kraft. In September 2003, Stan Kroenke broke the league's losing streak with investors, taking over in Colorado. In less than three years, MLS had added five more—Chivas in Los Angeles, Checketts in Salt Lake City, Red Bull in New York, MLSE in Toronto, and the OnGoal group in Kansas City. Wolff had an option to revive the Earthquakes in San Jose to make it six.

Anschutz's investment, once half the league, had dropped to four teams —Chicago, D.C. United, Los Angeles, and the "new" Houston team. Hunt was down to two.

Not that all the investors were finding it easy.

TROUBLE IN UTAH

The league's hardball approach was put to the test again over the summer when Real Salt Lake's stadium plans collapsed amid bickering between city and county boards. On July 11, the county council voted down a plan to put the stadium in the town of Sandy.

Within two days, relocation talk had blossomed. Rochester and its new PAETEC Park were once again in the thick of it, with Garber telling the Rochester *Democrat & Chronicle*'s Jeff DiVeronica he expected a meeting between RSL execs and Rhinos president Frank DuRoss.

DiVeronica said Rochester had heard something similar two years earlier about the Wizards. But this one had a greater sense of urgency—and nastiness. Among the political forces at play:

County councilman David Wilde cast the deciding "no" vote on the Sandy vote because, the *Salt Lake Tribune* reported, the total package of "$30 million for the stadium, $45 million for downtown and $15 million for westside parks and baseball fields" came up $4 million short of what he was seeking for the west side.[10]

Checketts was feuding with Larry Miller, owner of the Utah Jazz. Checketts had once been team president but had fallen out with the owner. After the Sandy vote, Checketts claimed Miller was working against the stadium for fear that it would take concerts away from the Jazz's Delta Center, a charge Miller vehemently denied.

Sandy Mayor Tom Dolan called the vote "anti-Sandy" and spread part of the blame to the news media, the *Tribune* reported.[11]

Prospective suitors, in addition to Rochester: Portland, Oregon; Phoenix; and St. Louis, where Checketts already owned the NHL's St. Louis Blues.

Salt Lake City Mayor Rocky Anderson preferred to steer the team to the state-owned Fairpark. Other Salt Lake officials touted downtown sites.

Anderson wasn't talking to the *Deseret News*, one of two major dailies in town, disputing a report on his travel spending.

One late suitor to enter the mix after the Sandy vote—Anderson Geneva, which owned an old steel plant well south of Salt Lake City and was willing to hand over land at no cost.

Checketts said he would only own the team if he could keep it in Utah. If he had to move, he'd sell first.

The antitax force brigade was out in full force even though it didn't seem that the stadium would draw much from local taxes. Checketts and company were planning to foot most of the construction bill for the whole project, of which the stadium was only part. The team just needed local authorities to help with parking and infrastructure. Even that money was earmarked from a hotel-room tax that wouldn't affect many Salt Lake metro residents, and it wasn't available for many other purposes. That didn't stop the usual "Schools, Not Stadiums" sloganeering.

Checketts set an August 12 deadline and checked out the Geneva site. The *Deseret News* showed public support for that site and opposition to public funding, though it's not clear how much the public fully understood the tax mechanism.

At the deadline, Real Salt Lake and County mayor Peter Corroon worked out a deal—at least the framework of one. Salt Lake County would contribute $20 million of hotel taxes. Sandy would contribute $15 million. The team would share a parking garage and would pay the county $27.5 million in "cash and in-kind contributions," the *Deseret News* reported. The deal also had a couple of clauses to mollify those who thought MLS might go belly up—the team was locked into Salt Lake County for 30 years and would owe $10 million if it went out of business.

Coincidentally, the other Real—Real Madrid—was in town. The deal came just in time for David Beckham, Roberto Carlos, and coach Fabio Capello to join a band of Salt Lake and Utah dignitaries whose names they surely had never heard for a groundbreaking ceremony on the Sandy site.

As it turns out, the groundbreaking still wasn't the last word. The deal would be reworked the next year after another round of threats and hair-pulling. Real Salt Lake stayed put, but the brutal process showed just how much persuading some local bodies would need, even for a well-supported team in a league that showed every sign of being stable and sound.

With each local standoff, the league was gambling its greatest asset—the reputation for staying power that had eluded every other U.S. soccer league and most leagues in other sports. Through 11 seasons, MLS has had stable operations in Washington, New Jersey/New York, New England, Colorado, Columbus, and Los Angeles. Dallas had a difficult road to a new stadium but was rewarded for staying the course. Chicago was firmly entrenched after nine seasons. Kansas City, perhaps the next stage for a league skirmish against local politicians, was shaky but could still claim 11 straight seasons of operation. Yes, two teams folded when the league hit its low point in 2001, but until San Jose failed to meet the ultimatum, no team had packed up and moved.

The solid foundation would prove especially useful after the league saw less of a boost from the world's biggest tournament than it had seen four years earlier.

WORLD CUP

After the success of the U.S. team in 2002, MLS built a marketing campaign around league players who would suit for the USA in the 2006 tournament in Germany. Landon Donovan and Pablo Mastroeni were shown in their MLS team colors—which would then be superimposed on their faces—and then together as U.S. teammates. The campaign: Embrace the Colors.

And why not be optimistic? Donovan and DaMarcus Beasley, so impressive as 20-year-olds in 2002, were now 24. With Donovan driving the offense, the USA had qualified for the World Cup in impressive fashion with a couple of games to spare.

But a team like the United States, full of solid players but lacking world-class stars, needs a bit of luck to make a run to the quarterfinals—a good draw, good health, and perhaps a couple of breaks. Not this time.

The draw was murderous—a team that had been surging in recent European play (Czech Republic), a perennial contender (Italy), and the best team in Africa (Ghana). Claudio Reyna and John O'Brien were banged up, and Frankie Hejduk and Cory Gibbs were injured after being named to the original roster. Donovan and Beasley were slumping. The breaks? Forget it.

In Germany, the 2006 Cup was the anti-2002 from the start. In 2002, O'Brien had put the USA ahead of Portugal in the fourth minute, and that lead became 2-0 and 3-0 in due course on the way to a 3-2 win. In 2006, big striker Jan Koller put the Czechs ahead in the fifth, and that deficit became 2-0 and 3-0. The Czechs came in with an aging, ailing team that had only one good spurt of action in the Cup, and the USA absorbed it in listless fashion.

The USA rebounded slightly the next match with one of the only breaks it would get, an own goal that gave the Yanks a deserved 1-1 tie in the first half. What followed—one red card for Italy, then two red cards for the USA—may have left soccer snobs sneering. But Americans love to see teams battling against all odds, and that's what they saw. Even reduced to nine men against 10, the Yanks attacked against Italy and even put the ball in the net on a Beasley shot, only to see it ruled out because Brian McBride was offside.

The underdog tale stuck in the public consciousness, at least for a few days. TV analysts and fans debated referee Jorge Larrionda's decisions to send off Pablo Mastroeni and Eddie Pope. The Italian red card wasn't the least bit debatable—Daniele De Rossi's wild elbow opened a big gash on McBride's face, and photos of the blood-splattered striker walking calmly to the sideline made a few soccer bashers reconsider the stereotype of soccer as some sort of sissy sport. *American Soccer News* columnist Dan Loney recalls:

> The incredible visuals of McBride leaving the field covered in blood, then returning after being stitched, may have saved American soccer. It was the absolute perfect metaphor for the American comeback against Italy after last week's disaster against the Czech Republic. The media loved it, of course. If it bleeds, it leads, and McBride is a leader. If your paper didn't run a picture of McBride wearing the crimson mask, you were probably reading *Baseball America*.[12]

If only that had been the final image. The USA still had one more game against Ghana, whose talent is readily apparent to soccer aficionados but not to those who think it unthinkable that the mighty United States should ever lose to a developing-world nation in anything. This time, the breaks were nowhere in evidence. Reyna stumbled, with an injury that would force him out of the game, and surrendered the ball to give up a breakaway that Ghana converted. Just after Clint Dempsey equalized off a Beasley cross, Ghana got a questionable penalty call. Stephen Appiah scored for a 2-1 halftime lead. The Americans needed a win to advance, but the strong African side killed the game with 32 fouls.

Given the respective talent levels of the teams, the slumps, the injuries, and everything else that went wrong, it wasn't a shock to see the USA emerge from the World Cup's toughest group with only one point. Try explaining that to the casual fan, or for that matter the soccer snobs who thought the 2002 performance was a fluke.

The harsh media climate didn't help. The Olympics earlier that year in Torino had seen the old media cycle—build up U.S. athletes and tear them down—moving with ruthless efficiency. That cycle is easy to measure with a few LexisNexis searches. Women's snowboardcross favorite Lindsey Jacobellis, who wiped out with an overly enthusiastic jump on the last hill of the final and settled for silver instead of sure gold, was mentioned more than 3,000 times in U.S. newspapers in February and March. Men's snowboardcross gold medalist, American Seth Wescott? A mere 342. Searching only magazines (newspaper mentions are far too numerous) for Alpine skiing—brash multimedal favorite Bode Miller was mentioned 71 times, while the surprise gold medalists in women's giant slalom (Julia Mancuso) and men's combined (Ted Ligety) drew 9 and 14, respectively. The finger-pointing after failures far outweighed the celebration of success.

Forget "Embrace the Colors" for the moment, and forget a post-Cup whirlwind of talk shows. Critics brayed about Arena's tactics, Donovan's mental toughness, and the state of American soccer in general.

Arena lost his job and was promptly snapped up by the Red Bulls. He then told Grant Wahl he didn't think the league as a whole was as good as it had been a few years before.[13]

Every league debates quality of play. MLS, still in its relative infancy, had other issues, and the news leading into its summer showcase would address a few more.

READY FOR PRIME TIME

For more than a decade, MLS got games on TV but no substantial revenue from it. This year, that would change. In the 10 days leading up to the All-Star Game, MLS would reveal two landmark broadcasting deals.

First up was Fox, with a five-year deal for Fox Soccer Channel, Fox Sports en Español, and some overseas affiliates. Then came an eight-year deal with ESPN and ABC. The broadcasts would move back to Thursday night, out of competition with ESPN's nonstop college football coverage on Saturdays, and would be produced by the networks rather than the league.

Two months later, the league would sign an eight-year deal with Spanish-language Univision and its family of networks. Add the existing HDNet deal, and MLS had four national networks paying to broadcast its games, as well as local networks and their feed into the MLS Direct Kick package. Many games were also available to subscribers online.

All told, MLS was pulling in around $20 million a year through the national deals. That's nowhere close to the billion-dollar deals that baseball and the NFL enjoy, and it's still a fraction of the money Versus pays to broadcast the National Hockey League, which some MLS fans see as vulnerable in the mythical race to be America's "fourth sport." But the league was able to boast broad exposure for its games without shelling out its own money, surely a sign of progress.

The deals also were a sign of Soccer United Marketing (SUM) flexing its muscles. Most of the contracts included a few international games, and Garber had helped steer the next World Cup contract to ABC and ESPN. The next Cups were almost lined up for NBC and Telemundo before Garber's intervention, said the *San Diego Union-Tribune*'s Mark Zeigler, and the ABC/ESPN deal was as much a "thank-you as a genuine investment in MLS."[14]

Dave Checketts saw the TV deals as a critical crossroads. "Don [Garber] is one of the reasons I invested so much in the league," he told *SportsBusiness Daily*. "He absolutely held the board together during the TV negotiations, when NBC was going after World Cup rights, which could have meant the end of SUM and perhaps MLS."[15]

While the broadcast news leading into the All-Star Game was good for the league, the game itself hit a snag, as it had a few times in years past. Ante Razov, Clint Dempsey, and Shalrie Joseph were selected to the team set to face Chelsea, but the Chivas USA and Revolution players couldn't actually play because of a domino effect in scheduling. The All-Star Game was moved back one week from July 29 to August 5 to accommodate Chelsea and an English rule that players couldn't take part in games within 30 days of the World Cup. Other MLS games could be juggled, but a scheduled Chivas-Revolution game wasn't moved because it was part of a doubleheader with Chivas (the Mexican parent club) and Spanish giant Barcelona. These doubleheaders had become far too valuable to skip.

Even without doubleheaders, MLS had learned to profit from European teams' tours. With ChampionsWorld out of the picture, SUM played travel agent for European clubs. Whether Barcelona faced Chivas of Mexico before an MLS game or simply took the field against the New York Red Bulls, MLS and SUM stood to gain. In 2006, D.C. United traveled thousands of miles from Washington, D.C., to Washington state, just to face Real Madrid in Seattle. The doubleheaders helped MLS's attendance figures. The MLS-vs.-Europe exhibitions weren't counted in the league averages, but it was hard to argue with the cash influx or the prestige value.

So without Razov, Dempsey, and Joseph, the All-Stars took on Chelsea at Toyota Park, the Fire's new stadium in Bridgeview, Illinois. The defense held together against the English champions, many of whom were just finding their legs after playing for various countries in the World Cup. Dwayne De Rosario, ever the clutch scorer, ripped the game's only goal into the net in the 70th minute, and the All-Stars won 1-0.

The summer showcases were over at last, and everyone returned to an intriguing regular season.

POWER SHIFT

D.C. United, anxious to start a second run of dominance, played a sublime game through the first two-thirds of the season. Troy Perkins, known more for his part-time job at a bank than his past success, took over the goalkeeping job from the injured Nick Rimando and never gave it back, ending up as the league's Goalkeeper of the Year. Bobby Boswell, also not a college or youth national superstar, was Defender of the Year. Freddy Adu moved out to the wing, probably his third-best position, but learned to play enough defense to keep a starting job, while Christian Gomez, in the midst of an MVP season, manned the center behind Jaime Moreno and Alecko Eskandarian. A 14-game unbeaten streak pushed United's record to 13-1-5. The team showed plenty of swagger—after a goal against the rebranded Red Bulls, someone tossed scorer Eskandarian a can of the team's namesake drink. He took a swig and spat, earning a small fine.

United's possession game wasn't disrupted by their home field, which had been nearly pristine but now had temporary pieces of sod laid over the pitcher's mound and base paths of the Washington Nationals infield. While the baseball team shared the stadium, some of the signs on the concourse still advertised the Washington Freedom, which still existed but not in the incarnation that had played in RFK.

Houston, changed little from its San Jose incarnation, nearly matched United's pace in the summer with a 10-game unbeaten run. Then the bottom fell out for both teams. United's lead was too big to be threatened, but Houston would find itself in a fight for the West.

Going in the opposite direction was Los Angeles. While Donovan and Chris Albright were away on World Cup duty, a two-game losing streak became seven. Even with Yallop taking over from Sampson as coach, the Galaxy didn't win again until Donovan's return. Then they were a different team—9-5-3 in their last 17 games, with Donovan netting 10 of his 11 goals. The Galaxy went 525 minutes, including the entire month of May, without scoring a goal, then turned around two weeks later and went 521 without conceding one thanks to Albright and the still-reliable Kevin Hartman in goal.

The divergent paths crossed in an August 27 game at RFK Stadium. United fans taunted Donovan with a banner: "World Cup match tix: $100. Airfare: $1,000. Landon in Germany: Worthless." Donovan responded with two goals and helped create two more in a 5-2 rout. Donovan waved to the crowd of 24,159 to bring it on. United recovered to win their next game against Chivas, then won only once more the rest of the way.

While the Galaxy challenged for the playoffs, Dallas pushed its new in-state rival Houston for the West lead behind the formidable forward tandem of Ruiz and Kenny Cooper, who replaced the departed Eddie Johnson. Dario Sala, sometimes prone to mimicking Jorge Campos's "keeper-sweeper" style with adventurous runs out of his own box, held the goalkeeping job even after the late acquisition of Shaka Hislop, a one-time Howard University star who had a long career in England and had just returned from a shining World Cup performance with Trinidad and Tobago.

Also in the mix out West was the reconstituted Chivas USA. The inexperienced Mexican players were gone, and new coach Bob Bradley brought along two of his former charges in Ante Razov and Jesse Marsch. They meshed well with Mexican stars Juan Pablo Garcia and Francisco Palencia, while young keeper Brad Guzan grew into the job. Versatile defender Jonathan Bornstein wound up as Rookie of the Year; Bradley took coaching honors.

The battle for the final playoff spot in the West would come down to three teams. The surging Galaxy, all but mathematically eliminated after the World Cup, contended until the next-to-last week, losing 2-1 at Dallas. For good measure, the Galaxy pummeled Dallas 5-2 in the season finale, but it was simply too late.

Real Salt Lake gave up Clint Mathis for Jeff Cunningham before the season and wound up much the better for it, with Cunningham nearly managing an improbable league lead in both goals (first with 16) and assists (tied for second with 11). The Utah club hadn't improved as rapidly as its fellow expansion team Chivas, but they contended until the last weekend.

But the spot would go to Colorado, where Fernando Clavijo continued to work his strange magic. After dealing Jean Philippe Peguero to New York, the Rapids had no reliable forward. Joe Cannon, playing behind a retooled defense, was uncharacteristically close to the bottom in goals allowed. Somehow, winger Terry Cooke led the league in assists with 12, keeping the Rapids competitive. While Salt Lake anxiously awaited a Sunday game on the final weekend, the Rapids traveled to Houston and clinched the spot with an improbable 3-3 draw. With a league-worst minus-13 goal difference, the Rapids finished 11-13-8, two points ahead of the Galaxy and Salt Lake.

The East was less suspenseful. Taylor Twellman, a controversial omission from the World Cup roster, had 11 goals and Matt Reis saved 141 shots as the Revolution cruised into the playoffs in second place, one point ahead of Chicago. The Fire coped with its long season-opening road trip before settling into its Bridgeview home and finally benched longtime keeper Zach Thornton in favor of Matt Pickens.

Columbus was out of the mix, with the departures of Simon Elliott (Fulham, joining Brian McBride) and Robin Fraser (retired), leaving new coach Sigi Schmid too many holes on his roster. An injury bug swept the team and forced the Crew to use five goalkeepers, once calling Dan Popik out of retirement.

That left two teams that had changed ownership and coaches in the past six months. The Wizards—who suffered without national teamers Johnson, Josh Wolff, and Jimmy Conrad and failed to regain composure when they returned—let Bob Gansler go while the team stood at 6-10-2. Brian Bliss took over on an interim basis and steadied the team to battle the Red Bulls, who had swept aside Mo Johnston in favor of interim coach Richie Williams before handing the reins to Arena.

The Red Bulls never seemed likely to make a run. Youri Djorkaeff had shown plenty of class since arriving at Giants Stadium, but he mimicked Lothar Matthäus with a curious absence, claiming a family matter but turning up instead at a World Cup game in Germany. The team was 2-9-9 with Tony Meola in goal, leaving the job ripe for Jon Conway to seize while Meola battled illness. But the scrappy team got the occasional boost from up-and-coming stars such as Jozy Altidore and remained in contention.

The Wizards and Red Bulls went head-to-head for the last spot in the season finale in Giants Stadium, with the Wizards needing only a draw. They took an early lead, but Amado Guevara converted two penalty kicks on his way to a hat trick. Scott Sealy's late goal made it 3-2, but the Wizards wouldn't get the equalizer.

The Red Bulls had another piece of good news late in the season. After years of negotiation and frustration, the team broke ground on a new stadium in Harrison, New Jersey. The new site wasn't just an aesthetic and economic improvement like other league stadiums—unlike at Giants Stadium, mass transit would be simple.

The Open Cup once again wrapped up before the playoffs and once again went to the Fire, which beat four fellow MLS sides, finishing with a 3-1 win to deny Los Angeles a consolation trophy in a difficult year. Chicago took the Cup for the fourth time.

PLAYOFFS

The compelling matchup of Bruce Arena's Red Bulls against his former team, always unconvincingly downplayed by the coach himself, swung in the balance until the final minutes at RFK. United, still figuring out an answer to the late-season futility, took a 1-0 lead in the first leg through an impressive Moreno-Gomez combination. New York stunned United's faithful, once again turning up in strong numbers, with a powerful attack and a breakthrough from Altidore in the 70th minute. Gomez conjured up a winner in the 86th, poking the ball into the net amid chaos in the Red Bulls box.

That was the only first-round series without a lead change.

Chicago had New England beaten for much of the series. Justin Mapp's free kick and Matt Pickens's eight saves gave the Fire a 1-0 lead after the home leg. At Foxborough, Chicago extended the aggregate lead to 2-0 on a Nate Jaqua goal. From there, the Fire defense folded. Twellman cut it to 2-1 just before halftime. Pat Noonan tied the series early in the second. Pickens, once again busy, kept it even from there.

As well as Pickens played in regulation, Reis outdid him in penalty kicks. The big Revolution keeper saved Thiago's shot, scored one himself, and saved another from Ivan Guerrero. The four New England shooters converted, with Twellman appropriately finishing off the series as Pickens, the player least deserving of blame, crumpled to the field.

Houston also went home with a one-goal deficit after Chivas's Brad Guzan stopped a Dwayne De Rosario penalty kick. Chivas kept the advantage through an hour in Houston before the game turned in a fit of nastiness. Francisco Palencia saw yellow for a foul on De Rosario in the 57th minute. Then Palencia got involved in some shoving with several Houston players. The Dynamo's Ricardo Clark drew yellow; Palencia drew red. A few minutes later, De Rosario fell in the box, and Brad Davis converted the penalty kick to level the series. Deep into stoppage time, De Rosario took on a couple of defenders along the side of the box and sent a high cross to Eddie Robinson, who headed the ball almost straight down. It bounced and hung in the air. Brian Ching rose up and knocked the series winner into the net.

As the final whistle was blown, Chivas's Juan Pablo Garcia slid violently into the back of Brad Davis's legs. He would be suspended for the first two games of 2007. That was nothing compared to what happened in Frisco, where Dallas faced perennial playoff nemesis Colorado.

Dario Sala, getting the call in goal over Hislop, made sure Dallas came back to Pizza Hut Park with a lead. Carlos Ruiz and Abe Thompson scored road goals for Dallas, while Terry Cooke's goal was all the Rapids could show for their statistical dominance in front of an anemic home crowd of 4,176.

After a scoreless first half at home, Ruiz extended Dallas's series lead, only to see Nicolas Hernandez score twice for Colorado. In overtime, Clarence Goodson scored early to give Dallas some relief, but Clint Mathis—who seemed to have bottomed out in a four-year slide since the World Cup—drilled a stunning 25-yarder past Sala.

For the second straight year, the Rapids forced Dallas to penalty kicks. Greg Vanney's miss on Dallas's fourth kick put Colorado on the verge of clinching, but Sala saved the fifth kick from Aitor Karanka.

Sala stepped up to take the sixth kick himself, but Joe Cannon came up with his first save. Pablo Mastroeni coolly finished, and the Rapids had knocked out Dallas in Pizza Hut Park for the second straight year.

It didn't quite end there. Colorado had been developing a reputation for taunting opposing fans. In Salt Lake City a few weeks earlier, Real owner Dave Checketts wound up confronting Mastroeni on the field, accusing Colorado players of making obscene gestures as they took the Rocky Mountain Cup. Mathis, who had hopped over the Rockies in the off-season, separated the two.

This time, with the Rapids taunting Dallas fans, Sala rashly decided not to take it. He came in swinging, hitting Jovan Kirovski and Hunter Freeman. Mike Petke responded with a flying kick. Order was quickly restored, but Sala would find himself suspended for the first six games of 2007 and $3,500 poorer. Petke paid a $500 fine.

THE FINAL FOUR

Colorado's passion carried over into Houston, where Kirovski gave the Rapids a fourth-minute lead. It wouldn't last. Neither team got much space, combining for 11 total shots, but the Dynamo converted three chances, two from Paul Dalglish. The former Earthquakes would play for another MLS title in their first year in Texas, conveniently within their new home state at Dallas's Pizza Hut Park.

In Washington, New England also took a fourth-minute road lead thanks to Twellman, who took a few steps back in the box to get to a Noonan cross and cranked his body at an awkward angle to slam the ball inside the post. The Revolution wouldn't have another shot on goal. They wouldn't need it. The Revs defense clamped down on Gomez, Moreno, and Eskandarian. United threw all of its offensive might forward, but Reis came up with eight saves, including one on a looping Ben Olsen header high above his head.

Freddy Adu had been one of the more effective United attackers, which made it all the more curious that Peter Nowak took him out in the 65th minute for Matias Donnet. While Adu sat down and put his head in his hands, Donnet added nothing. When Gomez somehow cramped up on a cool 50-degree day a few minutes later, United had no creative forces left. Only Olsen, by sheer force of effort, managed to keep pressing the attack.

Adu, who had previously made the occasional youthful complaint over his playing time, said nothing impolite after the game or in our interview nearly 18 months later. "It was a tough situation," he says. "As a professional, you just deal with it. I was disappointed. I felt like I was being active. Maybe Peter saw something different. And that's what he went with."

But his future in D.C. was clearly in doubt. Adu and the league were always able to deflect rumors of a European move by pointing to rules limiting opportunities for anyone under 18. At age 17, Adu wasn't that far away from being "legal." He also didn't need a ride from his mom anymore. Under Nowak's stern guidance, Adu had clearly improved—his defense was stronger, and he wasn't dispossessed as easily. Yet the awkward marriage of Gomez, Moreno, and Adu—all players who do their best work running at the goal with the ball at their feet—was always combustible.

The Revolution moved on to their second straight MLS Cup, third in five years. As if inheriting the mantle of New England agony from the Red Sox, they would once again fall agonizingly short in the November 12 final.

Once again, the Revolution played to a scoreless tie in regulation and went into overtime. But in the 113th minute, Khano Smith found Twellman in some space. The striker's perfectly placed shot to the far post gave the Revs their first goal in 346 minutes of play over three finals, and New England started to celebrate.

That celebration lasted less than a minute. Brian Mullan crossed to Ching, who towered in the box and headed it down for the tying goal. For the first time, MLS Cup would be decided on penalty kicks.

As always, Reis came up with a save and powered home a shot of his own. But Pat Noonan's shot went wide, and Pat Onstad saved the fifth shot from Jay Heaps. Texas had its first MLS Cup winner. Houston fans joined D.C. and Chicago fans in celebrating a title in their first year with a team.

A few weeks later, the league mourned one of the men whose faith in the game had kept it in business. Lamar Hunt passed away in December at age 74.

From the World Cup to the stadium sagas to the action on the field, the year had been dramatic, to say the least. The league's evolution was never clearer, from expansion to stadium-construction to slow erosion of the micromanagement from league headquarters. The media had noticed part of the story. In 2007, they'd pay much more attention.

11

Beckham and Blanco

Of all the European stars linked with MLS in the continent's rumor-hungry media, David Beckham always seemed the most likely to hop across the pond and get noticed. The English superstar's love of the United States was so well-known that the name of his first son, Brooklyn, was linked to a trip to New York nine months before his birth, though that story has been disputed. Beckham also had opened a branch of his soccer academy in Los Angeles at the Home Depot Center.

Of course, getting Beckham to MLS wouldn't be cheap. The league had bent its budget rules on stars of the past—Jorge Campos and Lothar Matthäus were among those widely reported to have a few extra inducements. The 2006 salary list released by the union had a few notables making well over $300,000, including Landon Donovan ($900,000), Eddie Johnson ($750,000, up to $875,000 with bonuses and other compensation), Freddy Adu ($300,000, bumped to $550,000), and two Chivas players—Juan Pablo Garcia ($624,250 including all compensation) and Francisco Palencia (grand total of $1.36 million). Beckham, though, was on a different scale.

MLS had landed players of significant stature before. Campos and Carlos Valderrama were genuine Latin American stars, and Mexican strikers Luis Hernandez and Carlos Hermosillo had passed through. Matthäus, though pushing 40 upon his arrival in MLS, had once been FIFA Player of the Year. Hristo Stoitchkov was twice runner-up, as was Beckham at his playing peak in 1999 and 2001. But in 2007, Beckham was still a relatively young player, turning 32 just before his MLS career would start. His long reign as England captain had run through the 2006 World Cup, and he played his club ball for star-studded Real Madrid.

Beyond that, Beckham had a celebrity appeal that transcended sports. Show anyone unfamiliar with soccer a picture of the scowling Stoitchkov side-by-side with the gently smiling Beckham, and it's easy to guess which one draws attention. He had endured a rollercoaster career—breathlessly hyped Manchester United phenom, red-carded villain of the 1998 World Cup, hero of England's 2002 World Cup qualifying—with grace and disarming charm. English tabloids surely would track his every move even if he were not married to a former member of the Spice Girls. Commercial endorsements had made him wealthy beyond any soccer player's dreams, and yet the appetite for all things Beckham was so great that London's National Portrait Gallery showed a film of him sleeping. The film *Bend It Like Beckham* portrayed him as a role model for a teenage girl learning free kicks and even alluded in a minor subplot to his status as a gay icon.

He wasn't quite the player Pelé was—it's impossible to have a discussion of the world's all-time best without the charismatic Brazilian who finished his career in the NASL. But in terms of name recognition, he was nearly Pelé's equal.

So when word spread that MLS was considering a salary-cap exemption to allow teams to sign marquee players, the informal name was obvious. Well before the league passed the rule and long before any reliable report suggested the man himself was on his way to an MLS team, fans talked about the "Beckham rule." Ivan Gazidis recalls:

> The first time that I remember us seriously discussing it was going into the board meeting in November 2005. We had a discussion at the board level about it then. There were proponents of it, and there were those who didn't feel the time was right for it. The board decided not to do it then. The thing with the designated-player rule has been our ability to capitalize on it. Until we had a critical mass of stadiums and TV contracts, sponsorship deals and those types of things, we weren't ready to sign a player like David Beckham. We've always been in the fortunate position that our owners have the financial capacity to do these things if they make sense. But they're not going to do things that don't make sense.

The issue was not a big clash of principle. The question is when is the right time to take this step, to elevate ourselves and bring in some very high-profile new players. . . .

The question, from 2002 onwards, as we entered into a very vibrant period of our development, was when would it make sense to bring in some real star power. For the 2006 season, the board decided we weren't quite there yet. By 2007, they believed we'd crossed the Rubicon.

In November 2006, the rule became reality, officially on an experimental level. For "designated players," MLS would pay the first $400,000 of the salary, and that would count against the cap. The team could then pay a little extra— or a lot. Each team would get one but could trade for a second $350,000 slot. Donovan, Johnson, and others with salaries already exceeding that threshold would be "grandfathered" for one year.

The Beckham rule, though, brought no guarantee that its namesake would show up. His tenure at Real Madrid hadn't been a smashing success, but he was still expected to hang around European soccer for a while longer. And so the announcement that Beckham had signed a five-year deal to join the Los Angeles Galaxy at the end of Real Madrid's season came as a bit of a surprise. It certainly surprised Real Madrid coach Fabio Capello, who vowed that Beckham wouldn't play again for his side.

Beckham made the publicity blitz on the U.S. airwaves, smiling and answering questions politely via satellite, while the European media wrote his soccer obituary. Then a funny thing happened. Beckham continued to train with Real Madrid, giving nary a hint of sulking. He trained hard and played well. Finally, Capello relented. Real Madrid—with Beckham on the field— would end up chasing its first La Liga title in the English megastar's four-year stint with the club.

ANOTHER SALE, ANOTHER LEAGUE, ANOTHER UTAH TWIST

The Beckham news came in the midst of a flurry of league news on either side of the draft. First, Anschutz unloaded another team—D.C. United, still a powerful team but still without a stadium. The buyers were an eclectic group of shrewd investors. Will Chang was the boss of a diverse investment company. Victor MacFarlane was primarily a real-estate man. Brian Davis and

Christian Laettner, teammates on Duke's back-to-back basketball champions in the early 1990s, had started their real-estate careers with a venture not far from their alma mater in Durham, North Carolina, and bought a small stake along with Chang and MacFarlane in the club near Davis's suburban Maryland roots.

After the draft, in which University of Maryland midfielder Maurice Edu was the first pick, MLS and Soccer United Marketing (SUM) announced a new venture—the SuperLiga, a summer competition pitting MLS teams against Mexican opposition. The countries' best teams already faced off in the CONCACAF Champions Cup, but that competition had never quite attained the stature that a good USA-Mexico showdown would expect. Also, since the Cup was played in the MLS preseason, league teams generally struggled against in-season opposition from Mexico and Costa Rica. This would be an MLS-Mexico matchup on MLS's terms.

Just as the league was moving forward, Utah politics reared its ugly head once again. Beckham had been there for the groundbreaking, but Real Salt Lake fans had reason to worry that he might not make many more trips to the region.

On January 26, a local debt review committee gave Real Salt Lake's Sandy stadium plan a thumbs-down. From the *Salt Lake Tribune*:

> The DRC insisted RSL's paid-attendance numbers are "overly optimistic," as are its concert projections, which the committee cut in half to mesh with the "real world." For example, the DRC foresees the stadium snagging four to 11 concerts a year that draw about 11,000 fans apiece—far short of RSL's vision of up to 18 big shows, averaging 17,500. The county panel also expects paid game attendance to lag about 2,000 to 5,000 behind the team's projections.[1]

Three days later, Salt Lake County mayor Peter Corroon said no. His reasoning, again from the *Tribune*:

> 1. The project as presented does not demonstrate that it is clearly financially viable. While I respect the experience of Dave Checketts in sports management and event promotion, even fairly optimistic but realistic projections show that the team would lose money.

2. The amount of debt required for this project would put RSL in default with only minor shortfalls in ticket sales.[2]

Once again, alternative venues popped up. Anderson Development again offered to buy the team and build on the former Geneva Steel site near Utah Lake. Salt Lake City mayor Rocky Anderson revived the Fairpark idea.

Real Salt Lake may well have packed up and emerged in some other city, but one man remained on the team's side—Gov. Jon Huntsman. Under his leadership, the state stepped in and reminded the locals why they had that money in the first place, tossing aside the skepticism of local politicians and the media. "Without the governor's involvement, there's widespread agreement that the proposal to use tourist taxes to buy the land needed for the project likely would never have won approval," the *Deseret News* said.[3] Local opposition persisted but didn't scare MLS.

"I wouldn't call it grassroots opposition," MLS commissioner Don Garber told *USA Today*. "I'd say it's one particular person in a pickup truck, trying to get the community exercised about what he's claiming is a diversion of tax dollars, which is entirely not true."[4]

Real Salt Lake could concentrate instead on its new acquisition: Freddy Adu was coming to town. In December, the team dealt a major allocation (rights to a future big-name player, though not necessarily a Beckham-esque "designated player"), future considerations, and goalkeeper Jay Nolly to pick up the phenom and goalkeeper Nick Rimando from D.C. United, where he had improved over his three-year run but had finished in disappointing fashion, holding his head on the bench while his team lost in the playoffs.

United made the deal even though the team was changing coaches as well. Longtime assistant Tom Soehn was promoted to replace the departing Peter Nowak, who was joining Bob Bradley with the national-team program.

Bradley had been named interim national-team coach and head coach of the Olympic team, creating a vacancy at Chivas USA. They also promoted from within, moving Preki to the top spot. The new trend around the league was to hire former MLS players as head coaches, one sign that MLS had indeed put down firm roots.

Another sign was the continued run on new stadiums. Toronto would have no interim home, starting right away in BMO Field, where 14,000 season tickets sold out by mid-March. Colorado would open Dick's Sporting

Goods Park on the first national broadcast of the year as the Rapids hosted D.C. United.

Meanwhile, the Beckham rule brought more than Beckham. Ignored by the English-speaking media but perhaps just as important, Cuauhtémoc Blanco left Club America to join Chicago. Though he, like Beckham, would finish out the season with his current club before joining MLS, Blanco made a quick trip to a Chicago news conference that drew more than 5,000 fans.

The Red Bulls, intent on making a big splash, picked up a second designated–player slot by dealing Amado Guevara to Chivas USA, then used both slots. Claudio Reyna, the New Jersey–bred midfielder who had been overseas since playing for Bruce Arena at Virginia, reunited with his college coach. Then New York landed Juan Pablo Angel, a prolific Colombian striker who had fallen out of favor at Aston Villa.

All four players were paid more than $1 million, according to the union's figures. Reyna was the cheapest at the curious figure of $1,000,008, with $250,000 more in other compensation. Angel stood to make $1.5 million with just a bit more in bonuses. Blanco would make substantial money—almost $2.5 million in salary, up to nearly $2.67 million overall.

Beckham's deal had come across as inflated. The reports harped on the staggering figure of $250 million for five years. That wasn't quite true. Beckham stood to gain that much when all the various marketing and commercial opportunities were added together. But the union pegged his annual salary from the Galaxy at $5.5 million, bumped up to $6.5 million with other compensation. That was far and away the most in league history but hardly outlandish compared with the megamillons paid to European stars—or to mediocrities in American sports. Like Michael Jordan or Tiger Woods, he would stand to make much, much more with his ability to move merchandise.

The English media continued to fret over Beckham's ability to hop back and forth across the Atlantic and play for his country, forgetting that plenty of people had managed to do just that in the past. Roberto Donadoni played his way back onto the Italian team for Euro 1996. Lothar Matthäus and Miklos Molnar played in Euro 2000. American players overseas coped with the transatlantic travel all the time, hopping from glittering European cities to obscure fields in Central American jungles. In the last World Cup, MLS had supplied roughly half the U.S. team, plus two players for Trinidad and Tobago

(Cornell Glen, Avery John), one for Costa Rica (Douglas Sequeira), and one for Mexico (Claudio Suarez).

MLS players would again be busy with international duty in 2007. The U.S. team was due to play CONCACAF's championship, the Gold Cup, before heading to South America for a rare appearance in the Copa America. Young stars would be busy in the Under-20 World Cup.

The tournaments would be one of the league's scheduling quirks in 2007. Another was the odd number of teams with Toronto's entry. Another was the Thursday night TV game, putting several teams through a frequent Thursday-Sunday doubleheader. The SuperLiga and Copa Sudamericana added to congested schedules for a couple of teams. The Galaxy would play in Super-Liga and deal with a back-loaded schedule designed to get Beckham in front of as many fans as possible after he finished his duties with Real Madrid, where he was still in a thrilling title chase.

While much of the media waited on Beckham, MLS kicked off Season 12.

SEASON 12

The Galaxy dearly wanted to avoid a repeat of 2006, digging a deep hole and hoping their stars could bail them out in the second half. But that's exactly what happened. Beset by an early wave of injuries, including the devastating absence of Chris Albright, the Galaxy started 1-4-3. Donovan was given a pass on the Copa America, where Bob Bradley took a young team, and rejoined in July to give the team some momentum before taking a month off from MLS play for a couple of high-profile friendlies and the SuperLiga.

In mid-June, Beckham celebrated his first Spanish title with Real Madrid. One bit of bad news—he had tweaked his left ankle along the way. While Alexi Lalas revamped the roster, adding Premier League veteran Abel Xavier and Gold Cup leading scorer Carlos Pavon, the injury bug kept infecting the team just as the world was starting to pay attention. And the Galaxy were entering the busy part of the schedule.

D.C. United, the Supporters' Shield winner and frustrated playoff semi-finalist, also started slowly. With Adu and Alecko Eskandarian gone, United went almost completely South American in the attack, with Brazilians Luciano Emilio and Helbert Frederico Carreiro da Silva ("Fred") joining the club. Soehn also made a tactical change, floating Ben Olsen out to the wing. Soon after losing their first three and tying the next, Soehn switched from three defenders to four. Emilio set a torrid pace, Olsen evolved into a surprising scoring threat, and United went on another summer tear.

More surprisingly, defending champion Houston started slowly despite returning virtually intact from the title run. After forcing Mexican power Pachuca to overtime in a thrilling CONCACAF Champions Cup run, the Dynamo started 2-5-1. The team hit bottom while celebrating their 2006 triumph, combining a trip to the White House with a loss at D.C. United. The team closed the door to the locker room in defiance of MLS media policy, hashing things out over 40 minutes. Dominic Kinnear righted the ship with that wake-up call and three low-profile but valuable acquisitions—Nate Jaqua, on the verge of journeyman status; Joseph Ngwenya, a skilled forward who had been a top pick a couple of years earlier; and the prodigal Richard Mulrooney, a versatile midfielder-defender rejoining his former San Jose teammates.

The other West contenders, Dallas and Chivas USA, thrived with newcomers and new coaches. Dallas coach Steve Morrow astutely saw great promise in Colombian midfielder Juan Toja, who caught attention with his classic rock-style mullet and kept it with his rare mix of work rate and skill. (The great soccer blog Du Nord called him "Freddie Mercury reincarnated as a bulldozer.") At Chivas, Preki and team management gambled by parting ways with the disgruntled Amado Guevara, for whom the team had given up its designated-player spot, and saw Cuban defector Maykel Galindo emerge as a potent strike partner for the rejuvenated Ante Razov.

The East would be a free-for-all, with three points separating first through fifth halfway through the season. In Columbus, Sigi Schmid's Crew picked up Argentine midfielder Guillermo Barros Schelotto and immediately leaped into contention. New England lost Clint Dempsey to Fulham, Americans' favorite outpost in the Premier League, but got the usual sterling performances from Taylor Twellman, Steve Ralston, and defender Michael Parkhurst. In New York, Juan Pablo Angel more than justified the "designated player" money, teaming with big phenom Jozy Altidore in a punishing attack. New Kansas City coach Curt Onalfo infused the Wizards with an aggressive, attacking mentality, which inspired Eddie Johnson to a 15-goal season despite missing time on national-team duty.

The Wizards also benefited from their devoted new owners. "When [Lamar Hunt] decided to sell the team . . . we became once again the ugly red-headed stepchild," Jimmy Conrad told *USA Today*.[5] The new ownership, not distracted by two other teams or an impending sale, made the players feel more comfortable.

With an imbalance in the conferences, MLS went to a wild-card system in the playoffs. The top two teams in each conference would qualify, followed by the four next best teams. Midway through the season, the eight spots seemed all but set—five East and three West.

The teams likely to miss out in the East were expansion Toronto FC, where "Trader Mo" Johnston tried to deal his way into the mix after realizing that the collection of English league veterans that debuted with the club couldn't cut it. Chicago, like the Galaxy, simply couldn't wait for its designated player to show up—a 1-8-3 run through spring and early summer brought down the ax on Dave Sarachan.

Out West, Colorado also skidded in June with a 10-game winless streak to leave Fernando Clavijo hoping for another late miracle while rumors of his imminent departure swirled. The Galaxy tried to limit the damage until Beckham's arrival. Real Salt Lake was never in it, starting with an 11-game winless streak that saw John Ellinger ousted and replaced by Jason Kreis, who immediately traded his uniform for a nice suit.

Ellinger's presence was one of the lures that had drawn Freddy Adu to Salt Lake. He had coached Adu while making a name for himself with the U.S. youth program. With Ellinger gone and Adu's impending 18th birthday set to ease the transfer process, MLS fans braced for the inevitable—Adu would soon head across to Europe.

The rumors of a pending move had never really stopped. Adu was always linked with the top clubs in Europe. But Gazidis says the talk was never serious, with clubs willing to wait until the critical birthday: "During the time Freddy was with MLS, no," he claims. "At that point, before he was 18 . . . clubs were always interested and monitoring him, but we didn't have any serious approaches for transfers."

Adu's agent at the time, Richard Motzkin, heard some interest but agrees that he was never likely to look for a loophole in FIFA regulations: "Once he was in MLS, I think there was sort of an understanding he would spend some time here. There was interest from other clubs. It still made more sense for him to continue. . . . The right time for him to leave was after he turned 18 and after he had a good U-20 tournament in Canada."

The swirl of rumors had intensified in the off-season when Adu trained with Manchester United. Plenty of observers assumed it was a tryout—a faulty assumption, says Adu: "It never was a tryout. . . . They can't do anything about me right now. I played really well when I was over there. I'm not 18—it's just too hard with all the rules and whatnot. . . . I want to go to Europe after this season. I really do. The goal has always been to play four years in MLS and then go to Europe."

Make it three and a half. After being linked with the usual suspects—Scottish giant Celtic, Dutch overachiever PSV Eindhoven, half of the Premier League, etc.—Adu landed at Benfica, a Portuguese club with a proud history. Adu's farewell was under cover of relative darkness compared with his arrival in MLS nearly four years earlier. The spotlight had shifted to the Beckham rule players. Even among the young phenoms making their way to MLS, Adu shared the glory with Altidore. The national team had no shortage of midfielders and withdrawn forwards who would compete with Adu for years to come; U.S. fans gazed upon Altidore to fill a more pressing need, a long-term replacement for Brian McBride up front.

Altidore, though, faced less pressure than Adu, who balanced his playing career with considerable commercial commitments. Adu recalls:

> That was the tough part. I had a lot of endorsements that first year and a lot of obligations as far as doing photo shoots, commercials, all that stuff and doing other things for the league. You go to training, then you have to go do something. It was tough on me. I didn't know how to balance it, I didn't say no to anything because I'm young and it's part of your job, I get paid for it, I've gotta put in my time. It's just one of those things where everything just sort of happened so fast and you have to adjust as it went on. You had to experience it and learn from that and adjust to it. That's how it was.
>
> The second and third season, it became very limited. I said no to a lot of things. I told them I just want to concentrate on playing. At the end of the day, being a soccer player is the most important thing. I'm a soccer player first.

Still, Adu notes with pride that he didn't need multiple takes to do the ball-flipping, spinning-volley trick in Nike's "Go Tell the World" ad, despite the looming presence of a helicopter: "It was a little bit harder when the helicopter was blowing the ball all over the place. It moved the ball all over the place, and I had to adjust to it. I almost fell over a couple of times. When you have a helicopter 20 feet above you, it is scary. I'm not gonna lie, it is scary."

He was still the league's biggest pre-Beckham celebrity. Like Beckham and Donovan, he dated someone from the entertainment world—young pop sensation JoJo. In a bit of awkward timing, JoJo made a video—released soon after their breakup, but filmed well before—in which her boyfriend doesn't devote enough attention to her. The boyfriend bore no physical resemblance whatsoever to Adu but just happened to be a soccer player. (Coincidentally, the "boyfriend" in that video, UCLA player Mike Zaher, joined D.C. United in 2008.)

While the breakout season of double-digit goals or assists never came for the charismatic phenom, Adu's improvement was apparent to those who watched him closely. He made better decisions, learning when to be aggressive and when to be cautious. He could take over a game at times but was cognizant of his role when a teammate was in control. In each season, he had spectacular moments, but by his last season he was also a solid professional.

That's hard to explain to pundits such as CNBC's Darren Rovell, who wrote in April as the MLS season started: "I want to be the first—the first to call Freddy Adu a failure."[6] Strong words considering the player in question was still too young to be an NBA rookie.

Even within the soccer media, some had turned on him, thinking he had never lived up to the hype. But he continued to excel in youth internationals, and he made an impression when given playing time at Benfica. Perhaps Adu had never been a true star in MLS, but he had learned enough to become one. Motzkin says:

> There's a lot of different ways you can view and analyze the Freddy Adu time in MLS, both in terms of on the field and off the field. From my perspective, there are a lot of positives that emanated from the Freddy situation. There were trying times as well, but overall, he left MLS as a far better player than he was when he entered MLS. He ended up economically doing well for him and his family. From an exposure standpoint, he became almost a cultural icon in the States and probably to

this day is the one name that people know. People lose sight of the fact that, as we sit here today [spring 2008], he's still a very young player—he's 18 years old and is at an age where he's already had four years of professional soccer when most people are at the early side starting their professional career. Everyone just needs perspective.

It was a unique situation when he started. In a way, it was extremely unfair that he, unlike most sports stars who gain their fame as a result of their on-field accomplishments, because of Freddy's unique story, because of his youth, here was somebody who became a star before he ever played pro soccer. . . .

Most rookies don't even make it past a year, most rookies barely play. He played in almost every game for which he was available, he scored a handful of goals. When he played for the youth national teams, he generally speaking did pretty well.

Ben Olsen sympathizes with his former United teammate:

I think it was unfair for Freddy. Some unfair expectations were put on him through all this exposure, but that's stuff that comes along with being the first and being the youngest guy, having all this hype on you, making the million-dollar Nike contracts and all that stuff. Nowadays, that's what comes with it.

The hype got so big that people thought he was going to be this player that he couldn't live up to. Everybody in the soccer world knew that he wasn't going to come in and score 10-15 goals, get 15 assists and be the MVP of the league. It just wasn't there. Most people knew that were educated in soccer. When it didn't happen, people reacted a little negatively toward Freddy. I think Peter [Nowak] did a pretty good job with him, but it was a tough task. Peter held strong to his beliefs. Sometimes he wasn't ready to play at that level and wasn't helping the team, so he'd put him on the bench and have him come in and teach him some lessons that a lot of young people need to learn.

I love Freddy, I think he's a great kid, I'm so happy to see him now [in Europe]. I've been enjoying watching him with the nationals as well. . . . Something like that is much needed on the national team now, someone with some unpredictability and some pizzazz.

Was Adu able to develop as he liked? Adu remembers:

Yes and no. I developed in a way that I learned how to be a professional. Because of everything I went through in D.C., I did learn how to really deal with pressure. Everybody expecting you to score two-three goals a game, and it just doesn't happen that way. I don't care how good you are.

Going through that, learning that every time I stepped on the field, I should just worry about helping the team instead of trying to please everybody else. I learned to just calm down.

Meanwhile, Kreis started retooling Real Salt Lake, landing a trio of talented Argentines, but he was building for next year. Elsewhere, the league's new stars would shake up the playoff race.

THE STARS ARRIVE

The league's All-Stars faced Celtic on July 19 at the Rapids' Commerce City home. Two of the league's brightest newcomers, Juan Pablo Angel and Juan Toja, scored the goals in a 2-0 win. Yet the spotlight was on a man who wasn't playing.

Beckham, always willing to do his share of promotion, turned up to award a trophy to D.C. United's Under-17 squad, which had won a tournament of league-affiliated youth teams. He then smiled his way through a half-time interview dominated by one crucial question: will you be ready to play Saturday against Chelsea? The answer was a definite maybe.

ESPN had cameras all over the Home Depot Center for the Galaxy-Chelsea match, and the "will he or won't he" question added suspense to an otherwise meaningless friendly. He got up a couple of times to test his ankle and warm up. Finally, in the 78th minute, Beckham stepped onto the field in a Galaxy uniform for the first time. The world's most recognizable star was officially an MLS player.

His debut would set the tone for many of his appearances over the season. Beckham had a few moments of rare class, making passes that few MLS players would have the vision to see. He would also play hard, not shirking out of tackles like some pampered celebrity.

Perhaps he should've pampered himself a bit more. Beckham faced a tough tackle from Chelsea's Steve Sidwell and seemed to come out of it a little worse than he came in. Everyone insisted that he hadn't reaggravated the injury.

But Beckham's ankle wasn't really in game shape. He could manage a few minutes in a friendly, but he wouldn't appear in the Galaxy's SuperLiga matches and limited air travel to combat swelling. That meant he missed his one chance to appear in Dallas, angering a few unsympathetic fans and pundits. "The league has erred in tying its marketing campaign to a man whose concession to celebrity is that he'll let you take his picture," said *Dallas Morning News* columnist Kevin Sherrington, who said Pelé traveled to Dallas and played hurt on his first tour with the Cosmos.[7] Between local media demanding his presence and English media fretting that their longtime captain was reaggravating his injury, Beckham couldn't please everyone.

And some skeptics had always doubted Beckham's impact on MLS. One was Jim Paglia, the one-time bidder for Division I status with League One America:

> One of the pieces I wrote for *Soccer America* dealt with Beckham coming to the United States and what I thought his impact would be on the pro game. It wasn't a particularly flattering piece, although I admire Beckham a lot, think he's a great player and will continue to be. My prediction was he'd be more of a celebrity than an impact to the pro game, he'd travel around much like Pelé did, the first time he goes into a city he'll be well-received, the second time they'll be less of an audience, and the third time nobody's going to care. His 15 minutes of celebrity will have passed at that point, and I don't think he's really going to have an impact on the pro game.
>
> I wrote all that and I summarized by saying his impact on the game would be the equivalent of his wife announcing she's reviving the Spice Girls in order to save American music. Two days later, she announced she was reviving the Spice Girls. And the *New York Times* picked up my article from *Soccer America*.

Beckham missed his scheduled MLS regular-season debut August 5 in Toronto, citing the artificial turf as one of the factors keeping him off the field. He then had to backtrack with a smile upon realizing that his academies used the same surface.

The media circus rolled on to Washington, where Beckham dutifully appeared in the sweltering under-stadium batting cage for a packed press conference the day before the Galaxy faced D.C. United. He still wasn't sure if he would be ready to appear.

The game was in many respects a typical August game in RFK Stadium, though the attendance of 46,686 more than doubled the usual crowd, but it wasn't just a collection of curiosity seekers or European-league snobs. D.C. United fans had long ago circled the date on the calendar, and their fanatical chanting mixed with the heat and heavy rain for the usual steamy atmosphere. Fans were eager to see Beckham but also take a few gentle jabs—"We Sing Better Than Your Wife" read one banner. Landon Donovan, so often dangerous against United, drew boos at every opportunity.

Luciano Emilio scored in the first half, the Galaxy's Kyle Martino was sent off in the second, and United seemed to be cruising to a routine 1-0 win while Beckham went through the warm-up motions. History of another sort was almost in the offing when Joe Cannon saved Jaime Moreno's bid for sole possession of the MLS career scoring lead, which didn't escape the knowledgeable crowd's attention.

All of a sudden, Beckham flipped off his warm-ups, put on a #23 Galaxy jersey, and walked to the fourth official. The crowd gasped. The reporters in the press box immediately tore up their stories and started fresh. Beckham was coming in.

And he played pretty well in 20 minutes of action, once again showing his superb vision and passing ability. United were lucky to escape when he sent a 50-yard pass to Donovan, who collided with goalkeeper Troy Perkins near the edge of the box without drawing a whistle.

Beckham skipped the Galaxy's next game, again on an artificial surface in New England, but his full-fledged home debut would be memorable. In the SuperLiga semifinal against the same United team, Beckham did what he does best, scoring on a free kick and setting up Donovan for another goal in a 2-0 win. Pity ESPN's armada of cameras wasn't there to capture it.

Yet league wins eluded Beckham and the Galaxy. They dropped a wild 5-4 encounter to the Red Bulls before 66,237 fans in Giants Stadium, then lost consecutive 3-0 decisions to surging Chivas USA and Colorado, which had snapped out of its summer swoon to keep its playoff chances alive.

The SuperLiga final at home against Pachuca seemed to be the Galaxy's best hope of picking up a trophy. The USL's Richmond Kickers had long ago knocked them out of the Open Cup, and their playoff chances seemed remote at best. The Galaxy would play well but suffer yet another setback. Beckham went in hard for a 50-50 ball in the first half and injured his knee. Somehow, the Galaxy's exhausted, injury-riddled team stayed in the game and forced overtime on a spectacular bicycle kick from Chris Klein, ensuring *Sports-Center* coverage if nothing else, but the Mexican club won on penalty kicks.

The loss and the injury seemed to be the final nails in the Galaxy's season. At this point, few could blame Beckham if he simply tried to get back in shape for crucial qualifiers in England's sputtering Euro 2008 campaign. In September, the Galaxy somehow made it interesting, embarking on a five-game winning streak. Beckham returned for the last two games.

The path to that last playoff spot would go through Chicago, where the other big-time player was making his presence felt. Blanco wasn't the only factor in the Fire's revival. New coach Juan Carlos Osorio spoke with an air of authority and experience, Wilman Conde followed Osorio to Chicago and helped to stabilize the squad, and Costa Rican forward Paulo Wanchope had at last made a long-rumored move to MLS. Blanco brought the gamesmanship people feared, diving to get fouls and agitating opponents like a hockey team's favorite pest, but he threw himself into each game with the commitment that a lot of MLS big names of the past had lacked. He simply made his team better, and it showed in a series of hard-fought ties and wins.

The playoff race that had seemed so clear-cut in July was suddenly frenzied. Four teams had pulled away—D.C. United claimed another Supporters' Shield with relative ease, New England sewed up second place, and Chivas USA and Houston dueled for the West lead. Dallas and New York hit late skids but had enough points to stay out of the fray. That left Los Angeles, Chicago, and Colorado on the verge of overhauling Kansas City and Columbus for the last two spots. A late injury to Schelotto effectively removed the Crew from the race, though he returned to spark a couple of morale-building wins over New England and D.C. United.

Three games on the final Saturday settled much of the season's questions. Kansas City shook off its late slump to beat Dallas 2-0 behind two Scott Sealy goals. Real Salt Lake took some consolation in denying Rocky Mountain Cup rival Colorado a playoff spot, winning 1-0 on a late goal by Robbie Findley, acquired in midseason from Los Angeles. Chivas USA clinched the West in an ill-tempered draw against Houston that saw coaches Dominic Kinnear and Preki exchange a few hostilities after the whistle.

That left the final spot down to the lone Sunday game. Los Angeles at Chicago. Two resurgent teams. Beckham vs. Blanco. Chicago needed just a tie; Los Angeles, which had tied New York 1-1 a couple of days earlier, needed to win their sixth game out of seven.

The game was a disappointment, particularly for Galaxy fans. The Fire kept the initiative much of the way, though Los Angeles could complain that a couple of close calls had gone against them. Beckham made his second appearance after his long absence, replacing Peter Vagenas in the 58th minute, but he couldn't change the tide. In the dying moments, the Fire counterattacked from a Beckham giveaway, and the unheralded John Thorrington put away the winner for Chicago.

Beckham would go on some postseason tours with the Galaxy. He played for England but couldn't salvage their Euro 2008 qualifying campaign.

Olsen, speaking early in 2008, maintained Beckham's signing was a sign of progress for the league: "I think it's a great situation. I've got some friends that play there, and I've heard nothing but good things about him. He makes them a better team. The money stuff—I think he's worth every penny. That's great."

Are the media too fixated on one guy? Again, Olsen:

That's something you have to ask the media. . . . It's not negative media, I don't think. A lot of it is excitement still. Is he the best player in the world? Probably not, but when I played against him I was pretty impressed with the passing ability and his all-around game. I think it's a good situation, I really do.

I think we need to keep getting forward now. We need to continue to get great players like Beckham. . . . This league will eventually become about soccer—who's winning, who's the best teams.

The playoffs would go on without Beckham. And a couple of the league's best teams wouldn't go far.

PLAYOFF UPSETS

Both conference winners went into the playoffs with injury problems. Chivas USA lost its strike force—Ante Razov was out, and Maykel Galindo wasn't at full strength. D.C. United saw Moreno and Luciano Emilio, the league's MVP and leading scorer with 20 goals, leave the season finale with injuries.

The worst news for United—they were playing perennial nemesis Chicago. In five prior playoff games against the Fire, United had been outscored 10-0.

Chris Rolfe made it 1-0 in the first leg in Chicago, then teamed with Chad Barrett to take a 3-0 aggregate lead in Washington. United pulled the ineffective Emilio and responded in the second half with goals from unlikely scorer Clyde Simms and from Christian Gomez, but Osorio's team didn't give up the equalizer. The Supporters' Shield winner was out.

Chivas USA went out with even less of an offensive bang against Kansas City, managing only to hit the woodwork a couple of times as Galindo gutted out the second leg. Davy Arnaud's first-leg free kick accounted for the only goal of the series.

The defending finalists both advanced, one with a frenetic comeback and one with a bit of luck. Houston fell behind Texas rival Dallas 1-0 in the first leg, then saw Carlos Ruiz double their disadvantage early in the second. Stuart Holden, capping a breakthrough season, started the comeback in the 66th minute, and Brian Ching tied the series five minutes later. The series went to overtime, where the Dynamo poured on two more goals.

The Red Bulls could claim a bit of misfortune in exiting so early. Claudio Reyna left early in the second leg with a hamstring injury. The New York defense shut down the cautious New England attack until Angel was hurt midway through the second leg's second half. Arena hesitated to send in a substitute while Angel tried to plead his way back onto the field, and Taylor Twellman scored the only goal of the series while the Red Bulls played with 10 men.

New England also scraped through the semifinals 1-0, though Twellman's goal was an attention-grabbing bicycle kick. Houston won convincingly, completely shutting down Kansas City and getting a goal in each half from Nate Jaqua and Dwayne De Rosario for a 2-0 win. The lone drawback: Brian Ching limped off with a calf injury.

Houston and New England, with teams bearing strong resemblances to the 2006 versions, would meet once again in the final November 18.

REMATCH

In the year of Beckham and Blanco, neither finalist had used its designated-player slot, an angle the media pounded in the run-up to the Cup. Perhaps this was unfair—Blanco had transformed the Fire, Angel earned his money, and Beckham was inspirational in his all-too-brief chances to play. But Kinnear and Steve Nicol had proved the value of keeping a solid core intact.

The Revolution found themselves on the defensive over their defensive approach. Nicol's teams had been in the final three times and played scorelessly through regulation each time. Twellman's overtime goal in 2006—quickly canceled out by Ching—was the only New England goal in three fruitless finals. And Twellman had been a one-man band, scoring all but one of the Revolution's goals over the past two postseasons. With Houston boasting the stingiest defense in league history—23 goals allowed in 30 games—no one was expecting a barnburner.

New England could at least point to a trophy at last, having won the U.S. Open Cup final 3-2 at Dallas. The Revolution fans who piled into one corner of RFK Stadium on a mild mid-November day had reason to be optimistic, while a surprisingly sizable orange-clad contingent took up residence near D.C. United's Screaming Eagles supporters' group.

The Revolution looked surprisingly ragged early. In the early minutes, the defense let a dangerous cross sail through the box. Matt Reis couldn't collect it cleanly, and Nate Jaqua had the first opportunity—a shot that deflected, to the Revolution's relief.

New England settled down quickly, and three of its stalwarts put together a combination of passes in the 20th minute. Shalrie Joseph played the ball from midfield ahead of Steve Ralston, running along the right of the box. As the ball rolled toward the end line, Ralston looked up and spotted Twellman. Cross. Header. Goal. New England had the lead.

The Revs nearly picked up a second, yet again through the indomitable Twellman. Khano Smith, New England's speedy left winger, stripped the ball from Brian Mullan and shredded the left wing, centering to Twellman. He couldn't quite get enough on the shot, and Pat Onstad, whose salt-and-pepper beard gave away his age, sprawled to make the save.

Houston picked it up in the second half, then scrambled for the equalizer. Dwayne De Rosario, once again impressive in a big game, got the ball deep in the box and played across to Joseph Ngwenya. The striker whiffed on his first shot. But the Revolution defense couldn't clear. Ngwenya regained his footing and punched the ball under Reis, away from Jay Heaps's despairing lunge. 1-1.

The crowd—undoubtedly relieved that the game wasn't the dreary encounter they had feared—raised the volume. Tempers flared after Smith and Craig Waibel leaned against each other and fell in the Houston box, drawing no call, to Smith's dismay. Waibel sniped at Smith on the way back toward midfield, and Smith leaned in, making contact with Waibel. Smith picked up a yellow card while Waibel stayed down.

The Revs shook off that incident and nearly repeated their scoring combination of Joseph to Ralston to Twellman. Onstad barely broke it up.

In the 74th minute, underrated Houston midfielder Brad Davis floated a cross into the box toward De Rosario. For all De Rosario's career heroics, he is not known for scoring with his head. Heaps, running behind De Rosario, would later say he thought the ball would float over his head. It didn't. De Rosario rose, snapped his body in an awkward but powerful spasm, and Reis couldn't keep it out. 2-1, Houston.

Things immediately got worse for the Revolution. Ralston, the game's prospective MVP until the Dynamo rally, left the game with cramps.

The Revs offense tried to conjure a goal from someone other than Twellman. Andy Dorman, entering the game for Ralston, immediately took a shot. Pat Noonan took a couple of shots from the top of the box, one off-target and the other easily saved.

So often, when a soccer team is frantically pushing for a tying goal, a shot comes ever so close to doing the job but signals to everyone watching that the game simply isn't going to go their way. That moment came in the 87th minute. Off a corner kick, Jeff Larentowicz headed the ball down, hard and straight at the goal. Onstad had little chance to get an eye on the ball. But his leg was in the way.

The day would end with the media getting a few celebratory comments from Kinnear, who lauded his no-name defense full of guys who weren't getting a shot with the national team. In the New England locker room, Twellman tried to take some solace by checking his messages while the media crept closer.

Outside that locker room, MLS had much to celebrate after 12 years. D.C. United's new owners, having hosted one last big event in RFK Stadium, kept pressing for a new stadium. In September, Anschutz had sold another team—investor Andrew Hauptman and Andell Holdings took over the Chicago Fire. Red Bull demonstrated its commitment to MLS by buying out AEG's interest in the New Jersey stadium, converting the plans along the way to eliminate a concert stage and keep the venue's focus on soccer. San Jose was planning to return to action in 2008 with the Oakland A's brain trust in charge of operating the team and finding a new stadium.

And another eclectic band of owner-investors—Hollywood mogul Joe Roth, longtime USL team owner Adrian Hanauer, megabillionaire Paul Allen, and comedian-turned-Galaxy-backer Drew Carey—had reached a deal to bring a team to Seattle in 2009.

MLS had even ventured into reality TV with *Sueño MLS*, a Univision show chronicling a long tryout process for a Chivas USA roster spot. Jorge Flores won the competition and even more impressively worked his way into the lineup for a couple of late games.

Some things never seemed to change, among them the revolving door at the club formerly known as the MetroStars. Red Bull parted with Bruce Arena, dissatisfied with the team's progress even though the veteran of D.C. United and the national team had created a good atmosphere. The Red Bulls could criticize each other without splintering, and they joked easily about developments like Juan Pablo Angel being named to *People en Español*'s "10 Sexiest Men" in the country.

"If Bruce Arena can't turn that franchise around, you have to think about reasons outside the coaching staff as to what the heck's going on over there," says Mark Semioli, the longtime MetroStar who had already lamented the team's inability to keep going in one direction.

"When I took the job there, I made it clear that this is going to be a three-year process," Arena says. "I didn't expect to do anything immediately. Having said that, we still made the postseason. That was the plan, to make steady progress. I think people lose sight of those things and get very anxious and want to win right away. With the roster and the situation in that particular franchise, it's going to take time. If you can't see that, you're never going to be pleased with anything in terms of the progress of the team."

The spillover effect hit Chicago. After only a few months with the Fire, one-time MetroStars assistant Juan Carlos Osorio jumped to New York. Years earlier, he had told Semioli he'd be back one day.

On the West Coast, the Galaxy kept loading up on stars, reacquiring Carlos Ruiz to go along with Beckham and Donovan. The Donovan contract had been "grandfathered in" so that he could get more than the maximum without counting as a designated player, and the league extended the exemption. Moving to the Home Depot Center's other occupant, Chivas USA, was apparently not an option. "I'm a Galaxy guy," says Donovan.

Whether the more globally famous star in the Los Angeles lineup would ever consider himself a true "Galaxy guy" would be a key question for the league over the next two years.

12

Beckham and Beyond

With David Beckham on board, the Galaxy had new frontiers to pursue. Plenty of people around the world wanted a glimpse of Beckham, and the team obliged.

While other MLS teams played in the playoffs for which the Galaxy failed to qualify, Beckham and company played a charity match against Hollywood United, a team of celebrities and former soccer players under the leadership of Anthony LaPaglia. Then came friendlies against USL teams in Minnesota and Vancouver. After MLS Cup, the team traveled to Australia to play a 5-3 loss before 80,295 fans in Sydney. Finally, on November 30, the Galaxy finished the 2007 campaign with a 4-1 win in Wellington, New Zealand. The off-season would be brief. The 2008 campaign, with internationally recognized Ruud Gullit taking over as coach, started February 20 in Hawaii in the new Pan Pacific Championship, where the Galaxy suffered a 1-0 loss to Gamba Osaka before avenging their loss to Sydney FC. Next stop: Seoul, then Shanghai and Hong Kong.

The Galaxy had toured like no U.S.-based team since the heyday of the New York Cosmos. But even if Beckham was the most globally famous soccer player since Pelé, the Galaxy weren't the Cosmos. Not in a league with a salary cap that limited L.A.'s options, even with the designated-player rule (or Beckham rule) exempting most of Beckham's salary and part of Landon Donovan's.

Alexi Lalas still managed to find six-figure salaries for a lot of players. Chris Klein, Edson Buddle, Eddie Lewis, and Peter Vagenas were well com-

225

pensated as befitting their MLS experience. More controversial was the money doled out to foreign defenders and midfielders—one-time European star Abel Xavier, young Brazilian Alvaro Pires, and unheralded Canadian Ante Jazic. Most controversial was the re-signing of erratic forward Carlos Ruiz, whose salary had been grandfathered into the designated-player rule along with Donovan's.

That left an imbalanced team, and a 4-0 loss at Colorado in the MLS season opener seemed to confirm the worst. But the Galaxy offense sprang to life, with Beckham and Donovan combining well with Buddle. The defense leaked goals, but the Galaxy often managed to make up for it at the other end.

Yet the Galaxy's bright start papered over a few weaknesses in the squad. The defensive lapses proved too costly and forced a few shakeups. Xavier was let go and replaced with Argentine Eduardo Dominguez, who also ate up a lot of the salary cap. Gullit never grasped the intricacies of MLS roster rules.

In the midst of an epic winless streak in August, the Galaxy cleaned house. Lalas was fired. Gullit resigned, realizing along with Galaxy management that he wasn't a good fit. Bruce Arena, so successful with D.C. United and the U.S. national team but recovering from being pushed out by impatient management in New York, took over as coach and general manager.

A year later, the full story came out. *Sports Illustrated's* Grant Wahl had followed the team through it all and captured all the frustrations. Wahl's book, *The Beckham Experiment*, painted a picture of a team that followed Beckham's advisers down the tubes. The coaching search that had brought Gullit, a great player in his day but a coach with a questionable résumé, had been conducted not by Lalas but by longtime Beckham associate and new Galaxy consultant Terry Byrne, Wahl reported. Beckham's quiet approach to team captaincy wasn't working, and by the end, Donovan was questioning Beckham's commitment to the team after Gullit's departure.[1]

While the Galaxy imploded and failed to make the playoffs once again, plenty of teams took big steps forward:

▶ Philadelphia, with the vocal supporters group Sons of Ben already making itself known around MLS, landed an expansion team to play in a soccer-specific stadium in Chester, Pennsylvania.

▶ D.C. United got a big-name jersey sponsor in Volkswagen, which also signed a leaguewide sponsorship deal.

- Houston found co-owners in boxing legend Oscar De La Hoya and business associate Gabriel Brener, who would share the team's operations with Anschutz Entertainment Group (AEG).
- Chicago landed Brian McBride, who returned to MLS after cementing a permanent place in the hearts of Fulham fans, leading the team to escape relegation from England's Premier League. Upon his departure, Fulham renamed one of its posh dining areas in his honor. A Fulham statement captures the club's sentiment:

In honour of Brian McBride, the all-American hero who captained the Club to the dramatic Great Escape of 2008, we are delighted to announce that our SW6 Sports Bar will be renamed McBride's from next season.

The American striker, who was twice named Fulham's Player of the Season during his time at Craven Cottage, made over 150 appearances for the Whites and scored 40 goals. He bid farewell to Fulham at the end of the 2007/08 season after four and a half years outstanding service.

The Lounge is a fitting tribute to Brian McBride, whose unquestionable commitment and bravery earned him the respect of everyone associated with the Club.[2]

- New England, which had overcome years of near misses to lift a trophy in 2007 through the U.S. Open Cup, won another one in 2008, beating Houston on penalty kicks in the SuperLiga final. That was one of two successes for MLS teams over foreign competition. The second came in the All-Star Game, when Dwayne De Rosario converted a game-winning penalty kick as the MLS All-Stars beat England's West Ham United 3-2 in Toronto.
- San Jose, returning to MLS with coach Frank Yallop back at the scene of prior championship runs, started slowly but looked competitive down the stretch with Englishman Darren Huckerby added to the squad.
- Real Salt Lake moved into Rio Tinto Stadium after years of bruising political battles, then got a 90th-minute goal from Yura Movsisyan in the season finale at Rocky Mountain Cup rival Colorado to claim the Cup and snatch a playoff spot—Real's first—away from the Rapids. Real followed up by fighting past Chivas USA to reach the West final.

▶ New York backed into a playoff spot when D.C. United lost, then made the most of the opportunity by shocking Houston 3-0 on the road to win on 4-1 aggregate. The Red Bulls then shut down Real Salt Lake in Rio Tinto Stadium to reach MLS Cup for the first time, along with the geographically questionable title of West champion.

Columbus took the biggest leap of all. League MVP Guillermo Barros Schelotto dissected defenses with incisive passes. Frankie Hejduk, whose energy level just seemed to rise with age, showed the bond between players and fans with beers and songs at a pregame tailgate while he was suspended, winning more fans when videos of the tailgate circulated on YouTube.

The Crew cruised through the season, claimed the Supporters' Shield and disposed of Kansas City in the playoffs. Chicago, bringing plenty of momentum into the playoffs, took a 1-0 lead in the conference final on a McBride goal, but the Crew fought back for a 2-1 win.

Columbus had a slightly easier time in the final November 23, taking a 1-0 halftime lead on an Alejandro Moreno goal set up by Schelotto's alert defensive play and precise pass. Long-serving New York forward John Wolyniec tied the game shortly after the break, but Chad Marshall instantly restored the lead off a Schelotto corner kick. Schelotto struck for his third assist to clinch it late, chipping the ball to the overlapping Hejduk for a header and an insurance goal.

Coach Sigi Schmid celebrated the fruits of his long rebuilding effort, then confirmed what many had suspected—he was moving back to the West Coast as the first coach of the Seattle Sounders' new incarnation in MLS.

Also on the move was Ivan Gazidis. One of MLS's original executives, the deputy commissioner returned to England as chief executive officer of Premier League power Arsenal.

Gazidis left behind a league that had taken *SportsBusiness Journal* and *SportsBusiness Daily* honors as 2008 Professional League of the Year as it prepared for more expansion. Ownership groups from seven cities bid for two expansion slots in 2011, giving MLS plenty to ponder in the off-season.

NORTHWEST AND EUROPEAN PASSAGES

Yet the off-season gossip once again revolved around the Galaxy. Beckham went on loan to AC Milan, at first insisting that the move was temporary but later expressing interest in staying longer. Donovan went on loan to Bayern Munich for a third go-round in Germany.

Donovan fared well by most reports but was miscast as a forward and left in an awkward auditioning position, trying to get playing time on a team that wasn't sure if he'd stay until the end of the season. He duly returned to the Galaxy at the end of his loan.

Beckham played better than almost anyone expected at Milan. The traditional Italian power exchanged negotiating stances with MLS through the international media, surely losing something in translation. In the end, Milan was allowed to keep Beckham through the end of the Italian Serie A season in exchange for a few concessions, most notably a change to Beckham's contract in which he would incur penalties if he exercised an opt-out clause at the end of the 2009 season—a clause Beckham hadn't admitted in the past but which had been unearthed by Wahl.[3]

Many MLS fans weren't impressed that Beckham was able to dial up his performance level in Italy, and he didn't seem prepared for some of the hostilities he encountered upon his return to MLS. He confronted fans, starting in Los Angeles, where he pointed as if to invite a fan to hop onto the field and meet him face-to-face. One fan did so, earning a lifetime ban from the Home Depot Center.

Beckham worked through the tough times and interceded to help overturn the fan's lifetime ban. Beckham and Donovan also made peace over Donovan's criticism and combined well on the field again. Fans didn't turn out in the overwhelming numbers that had greeted Beckham's first tour of the league, but the attendance for Galaxy road games with Beckham in tow was still a considerable improvement over the league average.

The story was far worse in New York, where the Red Bulls' MLS Cup run didn't carry over into regular-season success. The team seemed cursed by the trade of winger Dave van den Bergh to Dallas, near his wife's family. As the team fell to 2-16-4, flirting with the worst record in league history, Juan Carlos Osorio threw in the towel and resigned. The only good news for long-suffering New York fans was the slow but steady rise of Red Bull Arena, whose impressive structure was clearly visible from trains heading out of the city through New Jersey.

New York and other markets had plenty of soccer distractions, though, in what MLS dubbed the Summer of Soccer. On the heels of the U.S. national team's astounding Confederations Cup performance, beating Spain to reach the final, the USA hosted the Gold Cup and many international friendlies, some under the auspices of MLS and corporate sibling Soccer United Marketing (SUM), some not.

The World Football Challenge, though, didn't pose the same threat to MLS as ChampionsWorld and MLS-baiting Giorgio Chinaglia had posed a few years earlier. Don Garber said SUM had a chance to be involved but was too busy with the Gold Cup. And in any case, a couple of the teams involved added MLS visits to their tours—Chelsea played at Seattle, Club America played a couple of friendlies against MLS teams throughout the year, and AC Milan took on the Galaxy in a meeting of Beckham's two clubs.[4] And MLS was indeed busy with its own friendlies—on August 1, Los Angeles hosted European champion Barcelona at the Rose Bowl and drew a crowd of 93,137.

The league also enjoyed friendly relations with the new women's league, Women's Professional Soccer, which made a low-key debut in 2009 and met its modest attendance goals with an average crowd near 4,500.

The story of the season was in Seattle, where an eclectic ownership group combined their strengths perfectly. Hollywood mogul Joe Roth and Microsoft co-founder Paul Allen gave the team firm financial footing. Adrian Hanauer brought his experience from the Sounders' incarnation as a USL team. And comic Drew Carey brought charisma, a fan's zeal, and clever ideas borrowing from European tradition. Sounders fans, most of them brandishing green scarves, would meet at a downtown park and march behind a band to Qwest Field. Fans could join the club's official supporters group and get a vote on many club matters, including a vote every four years on whether to retain the general manager.

The efforts paid off at the turnstile, with crowds around the 30,000 mark for most home games. And on the field, Sigi Schmid assembled a team capable of chasing trophies right away. Swedish star Freddie Ljungberg made an impact worthy of his designated-player status. Longtime USA goalkeeper Kasey Keller, who grew up in Washington, was still in strong form.

The Sounders are the first club to take a name and some staffers from the USL to MLS. They won't be the last. In March, MLS officials made a Northwest swing—expansion announcement in Vancouver, first MLS league game in Seattle, expansion announcement in Portland. In 2011, Seattle fans are scheduled to resume regional rivalries—and they'll have some feasible road trips.

Vancouver and Portland had outlasted the competition for the expansion slots. Miami, Atlanta, and Montreal were out of the running early. Ottawa had not yet backed an MLS stadium over a CFL stadium. St. Louis, a traditional hotbed of U.S. soccer, had a stadium plan, but the ownership group hadn't convinced MLS that it had the financial clout to run a league team.

Both expansion cities hit snags with their stadium plans over the summer. History was repeating. But league officials were unfazed. This league has experience.

This league has history.

THE AGENDA
So what's next?

Here's how Don Garber answered the question in early 2008:

I think we've gotten bricks and mortar in place, the foundation has been laid, we're on the right path, if we continue what we're doing we'll continue to grow and become more popular. Our franchises will grow in value and more people will care about soccer. Now it's about raising the quality of play so as the market continues to get more soccer-oriented, instead of turning their interest to Europe or Latin America they're going to turn their interest here. So it's thinking about what kinds of changes need to be, what kind of evolution do we have to our salaries, to our player budgets, what do we do with the designated player.

It's also in the next couple of years that we have a [collective bargaining agreement] coming up, and we've got to go through negotiations that will be very different than the ones we went through when we had just won a lawsuit against our players.

It's about growing television ratings and raising the quality of our productions and further engaging our broadcast partners in promotion and their support of the game.

A massive, massive focus on stadium development in all of our markets and continuing to build the infrastructure for the sport.

Expansion will be a major focus over the next five years. Certainly we'll be at 18 teams by then but it's possible that within the next five years we'll add more.

And it's the continuing evolution of our ownership group. The provocative, stimulating conversation around our board table will take this league into new directions. I don't know what those directions will be, but I know that it will change. I'm sure it'll change for the better.

Getting new investors, the league's most vexing problem for years, is no longer a concern. Anschutz, who once owned more than half the league, is down to Los Angeles and a share of Houston. Lamar Hunt has passed away, but Hunt Sports Group retains control of two teams in Dallas and Columbus. Soon, their ownership may be down to one. MLS has come a long way from the days of Anschutz, Hunt, and Kraft owning the entire 10-team league.

But the bricks-and-mortar work isn't quite done, and several longstanding questions have yet to be answered.

These are among the challenges MLS faces going forward:

1. Finishing the construction job

As of 2010, most existing and expansion teams are sitting pretty. Columbus has its cozy stadium. The Galaxy and Chivas USA share the Home Depot Center. Dallas, Chicago, and Colorado have newer venues. Toronto has christened its home with a season of boisterous fans. Salt Lake's new home has been a success. Kansas City is in a minor-league baseball park but has almost everything lined up for its own place. New York's long-promised stadium hit the occasional construction snag, but the Red Bulls stuck with it. Philadelphia will play in a stadium anchoring new waterfront development in Chester. That's 11 of the 16 teams as of 2010, all in soccer stadiums.

Seattle shares the Seahawks' NFL stadium, but the team is optimistic that it'll provide a better atmosphere and revenue stream than MLS tenants have found elsewhere. The stadium was built with the intent of switching between the two forms of football.

New England also is still sharing a stadium, though it too can hold a good-sized field and has the benefit of shared ownership—Kraft owns the Revolution and the NFL's Patriots. The atmosphere isn't ideal, with one side of the stadium left empty, and the team has looked into sites for something smaller.

That leaves three teams in various states of progress—three teams that account for more than half the league's championships.

The original San Jose Earthquakes moved to Houston in part because the team had made no progress on a stadium in the Bay Area. The team took up temporary residence at the University of Houston and is searching for something permanent. Early in 2008, a strongly worded note from Don Garber to Dynamo ownership was made public, stirring up some controversy in the stadium negotiations.

The new San Jose Earthquakes, under local ownership at last, had one false start and started the 2008 season playing most of their games in a converted college stadium at Santa Clara, with a couple of bigger games in Oakland's McAfee Stadium. Owner Lew Wolff has been working on deals to swap land without taking public money, but the sour economy has slowed his progress.

D.C. United reclaimed RFK Stadium for itself in 2008 as baseball's Washington Nationals moved to a palatial estate of their own. But that ballpark drained more than $600 million from the cash-strapped District, leaving little political capital to devote toward a public-private partnership for a soccer stadium. Talks on the District's Poplar Point area stalled, and United has started looking to the suburbs. During the delay, Victor MacFarlane sold his share of the club to co-owner Will Chang.

The other issue with stadium construction is the turf. FIFA has encouraged wider use of artificial turf, particularly a new generation called FieldTurf that is far more sophisticated than the carpets on which Pelé and the NASL played. Players—and, to some extent, fans—aren't convinced. When David Beckham arrived in MLS, he criticized the artificial surfaces in several league stadiums. He quickly apologized with an embarrassed smile when he realized his own academy used artificial turf, but he's not alone in his complaints. Players believe artificial turf can add to leg strain, and the ball is sometimes more difficult to control than on a nice grass surface.[5]

Some artificial turfs are better than others, and newer models are an improvement over a grass field torn up by a football team—see Giants Stadium in New Jersey before the artificial surface went back in to stay. New England's Gillette Stadium is a few steps above the unforgiving, foot-scorching Dragon Stadium turf Dallas endured for a season. Seattle has long sought a mix of football and soccer on Qwest Field and will surely strive to make sure their artificial surface is suitable for players and fans.

San Jose and Houston may be close to stadium solutions, and D.C. United may eventually force the city to pitch in or watch the team depart for the suburbs. That will leave New England and Seattle in football stadiums, playing on artificial turf. Down the road, the league will need to decide whether those situations are sound in the long term.

But the league doesn't just need a place to play on game days. Bruce Arena reaped the benefits of D.C. United's early training facility—which United had to abandon for a less ideal setup at RFK Stadium. He appreciated that facility even more after going to New York and finding his team and the front office nowhere near each other.

"[Early league executives] wanted to be involved in the sexy things, and the sexy part of the business is the players," Arena says. "The part they needed to get right was facilities. Most teams in the league didn't have training facilities. The stadiums we played in were poor. There were a lot of things that they didn't get right until this day. The league is still paying for it. However, it's obviously high on the things-to-do list. Now we see into Year 13 that there's a good number of stadiums, teams understanding the value of training facilities, all those kind of things."

2. Serving the right mix of fans

The demographic challenges outlined at the league's inception are still around. Fans raised on European traditions don't always share the same interests as those raised on Latin American games, and neither group always sits well with families who want to bring kids without exposing them to profanity and hostility.

"Soccer at its best in the stands has gotta be a little dangerous," says Doug Logan. U.S. fans have done well to bring the passion without the danger—several supporters groups explicitly ban anything resembling hooliganism—but games sometimes have a hint of the troubles that mar the sport overseas. Salvadoran fans angry over D.C. United's trade of Raul Diaz Arce sometimes came to RFK Stadium and booed the U.S. national anthem. A parking-lot skirmish between a few Red Bulls fans and some agitators outside RFK made the rounds on YouTube in 2006.

But the supporters groups also say some stadium security forces go too far in dampening fan passion. One common concern among New York and D.C. fans: security at Giants Stadium is overbearing, removing fans with little to no reason.

Soccer fans are unique. They take action to ensure that the game belongs to them. One such action: creating their own competitions within the league.

On February 2, 2001, a charter was written to create a new trophy to award to an MLS team each year. The charter is meticulous, beginning with a "mission" and spelling out in precise terms how the trophy's winner is to be determined. MLS commissioner Don Garber didn't write the rules. No one from U.S. Soccer is named among the signees. The six people listed are fans—three for the Chicago Fire, three for the Dallas Burn. The trophy is called the Brimstone Cup, a play on the names of each team. (The trophy's name was not changed when the Burn became the less incendiary FC Dallas.)

The idea caught on, with D.C. United and the MetroStars establishing the Atlantic Cup. But that trophy was endowed by the front offices, not the fans. Not as cool.

When Real Salt Lake joined MLS in 2005, the fans took the initiative again, pairing up with Colorado Rapids fans to establish the Rocky Mountain Cup, overseen by "the Committee of 10." Colorado's Jeff Cunningham lifted the trophy October 12 in Salt Lake City and made a point of showing it to Real fans, according to the match report at ColoradoRapids.com. In the off-season, the Rapids traded Cunningham to Salt Lake. The USL's Minnesota Thunder also had a tongue-in-cheek claim to the Cup, having beaten both teams in the U.S. Open Cup.

The trophies and other prizes continue to spread. FC Dallas and Houston play for possession of a cannon nicknamed El Capitan. The Chivas-Galaxy rivalry has a sponsor, rendering it the Honda Superclasico. The two Hunt Sports Group teams, Dallas and Columbus, have played a preseason charity game for the Lamar Hunt Pioneer Cup. Columbus and Toronto now play for the Trillium Cup, named after a flower with official status in both Ohio and Ontario.

All of these prizes are establishing new traditions that European fans and Latin American fans can easily understand. Families may catch on, too.

Garber sees MLS catching up with a fourth audience—the general sports fan.

With Beckham coming in and that audience being engaged and excited by the World Cup, they're beginning to say, "Hey, soccer's pretty cool. My brother or sister plays it. My roommate in college plays it. My friend from Brazil or Mexico is into it. My friend who is a member of the [Toronto] Red Patch Boys took me to a game and there's no experience like it anywhere in North America." That audience is still the smallest target for us, and it's not something we've emphasized specifically in our marketing, but it's beginning to pay attention to us.

But Garber doesn't care about winning over those who are hostile toward the game. "I don't care about [that audience], I don't wanna care about, I don't wanna hear about any of our people focusing on it. That audience, the soccer basher—they don't care, they never will care. Any interest they have is negative, and we shouldn't be distracted by that."

Garber's stance clarifies one point that has gone back and forth in U.S. soccer history. The game itself isn't going to change. MLS and SUM are built to make money on the global game, not some Americanized version of it. Chasing the European and Latin American fans will be a constant challenge, but the league has at least solved a long-standing identity crisis in the sport.

3. Settling the schedule and format

There's no good time to run a soccer league in the United States. The winter months are off limits in Colorado, Toronto, New England, New York, and Chicago, where the weather simply won't cooperate. The league shares its late March–early April start time with the NCAA basketball tournament and the start of baseball season, rendering it invisible in the media. The late weeks of the regular season and the playoffs fall in the middle of football season, leaving no space for weekend TV coverage on ESPN's networks.

Fall games tend to do well, with hard-core fans drawn by the tension of late-season clashes and families planning activities after the school week. Playoff games, for which fans can't plan in advance, often don't.

Playoffs as a whole are another contentious point in the league. Traditionalist fans would rather see the league do away with the East and West divisions in favor of a "single-table" model. They'd like to scrap the playoffs. Then the ultimate step toward traditional soccer leagues: relegate the worst teams to a lower tier and promote the best of the lower group.

Promotion and relegation aren't feasible yet. Freddy Adu concedes the point: "The league is so new that it's hard to do all the stuff. We just don't have the structure here yet."

Ivan Gazidis says:

"Ever" is a long time. Would we ever see it? It's possible someday. But the way our business is structured and where we are in our development, it's very difficult to imagine it in any foreseeable time frame. We are focused on getting people to invest hundreds of millions of dollars in Major League Soccer—municipalities, states, individuals, sponsors. It's very difficult to imagine that money would be committed if there were any serious risk that teams could be ejected from the league. As a practical matter, regardless of any debate on the pros and cons of the promotion/relegation system, I don't see it happening while MLS continues to be in its growth phase.

Could I imagine once MLS is a very established league that has stadiums, potentially has a second division that MLS owns? I could imagine a system like that, yes, but not in any foreseeable time.

Scrapping at least part of the playoff structure is more feasible. Perhaps that move would add more meaning to the regular season, at least among the top teams. "The way things happen in this league—your 30, 32 regular-season games don't mean anything anyway," Bruce Arena told *USA Today*. "The idea is to get into the playoffs, and then everyone's on even terms. And that's in any league that has playoffs, anyway."[6]

Arena sees a possibility for a cup competition after the season. "We're in a culture that, when people view sports, they understand playoffs and then the ultimate winner. People still view [the MLS Cup winner as] the MLS champion. I believe you should have a playoff system, but I believe you should have a single table."

Gazidis sees an opening for a single table without playoffs:

It terms of single table, I think that's a very different issue. I think there is a belief that European soccer is the gold standard, and that everything that happens in Europe therefore must be the right way to do things in soccer. And I don't discount that because it's extraordinarily successful in Europe. If you discount things in Europe, you do so at your peril. So you have to look closely at it. But interestingly . . . if you speak to someone [in Europe], they're often more open to new ideas than purists are in the United States. The English love the shootout, for example. I'm not sure they would put it in the Premier League, but they do enjoy it.

We're seeing a movement around the world to look at playoff systems. It's been introduced in promotion/relegation, for example. It's been used for a long time in many parts of the world.

I think you can have an endless debate about whether it's better if Chelsea beats Arsenal twice during the year, both times 5-0, but Arsenal beats Wigan more often than Chelsea beats Wigan, Arsenal is the champion. In our system, if Chelsea beats Arsenal, Chelsea's the champion.

You could have an endless debate about which of those systems is fairer or more compelling. And I think what you find fairer or more compelling is really a question of personal taste.

It's not impossible that we would change. I think it would be a change in philosophy. It's not like promotion/relegation where I see there's no way I could conceive of it in the foreseeable future.

Scrapping the playoffs in their entirety also would do away with the league's biggest event, MLS Cup. Just as the NFL maximizes its Super Bowl week, MLS does what it can to take advantage of whatever spotlight it gets leading up to the final. The league announces its annual awards and lets the commissioner do a "state of the league" press conference that often includes news on expansion or other MLS business.

But the current format gives little advantage to the higher-seeded teams. The first round is a two-leg aggregate series in which the higher seed hosts the second game, an advantage only if the series goes to extra time and perhaps penalty kicks. Lower seeds frequently advance through the first round, and then they're one road upset away from MLS Cup. Los Angeles won the 2005 MLS Cup after posting the ninth-best regular-season record in the league, finishing ahead of expansion teams Real Salt Lake and Chivas USA, making many wonder if the Galaxy had any incentive through much of their schedule.

An advantage from an owner's point of view is that eight teams get at least one home playoff game. But given the difficulty of marketing games on short notice, that tends to be a reward for hard-core fans rather than a big-money, big-gate home date. And many of the hard-core fans are traditionalists who will watch the playoff games but would rather see a league without them.

The Supporters' Shield gives some incentive to regular-season games, and teams such as D.C. United insist that they take it seriously. But with the league still playing an unbalanced schedule—some teams play each other three times, some twice—one team can have an easier path than another. Aside from the Shield, the only incentive to finish first in the conference is a home date in the conference final—assuming the team makes it past the first round.

A number of options:

▸ A six-team playoff. Give the conference winners a bye to the semifinals. The second and third seeds could still play a quick two-game set, or perhaps just one game at the second seed.

▸ The Page playoff system, used in Australian rules football, sailing, curling, and a few other sports. In a four-team bracket, the first-round matchups are #1-#2 and #3-#4. The loser of the 3-4 game is eliminated, but the loser of the 1-2 game is not. The winner of the 3-4 game plays the 1-2 loser. The 1-2 winner gets a bye past that game and waits to play the next round at home. This system gives an advantage to each rung of the ladder. First place gets at least one home game and must be beaten twice to be eliminated. Second place must be beaten twice and would have a home game somewhere along the way. Third place hosts the first round. Fourth place is just happy to be in the playoffs.

▸ The WPS system. In the first season of the women's league, the first-place team got a bye to the final and the right to host it. The first round was #4 at #3. The winner played at #2 in the semifinal.

▸ Go straight to MLS Cup, with two division winners or the top two teams playing a single game. The league could still have playoffs for berths in CONCACAF tournaments or SuperLiga, just as many European leagues have playoffs for promotion.

▸ So far, MLS has tweaked the format without making any drastic changes. Without any momentum for an overhaul, it's not likely to happen.

4. Keeping labor peace

The first league's first collective bargaining agreement [CBA] drew little attention, and players—coming off the heels of the lost lawsuit—didn't make extravagant demands. Still, the process took more than 18 months. The MLS

Players Union was formed in April 2003, with Ben Olsen, Landon Donovan, Tim Howard, Alexi Lalas, and Chris Klein on the executive board. The CBA's official start date: December 1, 2004. It expired in January 2010.

"The initial goal of the union was just to get the first one done," says Ben Olsen. "We knew we didn't have the organization to have too much of an impact on the first collective bargaining agreement, but we thought it was important just to get the first one under our belt to one, just get the union formed. Seeing even the little things we did in that first collective bargaining agreement was a huge step. Historically, I think if you look back at first collective bargaining agreements in other sports, it probably wasn't too bad."

Those "little things" included a raise in the minimum for senior players, a 401(k) plan, and league-paid health insurance. The CBA, though, allowed a lot of players to play for peanuts, generating some harsh publicity for the league over the years. The senior players, limited to 18 per team, had minimum salaries that rose to $34,000 in 2009. Developmental players, excluding those who made more money giving up college eligibility to sign with Generation Adidas, made monthly salaries that maxed out at $1,575.

The developmental places, which dropped in number when MLS abandoned its reserve league for the 2009 season, could be seen as the MLS equivalent of minor-league baseball or perhaps an extended trial period. Yet these players, along with the lower-paid seniors, often work their way into key roles within a team. Every once in a while, the media stumble upon the salary information—released by the union—and produce a flurry of stories about players sharing apartments and working part-time jobs. With David Beckham making money on a par with top baseball or basketball players, the contrast is often too simple for journalists to ignore.

The players notice, too, the ones who are well compensated themselves. "I think if player salaries are a bit higher, then all the kids that stop playing soccer when they're 12 years old are gonna want to keep playing the sport," says Freddy Adu. "It's tough to live off some of those salaries that guys make. I played with guys like Troy Perkins, who had to get a job after training."

"Some people say, 'Do you think it's crazy to get paid that much?'" says Ben Olsen. "No, I don't. I think it's crazy that the developmental players are making $18,000. The roster size can be increased and the minimum could be raised. Ideally, your developmental players are actually just on the roster—

they're not called 'developmental players.' They're all making 50 grand. Your roster size is 30 people. So you essentially have a reserve team. And then you're developing players through your academies, which is going to be the next step, but that's more of a team thing."

From a coaching perspective, Arena wants to see younger players able to focus on playing competitive games instead of paying the rent:

> Let's be fair, a lot of people [owning teams] have absorbed a lot of losses. But I think more money needs to be put into the salary cap. The development side has to be expanded. Those minimum salaries need to be increased considerably.
>
> And I think you need to have a real reserve league. Your reserve players or your developmental players need to be trained separately and have their own competition in order for them to really develop properly. I believe right now that players who are not on the senior roster or not playing with the first team do not get the right kind of training and competition throughout the MLS season to develop properly. I think it's on a very minimum budget right now.

The older players say they're not looking for big bumps in pay, but they'd like to test their worth on a less restricted market within MLS. The league still doesn't have the equivalent of free agency, in which one team can bid against another for an out-of-contract player.

"The funny thing about the union, what we want—it's not money, it's freedom, freedom to go to another team and to get paid what you're worth in this league," Olsen says. "Right now it doesn't happen all the time."

Eddie Pope sums up the players' point: "Having a bigger voice into your career and how it unfolds and develops in determining your market value and your worth, having teams be able to fight over a player they think is great, not saying, 'Hey, we don't want to pay a million dollars but we'll certainly charge a million dollars for you.' Players want to be able to have more say-so. They want to have the opportunities and the freedom that their peers have overseas."

But the players aren't gearing up to challenge the single-entity structure itself. Attitudes have changed since the lawsuit days. Player-turned-executive Garth Lagerwey explains:

I think a lot of the attitude driving the lawsuit from the players' side in the beginning was that they felt the league wouldn't negotiate, wouldn't compromise, that there were things within the single-entity system that one could do if one chose to that could make it less onerous to the players without impacting in any way the financial and economic bottom line that it was set up to preserve.

You can't argue with a system that has kept the league afloat to this point and moved beyond the point of MLS surviving to multiple cities competing for MLS teams and that's certainly a good thing for MLS's future.

Agent Richard Motzkin says the structure is a challenge, but that it can be more flexible than it currently stands:

I would certainly prefer that it didn't exist. I think over time it's going to become less of an issue. . . . Ultimately, that agreement [the next CBA] and the ones that get negotiated down the road will probably make the structure of the league a little less relevant in the sense that the collective bargaining agreement hopefully will provide for things like more free agency for players and more ability for individual negotiations with teams and things like that. . . .

There's been modification all the time. Look at the Beckham rule. Individual teams have the ability to do unique things.

For me, my ideal is I'd rather be able to negotiate with every team individually. Do I see that happening tomorrow? No. But do I see down the road, something like that occurring as the league grows and prospers and there's more flexibility in the system? Yeah.

The MLS front office sees evolution in progress, with teams taking more responsibility.

Mark Abbott says, "Within the structure you can delegate the responsibility for certain functions to teams. That still doesn't mean you've changed your structure at all. It just means the structure has chosen to delegate certain matters. In the case of player scouting, within the structure of the single entity, we've determined that it's great for teams to go out and find the talent."

Ivan Gazidis says the league office's role is

to create a strategic plan overall for the league—how much we're going to spend on players, what type of focus we're going to have in terms of where players come from and what sort of players we have, but it's not so involved on selecting individual players. It is involved on every single player negotiation. It's still negotiating every single player contract. It's still administering the entire player pool centrally. But teams are given more ability to have their own identity and to do things in a unique way within that structure.

Jim Paglia, who proposed another single-entity league back in 1993, says the MLS version isn't really single entity, anyway: "I don't think they ever got single entity right. I think they did it in name only. I think that's why it failed. . . . It doesn't work today. They don't have single entity today. Eventually MLS broke it into ownership, because they didn't have a true single-entity mentality."

Meanwhile, the union is growing into its role. One recent hire: Eddie Pope, who moved into the union office shortly after retiring. "Who better do you want fighting for you than the American soccer icon?" Olsen says.

Pope says he was excited to stay in touch with the game and make a difference for players and their families. Outside of the CBA negotiations, he's already involved in helping players on a day-to-day basis.

There are a thousand little details in that. But what we want for them to do is worry only about playing. Not have to worry about anything else but go on the field and focus and concentrate on playing and not have to worry about off-the-field things. That's the biggest thing that's there for us.

If a guy is fined, and we don't think it's fair, obviously we're going to go to bat for him. At the end of the season, we hear guys' gripes that they pass on to us, and we say this is something in collective bargaining we're going to fight for. We'll collect all that stuff.

It's a daily management thing. Especially with me here now, I want the players to think, "There's someone I can pick up the phone and call any time I need anything. If I'm not being treated right or not being treated fairly, I have a player over there who's gone through [what I have]."

5. Strengthening the talent pool and developing stars

In the early days, skeptics thought MLS would be too reliant on the 1994 World Cup team. In fact, Marco Etcheverry, Eddie Pope, and Brian McBride had a far greater impact on MLS than Frank Klopas, Roy Wegerle, or most of that team. MLS has played a key role in developing players, including those who might not have stayed in the game. Pope, for example, was considering law school until pro soccer became a viable option, and Olsen might have been a teacher and coach.

Without duplicating the brazen shopping sprees of the NASL—surely impossible in the modern market—MLS has opted for a mix of international and domestic talent. U.S.-born players compose two-thirds of the league, and most of the recent imports hail from the relatively cheap but talent-rich South American market.

On top of that talent base, MLS is landing designated players, giving coaches an instant boost of talent and giving teams more marketing power. "I think really what the designated-player rule does is allow you to bring in the same type of player we had in 1996," says Jeff Agoos from his perspective as former player and current executive. "We brought in the Marco Etcheverrys, Roberto Donadonis—all these big names that played well—but now, the designated-player rule is allowing you to bring in the same players, but because of 13 years of market increases, you're having to pay a premium for basically those same players."

But the big names only go so far, Agoos says:

> I'd like to see more emphasis put into the product. I think it'll bring in more fans, it'll be a more entertaining game. We've got to increase our player budget. Obviously, I'm saying this from a sporting management position. I know the league will say we've gotta cut down cost. They do have a means behind what they're doing. But in the end, I think getting better players in the field will help this game overall.

MLS, like the United States at large, has been accused of having a vanishing middle class. Between young developmental players and established national-team veterans like Olsen lies a group of players that finds itself lured to Scandinavian countries where the professional leagues are growing enough financial clout to outbid MLS from time to time. Motzkin thinks the league should do more to reward those players:

> To me, that's a much bigger issue if I'm the league. Particularly if they're American players, the fact that the league is losing guys like that is what I would find very troubling. . . . The discrepancy between what they're willing to pay those guys and what those guys end up getting overseas is not a huge amount of money, yet the money they're going to spend to try to replace that guy, they're not going to get anywhere near equal value. The number of foreign players who come in and really make a good impact is greatly outweighed by the number who come in who are either not as good or far worse. It's one thing if you're selling players to England or guys leave at the end of the contract and the league can't compete with that. But to be losing them to Scandinavia, to first- and second-division Norwegian clubs, or whatever the case may be, I find that troubling.

Losing players of any caliber to Europe can hurt a team. Few could blame Brian McBride for departing to England, where he became Fulham's cornerstone, but Columbus wasn't the same on or off the field for several years after his departure.

And keeping a consistent roster from year to year has been a proven key to success on the field—Houston and New England reached two straight MLS Cups with the same core of players on each team. Now that many players and executives have MLS experience, teams can plan to avoid the salary-cap troubles that tore apart the D.C. United dynasty of the early years. Yet after that second MLS Cup, several players took flight—Houston lost Nate Jaqua and Joseph Ngwenya to Europe, while New England lost Pat Noonan and listened to Taylor Twellman grumble when a bid to take him to England was squashed.

Overall, though, most past and present players say the quality of play is rising. Ben Olsen remembers:

> I think we started off with . . . for a starting league, it seemed like a pretty high quality. Unfortunately, I think it kind of stayed the same for a long time. Certain teams got better, some got worse. Some got much

better, some got much worse over the next 10 years. I think the league got a lot younger, it's a lot faster, younger, more athletic now than when it was when I first came. I think the last two years, we've taken a step forward. I think the play was in danger of being the same . . . with some relief in the salary cap and the designated-player spot, I felt like it took a step forward last year. And I think it's going to do that again each year from now on. I hope it's going to progress a lot quicker than it did in the first 10 years.

Buying international players is one way to build the league's talent. The other way is to cultivate younger U.S. players, and the league has taken a long-term approach to that by requiring MLS teams to develop youth academies. Many of these teams play in U.S. Soccer's new elite national league, which it calls a Development Academy even though it's a competition between academy teams.

Arena, while thankful for several of the league's international players over the years, thinks teams are opting too often for the quick fix:

It's hard for me to be critical because I haven't spent any money on a soccer club. Sometimes it's difficult because the return on the investment isn't right in front of you. It takes many, many years. But I think the league and the clubs have got to come to grips with the fact that this is a real part of having a professional soccer league and professional clubs, and this is something that needs to be done. And I'd rather see that money spent on developing domestic players rather than saying we can go out and get second-tier players elsewhere that don't cost that much.

In New York, Jeff Agoos defines the Red Bulls' goals:

I think part of the way we can be successful in the club is really developing our academy players. I think we have to put a big emphasis on that side of it. The way the college game is right now—no disrespect to the college game—it's so limited in the amount of time they can spend per year developing players. They have a four-month season and a very limited spring season. Over the course of the year, it's really difficult to develop. We think we really have to ratchet up our academy setup and start developing players through that system.

I've told Bob Montgomery, our academy director, that I'm not really concerned with championships. I don't think it's that important. But what is really important [is] how many players you develop for the first team. We're really at the beginning stages of that part of it. We've got a couple of players who show there's a possibility they could be with the first team.

Agoos sees little hope in reforming college soccer because "it's governed by a body that doesn't really want it to succeed." But Eddie Pope still sees a role for the college game:

I think we have to be very, very careful as far as brushing off college soccer. For me at the time, where soccer was at, entering college, there wasn't MLS. For me, even at the end of my college career, when MLS was being established, I needed that four years of college soccer to start out with D.C. United. That helped to prepare me.

Do guys still need that four years? It's a good question. People want to look overseas and see how their systems work. . . . Maybe in college soccer, there's too much time off, because the season isn't that long and then there's a small spring season. There's a lot of time off where players aren't developing. There may be some truth to that. But having said that, I don't think you all of a sudden get rid of college soccer. Maybe college soccer gets tweaked a little bit, maybe the coaches are given more freedom to develop players. . . .

We have to look at the broader picture and see how great an opportunity it is for any individual to play soccer and get a college degree. A lot of guys are doing that. So the question is can you combine that with developing soccer players and having the time and the resources so maybe college soccer is something that becomes bigger than it already is.

The NCAA is more flexible with individual sports such as tennis and golf, in which players can often compete alongside pros as long as they decline prize money. Other sports have longer seasons. The NCAA would have plenty of room to reform, but it's not known as a fast-moving organization.

Even so, given the state of the developmental players in MLS, Arena sees college as a better option in some cases:

> I read today this example of this kid Matt Kassel in New York. He's offered basically $12,000 a year to give up a scholarship. And you know he's not ready to play, so there's a less than perfect training situation in New York. Their facilities are not comparable to a good Division I soccer school. He'll probably get a little bit more active training and obviously more games between now and the end of the year. So it's probably a better move for him to do that right now.

Beyond the college game, the MLS quality of play lies more and more not just with current players but with its alumni. Agoos, Lagerwey, Lalas, Peter Vermes, Mike Burns, John Doyle, Brian Bliss, Frank Klopas, Preki, Frank Yallop, Tom Soehn, Curt Onalfo, Jason Kreis, Paul Bravo, Mo Johnston, Steve Morrow, and Dominic Kinnear are among the players who have made the transition to coaching or the front office. Olsen followed in 2010.

The typical team front office is changing, giving former players another path to remain involved. "With the introduction of the technical director—we've started to separate the general manager into two positions, one guy doing soccer stuff only and another guy doing ticket stuff only—the evolution into that is necessary, and I think that's been a big reason why things have been moving a little bit smoother," says Jimmy Conrad. "In the past, when you talk to the general manager, they've got a million things going on. Not only are they thinking about the soccer side of things, they're thinking about contracts, they're worried about ticket sales, there's so much going on. Splitting that position in two has been a real big deal and I think is really going to help this league come along, and that's just come along in the past couple of years."

Yet the former players also will have a voice within the office to make sure current players are treated well, Conrad says, "The guys that are now in positions like Alexi, Peter Vermes, Jeff Agoos—they're going to apply what they didn't like or what they remember not liking to make it as efficient as possible and make sure the players feel wanted and treated well. The product on the field will be better. And when the product on the field's better, you can have more fans, and it all just has a nice ripple effect."

Agoos's official title with the Red Bulls, before moving into a scouting role after a house-cleaning before the 2010 season, was "sporting director," but he saw it as similar to the "technical director" job Peter Vermes has had in Kansas City. "I think it's a little more organized in terms of what teams are trying to do, how they're set up," Agoos says.

> You have teams that are investing in the playing side of things. This new position like mine and technical director position in other teams. You're really understanding . . . championship teams are created by having depth, and good players and team chemistry . . . I think there's more organization than there was in the earlier days. . . . Peter's a very intelligent guy, he's a guy that "gets it." I knew Peter would have a long history in the sport. I could've told you at that point he was going to be involved in the sport in some way.

Lagerwey's background is different, having gone through law school between his playing days and his front office job. He met Real Salt Lake owner Dave Checketts through a business transaction at Latham & Watkins, the firm from which several MLS founders sprang and the firm that hired Lagerwey out of school. Lagerwey is a vice president and general manager.

"I'm a technical director, but I'm much more than that," Lagerwey says. "I'm running the soccer side of our business—that's everything from the image of the team, the public relations of the team, how we communicate with our fans. . . . We have to have a winning team on the field, that is absolutely the number one priority. But we also have to be successful in the community. We have to be good neighbors, we have to be good citizens, we have to conduct ourselves in a way that encourages our fans to want to be part of us. So some of those off-field elements . . . are also important."

At the start of the 2008 MLS season, every team except Colorado had at least one former league player as a head coach, sporting director, technical director, director of soccer, or general manager. Seattle hired Chris Henderson as technical director 15 months before taking the field. Several more former players are assistant coaches.

"You do see a lot of inexperienced guys," Arena says. "But that's all part of the process. You have to let these young executives have time to grow. Let them make their mistakes."

6. Competing with other leagues on the field and in the marketplace

One challenge MLS faces that other primarily American leagues do not is that its quality of play isn't judged in a vacuum. Baseball, football, and basketball fans may have idle conversations comparing today's stars to those of yesteryear, but there's no debate that the American leagues are the best in the world today. The NHL can't always snare the best international players out of the murky world of hockey transfers, but at this point, no one can challenge its status as the world's best. MLS isn't the best soccer league in the world, and it faces a constant battle against regional teams on the field and the world's teams on the airwaves.

Since D.C. United's Interamerican Cup and the Galaxy's CONCACAF win, MLS teams in international competition have ranged from mediocre to woeful. At best, MLS teams have managed the occasional good result at home against Mexican teams and Costa Rican power Saprissa; on the road, respectable losses are all they have to show for their efforts. In the first CONCACAF Champions League, the rebranded and reorganized regional championship, MLS clubs were outperformed by their counterparts from the USL.

Mexico has a deeper talent pool, thanks to its longer tradition and money from TV and sponsorships. Saprissa takes the best of what Costa Rica can offer. If MLS pooled its best talent onto a handful of teams, perhaps they could compete. But the league, like most U.S. leagues, is geared toward parity.

Garber, atypically, admits to some uncertainty about balancing the need for a level playing field and the desire to have strong teams that fans either love or hate:

> Superclubs create national interest and helped launch baseball to its best year ever. It seems to work overall for the league. I'm not sure it works for Kansas City Royals fans or for Pittsburgh Pirates fans or even for their owners, but overall, it seems to work for the league. But they're a 125-year-old league. We're 12 years old.
>
> I still believe and feel very strongly that the future of the league in the short- and medium-term is going to be based by the strength of the clubs in their local markets. And in order to have that local market strength, the fans have to believe that you have a chance to win the MLS Cup. If they believe that they're subjugated to the big markets or to wealthier owners, there's no hope and no reason to support your team.

That might change in time. You could argue that the Premier League continues to generate massive revenue, but you're starting to see empty seats at some of the clubs. Even that deep passion wanes when you just don't win.

Yet the Premier League and a few other overseas leagues have enough passion to have fan bases that aren't yet won over by MLS teams. American soccer fans have nearly unlimited choice of viewing options from around the globe. College soccer, once the most serious soccer being played in this country, is broadcast far less frequently than the English, German, Spanish, Italian, or Mexican leagues.

Soccer United Marketing has a piece of this action through clever deals to get licensing and promotional rights. These deals give league investors a nice revenue stream, but another balance must be struck here so that the primary product—MLS—stands out in the marketplace.

7. Landing the next TV and sponsorship deals

The league needed to reach a new collective bargaining agreement when the old one expired in January 2010. The next key date is 2014, when the current Adidas and ESPN deals are set to expire.

Sponsors have plenty of options within MLS now that many teams have stadiums. Naming rights and prominent displays are for sale, and MLS often has the cash register. Even if Nike and Adidas were to back off from their constant battle for the soccer dollar, plenty of sponsors have stepped forward.

The TV deal could be trickier. MLS needed more than a decade to convince national broadcasters to pay for rights. Once the stadiums are built and those revenue streams hit a consistent level, broadcasting money could still be a growth area.

But no U.S. league can continue to assume that its next TV deal will bring more revenue. A flurry of overspending in the '80s and '90s has given way to more cautious spending and creative deals in a heavily fragmented marketplace.

The league and the soccer community at large have been creative in getting around the mainstream media gatekeepers. MLS came into existence just as the Internet started to reach the masses. The Web has been a vital medium for the league, both for fans and for the league's own efforts to get around the obstinate media. Fans created networks of sites to share information and act as an unofficial, semiprofessional medium from which several professional soccer writers have sprung.

A few players have joined the fray as well. When Grant Wahl took some time off from his SI.com column, he turned it over to Garth Lagerwey, who took an irreverent view of his employer and noticed some reaction:

> Indirectly, yeah. The cold handshakes and the stony glares. The turned backs. . . .
>
> The folks who were running the league then are many of the same folks running the league now, who I'm working with now and I've gotten to know a lot better. The people are all enormously intelligent people, smart people. As players, we didn't have an appreciation of the challenges the league was going through just to survive.
>
> The league didn't really appreciate some of the criticisms that I made. Stuff that I wrote that I meant to come across humorously was taken seriously. But as I've learned since I've joined the management ranks, there were serious threats to the league. It probably was a heck of a lot easier to laugh at some of the failings of the early league, and there is probably a lot of pride in undertaking such a massive enterprise.
>
> It wasn't well liked, it wasn't well received. Jimmy Conrad, writing after me, has been really well received. I'm proud that I've been a pioneer in that regard, that I kind of introduced the idea that personalities can help sell the league. Jimmy's a better player than I ever was, and it's always easier to market a star.

Conrad started writing when he needed to vent about his overseas experience:

> Garth kind of paved the way for me. He had the original slot. Once he got out of the league, I kind of stepped in and took over that spot. I had gone over on loan to Poland at the end of my second year in 2000. The regular season ended like mid-September, something crazy, so I went over. Wojtek Krakowiak, when I was at San Jose, he had something set up with his Polish team, Lech Poznan. They needed some other players.

Ian [Russell] and I said we could go. We ended going to an Internet café every day. We were there for 2½ months. It really took 15-20 minutes to write one e-mail because the connection was so bad. I finally got to a point where I was tired of e-mailing one person at a time, so I sent this huge group e-mail about how I'd just had it here, and just went off on Poland. I had sort of formulated ideas about this e-mail and how I wanted it to be kind of funny and tell a story.

Why not turn these e-mail rants into a column? Carie Goldberg, director of athlete marketing for Richard Motzkin's agency, championed that idea, and Conrad wound up first at SI.com and then at ESPN.com. He then put some effort into crafting his work, saying his early writing seems "raw" by comparison.

After a couple of years of hearing nothing from the league about his writing, Conrad learned that his columns were in circulation among league officials. They were receptive. MLSnet, the league's official but independently operated site, picks up a radio show Conrad does in Kansas City.

"If they were that insecure about something I'm writing, I'd be pretty disappointed," Conrad says. "And I've never really taken a shot at any specific person. For better or for worse, MLS has made decisions. That's just part of being a leader and running a business. . . . I had commissioner Garber say they'd like to have me in the broadcast booth at some point in the future, so I'm going to hold them to that when the time comes."

Conrad's columns are a way to give fans a glimpse of the game, though he says he's careful not to reveal too much of a team's inner workings. His writing is also therapeutic. "I love making fun of me," he says. "I think that's the best way to go. That's what I feel more comfortable doing, being self-deprecating. If I make a mistake in the game, it takes me a couple of weeks to be OK with it, but once I write, I actually feel like it's part of the process. Sometimes writing has been a good healing process. Writing's been a blessing in disguise."

Many players have been quick to jump onto social networks Facebook and Twitter. Houston Dynamo players are particularly adept at teasing each other on Twitter, and MLS alumni Freddy Adu, Maurice Edu, and Jozy Altidore use the microblogging site to keep fans apprised of their European adventures.

MLSnet also has ramped up its video offerings, and the league makes highlights available on YouTube and elsewhere. Getting highlights on the Web is a blessing for a league that has struggled to get highlights aired anywhere else. Various highlight shows on ESPN's networks and Fox Sports World (now Fox Soccer Channel) have come and gone.

"Whether you want to agree with it or not, the *SportsCenters* have tremendous influence on people," Arena says. "When on a daily basis your sport's not covered and many others are, it really knocks you down in terms of how the sport is perceived by the public. So I think that's a major flaw."

Those are the challenges: building stadiums, growing the fan base, solving scheduling dilemmas, keeping labor peace, strengthening the talent pool, winning on-field and off-field competitions, and making new lucrative deals to keep MLS on firm footing, with high quality of play in the public eye.

The rest of MLS's mission: maintain the steady growth. Ben Olsen said in 2008: "I think you see in the last two years, this league is moving pretty quick now. You can see in this next 10 years, this league is going to be moving pretty quick. People are getting in there, money's getting in there. Owners want to start to win. A lot of times, buying the right players and getting the money in there and getting the best stadium . . . It's a great time, I think, for this league."

MLS TODAY

If soccer is a religion, then Don Garber has the zeal of the converted. The commissioner didn't know much about the game when he was first sought out to join MLS, but he now counts himself as a committed fan:

> I have subsequently become a more passionate fan of soccer than I have ever been for any other sport I have ever been associated with. I worked for the NFL, I wasn't necessarily a big NFL fan, I didn't go to a lot of games, I didn't watch it intently on television.
>
> I grew up in Flushing, Queens, and I remember going to Jets and Mets games, but I never really had a deep, deep emotional connection with a sport like I have with soccer, and I don't think it has anything to do with the fact that I'm commissioner. This sport just has a way of getting into your bone marrow. It gets under your skin and in your heart and in your soul, and it just twists you all around and gets you to

be one of those soccer-crazed junkies, and I've become one. And that's a good one.

I don't necessarily think—I didn't think then, I don't think now—that you have to be that way to lead the sport. In essence it's a business job, it's a business task. You've gotta believe in it, you've gotta understand it, but you don't necessarily have to be passionate about it. I've been fortunate to be able to do that. . . .

It's been an interesting ride. It's certainly a different sport than any other sport in America. . . .

The most emotional I've ever been at a sporting event in my life was the USA-Korea match [2002 World Cup]. I can remember when Clint Mathis scored a goal, Lamar Hunt turned to me, almost in tears, and said, "Isn't this great? This is the best feeling I've ever had other than the Chiefs winning the Super Bowl, and that was a long time ago." I turned to Mark Abbott, who was at my side at this point, and said, "How cool is that?"

Garber's enthusiasm is also driven by the tangible progress MLS has made:

There are a couple of things that have been game-changers for us: expanding the ownership group, building soccer-specific stadiums, the television deal, the expansion and the formation of SUM. Those are the five things that have transformed the league from where it was from 2001 to where it is today. People paying for television rights, building stadiums faster than we can get teams into them, we have more demand for expansion.

Mark Abbott says interest in MLS expansion is at an all-time high: "A lot of it wasn't incoming requests when we started the league. We would fly around and try to talk to people. That's not what's happening now—people are calling us. . . . Also, the people that owned multiple teams are selling those teams off, which is also a very healthy thing for us."

And with SUM, Garber and company have united several interests that often competed and left the sport's fan base fragmented, an accomplishment of which Garber is particularly proud:

Here we have a sport that has struggled for its rightful place in the sports landscape and yet had so many different entities competing to both lead the sport and manage their own self-interests. Not personal self-interests but organizational self-interests.

If you look at soccer everywhere around the world, the professional game leads the sport. That couldn't have happened in the early days because there wasn't a professional league to do that. [Early on,] MLS didn't have the significance, the credibility, the legitimacy, or the success to assume that role. I believe the league is leading the sport today, and as such, is providing value to all of those other entities that felt they needed to satisfy their own interests. Today many of their interests are being satisfied by the league. You have a league now helping to develop players, helping the federation in building stadiums, representing the marketing rights with guarantees, providing great value to the federation, not the least of which is creating a fan base. . . .

We've been pushed to that position, basically, by the soccer community. And that's the ultimate validation of the credibility of the league. We're no longer fighting amongst ourselves. If it makes commercial sense for it to happen, we try to go after it hard, and everybody benefits by that.

Fourteen years after U.S. Soccer passed on his proposed league, Jim Paglia remained skeptical that the fan base for traditional soccer has grown:

A lot has changed in the past 15-20 years. Soccer fans have gotten more sophisticated. But what fascinates me is that those people who are true die-hard soccer fans—that number hasn't necessarily changed in my opinion. The generation that was going to grow up and be knowledgeable and adore the game—they're still what they were in my mind. They're participants, they're not spectators. Soccer is very much a participant game. It's not a spectator game for the reasons I've mentioned before. . . .

MLS inflates its attendance numbers as badly as NASL did. The numbers aren't accurate. There's still a core of 6,000–7,000 people who will continue to go and they're crazy about watching any kind of soccer.

The Columbus Crew against the Chicago Fire? Is that a game I want to watch? Most people would say, "not a chance." It's not good soccer yet.

Paglia isn't surprised that the league is still here, but he disagrees that it has turned a corner, saying that he felt all along that any league would need more than 10 years to prove its viability:

My wife said you're risking everything we have, every dime we have . . . when am I going to know whether it works or not? I said it'll be at least 10 or 15 years before anyone gets a sense of whether this will work or not. Both sides, MLS and us, are well funded enough that we can last at least 10 or 15 years. Then it'll be a question of whether it's worth keeping it afloat.

The next three years are going to be the determining factor for MLS. I don't think MLS has assured itself of survival at this point, and I don't think it's going to fade at this point. It'll be another two or three years before we know.

I don't think that they could declare themselves successful at this point, although they try to. I don't think they've proven they're going to succeed yet. I think it's going to be another couple of years. They're still at the formulative stage as far as I'm concerned.

Doug Logan agrees in the sense that MLS hasn't had an attendance boom aside from the surges caused by big events—doubleheaders, Beckham's presence, team debuts, etc. But he puts the core audience in a more positive light:

The reality is that this is a sport that—in its present professional configuration, if you take paid attendance starting with the 1996 season and extending through the 2007 season—has had relatively stable and relatively flat attendance. Some years up a 1,000, some years down 1,000. The reality is that for at least this generational period of time, that's what you're able to draw on a regular basis. Which is credible. It's credible in comparison to other leagues around the world.

It is what it is—there are far fewer, if any, breakthroughs from the standpoint of sports. No one goes from start-up to 25,000 or 30,000 or 40,000. All you've gotta do is read a little bit of history and see where all these other sports have been in the course of their genesis. I see them as minor fluctuations within a range. . . . That's a pretty narrow range.

So what exactly has MLS built? Garth Lagerwey sees a credible structure to build up the quality of play over time:

I think it's fair to say that the teams were more uneven (in '96). There was less thought put into them, it was the idea that you just had to field a team, you had to get a product on the field. It was the Wild Wild West, and you had to figure out all the rules of the single-entity structure and do it in a fair manner.

There's no question the league has grown by leaps and bounds in terms of its professionalism, from off-season training programs to complete coaching staffs to the reserve system to youth development. When you look back to '96 and look at where we are now—we've implemented, in 12 years, a full global soccer-style system of developing kids from 12 years old up through the first team. That's pretty impressive, that's pretty amazing.

Does MLS have its flaws? Sure it does. But at the same time, it's moving in the right direction. You have cities competing for franchises now, you have the league opening up to the international player market, you're seeing globalization impact the American player having opportunities abroad. Everyone's terrified about this group of players, but it mirrors a lot of the labor debate in the presidential race, and ultimately, players going to the best market for them benefits everybody. Free trade benefits everybody. If there's a market for American players abroad, that's money you can use to sell those players and then plow it back into youth development domestically. If you want to compete with the Premier League, with a payroll 50 times what an MLS payroll is, the only way to do that is to develop players domestically.

Richard Motzkin sees progress on the business front, building a stable foundation for a league set to grow into its fan base:

It's night and day. You look at . . . in the early years, you had no soccer stadiums, and now almost every team's got a soccer stadium. You had one guy owning 80% of the teams, and now it's almost an individual owner for every team, more or less. There was limited marketing support, there was no TV deal. The league as a whole has improved dramatically over the years. I don't think player compensation has improved at the rate the league has improved.

The question of "is the league going to be around and survive next year?" is not one that's asked anymore. . . . It used to be every year, will this league be here next year? The fact that this question doesn't even get asked anymore is a very clear reflection of how much the league has improved. There's so much positive momentum behind MLS when you look at the ownership group, the stadiums, the marketing partners, the fact that we're an immigrant population where soccer is the number one sport . . . there are tons of signs of success.

That progress on the business front came on the shoulders of investors who now have much more company in the boardroom, Sunil Gulati says:

The league has done a lot of right things in the past 12 years. Obviously some mistakes, for sure. But no one's asking the question and has asked in quite a while—is this league gonna survive. Now it's just a question of what it's going to take for the league to thrive. The strength of the league is still what it was from Day 1—the quality of the investors. It's absolutely a critical element for the league. People in that boardroom are hugely responsible for making it go. They stuck it out and made extraordinary, mind-boggling investments. That's a huge plus. And the people that are joining them at the table can only help to strengthen the league going forward. I think the league's made it through a lot of hurdles. Is it there yet with where the support wants to be? No. It's still a long way to go. But it's 12 years in, not 112 years in.

Jimmy Conrad sees the league growing secure in its niche, both within the American sports landscape and the world of soccer:

It's tough to compare us to leagues that have been around 70–80 years. If you look back at the NBA or the NFL in the '60s, they were onto something but it wasn't like where it is now, where they're well-oiled machines. For us to be competing against well-oiled machines in an Internet-saturated society now where there's so much information . . . I think we've found ourselves in a nice little spot and we continue to grow. The hard part is we get compared with the other great leagues around the world soccerwise, and they've been around for even longer than the NBA, NFL, and baseball. It's really hard to compete with that kind of rich history.

So how good can the league be? Alexi Lalas says the quality of play is already credible on a global scale:

> The overall quality of play has dramatically increased. The personality that maybe existed early on has unfortunately dissipated, but it's probably a logical evolution of having to compete in the international market and having to compete with a fan base that is constantly comparing and contrasting with the quote-unquote best leagues in the world. I still from Day 1 have maintained that we have an inferiority complex. I think it still exists. It's changing a little bit. We are as good if not better than much of the soccer around the world and much of what we hold out to be the "elite" soccer. I just don't buy that many of our games or players or teams are of lesser quality. I completely accept the fact that what goes on outside the field is very different from other cultures. I think unfortunately that taints everybody in how they view MLS. But that's something we're working on in terms of the stadiums, the Beckham rule and all that kind of stuff.

Richard Motzkin, admitting that he's looking from the perspective of an agent, sees investment in players as the next logical step: "As a guy with subjective self-interest in the players, I think both in terms of player compensation and the overall quality of play needs to improve, and there needs to be a bigger investment in the player side of things, because this ultimately is what the league's about, the on-the-field product."

Eddie Pope agrees:

> I think it's improved in that now we're starting to see soccer-specific stadiums. I think in the long run that's only going to benefit everyone,

including the fans. It's difficult for teams to play in 60,000–70,000 seat stadiums and have the right atmosphere. In that part, the league has obviously come a long, long way.

From a quality standpoint, certainly it's getting better. Games are a lot more difficult than the first year or second year. Teams are a lot better, coaching is a lot better, now you're starting to see players that are becoming coaches. . . . You're starting to see technical directors become involved. A lot of those technical directors are ex-players. Players need to get moving into the other positions, to, the front-office positions. It's gotta be a clean sweep. That's where it needs to be. Now a coach can come out on the field and show how it's supposed to look at the speed at which it's supposed to be done.

How players are treated . . . can always get better. It would always come back to the players having a voice and having more freedom, period. All of those things. I don't think anyone is satisfied with the way players are being treated. That's not to say things are absolutely horrible, but it is to say things can certainly get better, and I think that will happen over the next several years.

And Pope doesn't see a dilemma in choosing investment in facilities or investment in players:

It doesn't have to be one or the other, it can certainly be both. If you go and buy a team, you gotta know that the team needs a training facility. If you can't figure that one out, you've got a problem. You know the team needs a stadium. Now once there's a system to where teams can compete, then there can be sort of a bidding thing that lets players take control. . . . It should all come together, and every owner should want to do that. And a lot of them do.

The man who pressed MLS into existence, Alan Rothenberg, says the league hasn't progressed as quickly as he had hoped. But it has progressed nonetheless:

I think it's probably taken a few years longer than I in my rosy expectations thought, but I think it's in great shape. Our initial business plan contemplated soccer-specific stadiums and contemplated aggregating all the various marketing rights that had been splintered throughout the United States. It took a little while to get there. But now having the soccer-specific stadiums has meant all the difference in the world. The ability to pull in the promotion of the big international games worked hand in glove with the soccer federation . . . has uncluttered a previously cluttered market and has enabled the league to have a very attractive television package to offer to somebody without worrying about the fact that it didn't control some vital elements to what would be an attractive package.

I think if I would've sat there in '94, '95, '96 and said where do I want the league to be, I would've said pretty much exactly where it is now, though I would have probably hoped and expected that it would have happened a few years earlier than it has. But thank God it has.

THE MIRACLE OF STABILITY

Every few years, someone thinks he has a better idea for making money on soccer in the United States. Indoor soccer. ChampionsWorld. Rule-bending Americanized leagues. Integrated "club" systems (which many clubs are now doing). But no one has come up with a better idea than the combination of MLS and SUM in place today.

It's not necessarily poised to explode. MLS isn't built to provide a sudden Cosmos-style or World Cup–style boom, and it's not going to eclipse the NFL in our lifetime. It's poised to grow steadily and make smarter decisions that make the league attractive to sponsors, broadcasters, players, and fans. Richard Motzkin says, "In time, it's clearly gonna pass hockey and become probably the fourth biggest professional sports league in this country in the not-too-distant future."

Whether it passes the NHL or not, MLS is already entrenched more firmly than any other U.S. soccer league of its size and stature. The NASL averaged more than 10,000 fans per game for its last nine years, most of those during the Pelé and expansion boom years. MLS has done it for 14 years, with little turnover in its teams.

MLS fans have spent 14 years trading information and insults with other fans. Kids who can't remember a time before MLS existed are now wearing the teams' colors in youth games. A handful of kids who can barely remember MLS's debut are playing in the league itself.

Motzkin notes, "The test is that the league is still here, and we're still talking about it 15 years later." First commissioner Doug Logan: "I continue to be asked when is MLS going to make it, and I say it made it over 10 years ago. The only true validation of having made it is that it's still in existence and play is still going on."

And yet today, the standard has changed.

●

MLS opened the 2008 season with some good news and bad news on the field. Barely 11,000 people braved a chilly night in Foxborough to see New England dismantle Houston 3-0 in a rematch of the previous two MLS Cups. The patient Salt Lake fans posted the only crowd exceeding 20,000, only to see Cuauhtémoc Blanco's late strike deny them a win on the ugly Rice-Eccles Stadium turf that would serve as Real's home for another few months. David Beckham's presence helped Colorado fill Dick's Sporting Goods Park, but the Galaxy's weaknesses were on vivid display in a 4-0 loss. Los Angeles went through April mixing beautiful Beckham-Donovan combinations with a porous defense.

San Jose's new Earthquakes took to the road against old rival Los Angeles and lost, then dropped a frustrating home opener, then puzzlingly won in Colorado, which had been the surprise team of the first few weeks.

Over one April weekend, MLS posted three crowds of less than 10,000. That sometimes happens in April, with unpredictable weather and many fans not really gearing up until school's out. Yet it sparked some restlessness.

Los Angeles Times writer Grahame Jones, one of the longest-serving soccer journalists in the country, pounced upon the crowd of 6,733 in Columbus to hint that the Crew might want to seek greener pastures in some place like Montreal, where a couple of people had made noise about coveting an expansion team. Then a letter from Garber to the Dynamo ownership made its way into the press via Houston mayor Bill White. Garber expressed frustration over the lack of a stadium deal and hinted that another relocation wouldn't be out of the question.

Columbus had the league's first true soccer stadium. Houston had new investors, plus a strong fan base that filled the stadium with orange and traveled to MLS Cup. In 2000, these clubs would've been considered far ahead of the curve. In 2008, they were being asked to keep up.

Mere existence is no longer good enough by MLS standards. Fans are demanding better quality. Coaches are demanding better players and facilities. Players are demanding better salaries. The league office is demanding better stadium deals.

All these demands may cause headaches. Some, particularly the potential for labor strife, could cause the league to take a big step backward. But the demands show a league preoccupied with building a strong future, not nervously protecting its present existence. While nothing is guaranteed, particularly in this time of political and economic upheaval, MLS has put down firmer roots than any U.S. league ever has.

The collapse of the last major U.S. league is captured in *Once in a Lifetime*, the great documentary on the NASL's Cosmos that vividly captures the team's heyday and its fall. When longtime team executive Jay Emmett hears that Peppe Pinton, who in today's terms would've been called part of Giorgio Chinaglia's "posse," now owns the "Cosmos" name, he laughs, asking how recently anyone has seen the team play.[7] "Peppe owns the Cosmos," Emmett says with a smirk. "The Cosmos are nothing, today. So Peppe owns nothing."

Over 3 years of planning and 14 years of activity, MLS has been built to avoid that sort of implosion. The league has built a stable brand, particularly in the five years since retrenching. The league no longer faced questions of survival but rather what sort of league it will be.

The Cosmos, in the words of Jay Emmett, became nothing. Today, MLS is something. It has jerseys that kids wear in the stands and in competition. It has stadiums. It has rivalries. It has passion.

Professional soccer hasn't suddenly supplanted professional football as America's top game. It isn't swimming in money like NASCAR or golf were before the 2008 recession. Yet MLS has grown to 16 teams, all of which have put down roots in some tangible fashion, from a dedicated fan base to a strong youth program to a new stadium.

Whether MLS has "arrived" is a moot point. It's here. And it's healthy.

AFTERWORD

The 2009 MLS season ended on November 22 in Seattle, where the league had plenty to celebrate. The host Sounders weren't playing, but they had a trophy to show off thanks to their victory in the U.S. Open Cup in September. Fans marched to Qwest Field as they had all season. Through the days leading up to the final, league and stadium officials agreed to release more tickets, ending up with a total of 46,011.

They saw an exciting game with a festive atmosphere, showcasing Seattle's enthusiasm and some brilliant moments of skill, such as Landon Donovan's pinpoint pass to Mike Magee for the Galaxy's opening goal. But the game, and an improbable title, belonged to Real Salt Lake.

I had a chance to see a Real practice just before a World Cup qualifier in Utah. The team was intense. A couple of young academy players had been called in to fill out full squads for a scrimmage, and they must have wondered how they got into this. Jason Kreis's club had some bad luck and letdowns over the season but was determined to regroup. Real barged into the playoffs as the wild-card team, then rallied in Columbus for a shocking first-round win. Nick Rimando saved three penalty kicks in the tiebreaker after a scoreless semifinal draw in Chicago.

After Magee's goal in the final, Real took control. Emerging talent Robbie Findley's equalizer was no less than Real deserved. Rimando made two more saves in the tiebreaker, and Donovan uncharacteristically sent his shot high. The Utah underdogs had the 2009 championship.

U.S. soccer's dignitaries in attendance had plenty to celebrate. MLS and a smorgasbord of international games had drawn several million fans over the course of the year. The U.S. national team took care of World Cup qualifying and made global headlines in the Confederations Cup, breaking top-ranked Spain's 35-game unbeaten streak and taking a 2-0 lead in the final against Brazil before falling 3-2.

One thing they could not celebrate: a new collective bargaining agreement.

Nor did MLS announce a new collective bargaining agreement at the SuperDraft in January, which by a happy coincidence took place in Philadelphia with an enthusiastic group of fans whose wait for an expansion team was near its end.

The draftees expressed little concern about the prospect of a work stoppage when the old deal expired on January 31, just as preseason camps were getting under way. Teams went about business as usual, signing the usual batch of players from overseas.

In the long run, MLS may not have lost much more than a modest publicity boost by letting the labor talks go to the wire. But coincidentally, the rest of the U.S. soccer landscape was reminding everyone how fragile the enterprise of pro soccer can be.

The United Soccer Leagues, which had held together a couple of tiers of pro and amateur soccer for nearly two decades, was sold to a Georgia company called NuRock. The USL's top flight immediately splintered, with a group of teams announcing their intention to form a new league that would bring back the name of the old North American Soccer League. U.S. Soccer refused to sanction either group as a second-division league, forcing them to coexist for one year in a makeshift league administered by the federation.

Indoor soccer was in worse shape. The Xtreme Soccer League lasted one year before taking what it said would be a one-year hiatus. The Milwaukee Wave rejoined its old rivals from the Major Indoor Soccer League (MISL), who had founded the National Indoor Soccer League (NISL) but decided to reclaim the MISL name after one year as the NISL.

No one expressed such fears about MLS. The league kept moving forward, with plans to expand to Portland and Vancouver. As of 2010, no teams were in imminent danger of folding or being moved. Through tough economic times, MLS was still growing.

From a fan's perspective, the league has much left to accomplish. MLS can't be expected to rival England's Premier League or the other top leagues in Europe, but fans are tired of losing players to Scandinavia and losing games to Central American teams. The league took a hard-line stance in labor talks, perhaps missing an opportunity to loosen its wallet and become more competitive. And perhaps the league was overconfident in moving so close to the brink of a labor shutdown.

The league and the union announced a new collective bargaining agreement on March 20, 2010, just five days before the expansion Philadelphia Union was due to open the new season at Seattle, where the Sounders had sold 32,000 season tickets. Players gained a few concessions on guaranteed contracts and quality-of-life issues, but the new regulations aren't likely to attract a stronger talent pool.

But MLS already has come much further than any U.S. league has come. The stadiums are in place. A generation has grown up not knowing what it's like to have no top-tier pro league.

And because of that, soccer in the United States has changed. Permanently.

NOTES

Introduction: Past to Present

1. Simon Kuper, *Soccer Against the Enemy* (New York: Nation Books, 2006), 191.
2. Interview with Doug Logan. Unless otherwise noted, quotes are taken from interviews with the author from January 2008 to March 2008.

Chapter 1: Before Kickoff

1. Associated Press as posted at CNNSI.com, "From Obscurity to Respect: A Look at Rothenberg, the Man Who Put U.S. Soccer on the Map," posted August 20, 1998, http://sportsillustrated.cnn.com/soccer/news/1998/08/20/rothenberg_legacy/ (accessed August 7, 2009).
2. Roscoe Nance, "League's Plans Impress FIFA," *USA Today*, October 20, 1993.
3. Roscoe Nance, "U.S. Federation Selects Plan for Outdoor League," *USA Today*, December 6, 1993.
4. Mark Stewart, *Major League Soccer: A Celebration of 10 Seasons* (New York: Major League Soccer, 2005), 9.
5. Dave Wangerin, *Soccer in a Football World* (London: When Saturday Comes Books, 2006), 209.
6. United States Court of Appeals for the First Circuit, No. 01-129b, *Fraser V. Major League Soccer, LLC*, ruling issued March 20, 2002, accessed through FindLaw.
7. MLS, like the NASL, would run on a baseball-style schedule from spring to fall. Several U.S. leagues in the past used the fall-to-spring schedule familiar through most of Europe—at least, the parts that aren't too cold.
8. Frank Giase, "Harkes Hesitant on Assignment to Team," *Record* (Bergen County, NJ), October 18, 1995.

Chapter 2: The Launch

1. Michael Martinez, "Clash Boss Misses Seeing Winning Goal," *San Jose Mercury News*, April 7, 1996.
2. Michael Lewis, "Season 10: An Unforgettable Comeback," MLSNet.com, posted May 16, 2005, http://web.mlsnet.com/news/mls_news.jsp?ymd= 20050516&content_id=29924&vkey=news_mls&fext=.jsp (accessed August 21, 2009).
3. Jeff Bradley, "First XI: Amazin' Metros," MLSNet.com, posted March 1, 2005, http://web.mlsnet.com/news/mls_news.jsp?ymd=20050301&content_ id=23198&vkey=news_mls&fext=.jsp (accessed August 21, 2009).

Chapter 3: After the Boom

1. John Haydon, "Payne Blames Player Law Suit for Static League Salary Cap," *SoccerTimes*, posted January 31, 1999, http://www.soccertimes.com/ mls/1999/jan31.htm (accessed August 21, 2009).
2. John Harkes, *Captain for Life and Other Temporary Assignments* (Chelsea, MI: Sleeping Bear Press, 1999), 169.
3. Tobias Xavier Lopez, "MLS Says It Will Back Off, Let Teams Set Own Goals," *Star-Telegram* (Fort Worth), May 26, 2006.
4. Steven Goff, "Diaz Arce Is Traded: Revolution Sends United Three Draft Selections," *Washington Post*, February 5, 1998.
5. Harkes, *Captain for Life*, 226.

Chapter 4: Concrete Steps and Change

1. Peter Brewington, "Attendance Up, Losses Continue," *USA Today*, July 16, 1999.
2. Stewart, *Major League Soccer*, 9.
3. MLSnet, "Valderrama To Return to Tampa Bay," posted April 23, 1999, http:// www.mlsnet.com/content/99/tb0423valderrama.html (accessed August 25, 2009).
4. "With Trade Impossible, Valderrama Is Handed Over to Tampa Bay," *Soccer-Times*, posted April 23, 1999, http://www.soccertimes.com/mls/1999/apr23a. htm (accessed August 25, 2009).
5. Grant Wahl, "Inside Soccer," *Sports Illustrated*, June 14, 1999, posted at http:// sportsillustrated.cnn.com/vault/article/magazine/MAG1016162/ (accessed August 20, 2009).
6. Gary Davidson, "Logan Not Planning to Cancel SI Subscription," *SoccerTimes*, posted June 21, 1999, http://www.soccertimes.com/mls/1999/jun21.htm (accessed August 25, 2009).
7. Robert Wagman, "The Story Behind Logan's Ouster," *SoccerTimes*, posted August 4, 1999, http://www.soccertimes.com/wagman/1999/aug04.htm (accessed August 25, 2009).

8. Steven Goff, "MLS Eyes a Shorter Season: League Also Ponders Eliminating Shootouts," *Washington Post*, October 22, 1999.
9. Rodney Page, "Mutiny's Diallo in Limbo as League Reviews Play," *St. Petersburg Times*, August 19, 2000.
10. Ibid.

Chapter 5: The Lawsuit

1. Kent Somers, "Fun While It Lasted," *Arizona Republic*, July 29, 2006.
2. Michael Lewis, "Caligiuri: An American Pioneer," CNNSI.com, posted November 12, 1999, http://sportsillustrated.cnn.com/inside_game/michael_lewis/news/1999/11/12/caligiuri_flashback/ (accessed August 25, 2009).
3. United States Court of Appeals for the First Circuit, No. 01-1296, *Fraser v. Major League Soccer, LLC*, ruling issued March 20, 2002.
4. United States District Court, District of Massachusetts, Civil Action No. 97-10342-GAO, *Fraser v. Major League Soccer, LLC*, summary judgment issued April 19, 2000.
5. Ibid.
6. Ibid.
7. *Fraser v. Major League Soccer, LLC*, ruling issued March 20, 2002.
8. Partial transcripts of the court testimony have existed for several years on a website at http://www.geocities.com/combedge/ along with a logo implying association with the MLS Players Association. Veteran soccer commentator Kenn Tomasch reproduced those transcripts on his site for some time. I have also obtained some excerpts through official means, and I have asked several participants about their recollection of what was said. The transcripts and participants' recollections have been consistent.
9. Philip Hersh, "Rough Birth for Pro League: Losing Bidders Decry Winner's Conflict of Interest," *Chicago Tribune*, December 13, 1993.
10. Opening argument from case transcripts.
11. Paul Gardner, "Enough Already with the Court Cases," *Soccer America*, December 25, 2000, 6.
12. Ridge Mahoney, "MLS Goes to Federal Court," CNNSI.com, posted November 16, 2000, http://sportsillustrated.cnn.com/soccer/mls/news/2000/11/16/mls_trial_sa/ (accessed August 25, 2009).
13. Gardner, "Enough Already with the Court Cases."
14. John Kerr Sr., letter to Paul Gardner posted at http://www.williamsfc.com/commentaries/February01.shtml (accessed on March 1, 2008).
15. Bowers testimony from case transcripts; verified in conversation with Bowers. As of 2009, the Baltimore Blast still exists, while the MISL has disappeared and reappeared. The indoor game has gone through a rough transitional period. Bowers retired and went into coaching but planned to make a comeback indoors with the Professional Arena Soccer League's San Diego Sockers in 2009.

16. Ridge Mahoney, "Verdict for MLS May Not Be Conclusion," CNNSI.com, posted December 20, 2000, http://sportsillustrated.cnn.com/soccer/mls/news/2000/12/20/mls_suit_sa/ (accessed August 25, 2009).
17. Ibid.
18. United States Court of Appeals for the First Circuit, No. 01-1296, *Fraser v. Major League Soccer, LLC*, ruling issued March 20, 2002.
19. Ibid.
20. Ibid.
21. Ibid.
22. Ridge Mahoney, "MLS Goes to Federal Court," CNNSI.com, posted November 16, 2000, http://sportsillustrated.cnn.com/soccer/mls/news/2000/11/16/mls_trial_sa/ (accessed August 25, 2009).

Chapter 6: The Low Point

1. Tobias Xavier Lopez, "MLS Dumps Two Florida teams," *Star-Telegram* (Fort Worth), January 8, 2002, accessed through Knight Ridder/Tribune News Service.

Chapter 7: Building Back

1. "Wynalda's Season Appears Over After Apparently Tearing ACL in Charleston Exhibition against Revolution," *SoccerTimes*, April 15, 2002, posted at http://www.soccertimes.com/proleagues/usl/2002/apr15.htm (accessed August 28, 2009).
2. Kelly Whiteside, "Mathis Creates on the Field and at Home," *USA Today*, May 16, 2002, posted at http://www.usatoday.com/sports/soccer/cup2002/2002-05-16-mathis.htm (accessed January 24, 2010).

Chapter 8: More Groundwork

1. Grant Wahl, "2003 the Year in Sports: Soccer," SI.com, unknown date, posted at http://sportsillustrated.cnn.com/2003/magazine/specials/sports_year/ups_and_downs/soccer/ (accessed January 24, 2010).
2. Allison Ann Otto, "A Volatile Mix in Rapids' Goal," *Denver Post*, September 22, 2003.
3. Grant Wahl, "¡¡¡Es un clásico!!!" SI.com, November 10, 2003, posted at http://sportsillustrated.cnn.com/2003/writers/grant_wahl/11/10/mls.classic/index.html (accessed August 25, 2009).

Chapter 9: In the Spotlight

1. "Pryor Cashman LLP: William L. Charron," Pryor Cashman LLP, posted at http://www.pryorcashman.com/attorneys-33.html (accessed August 25, 2009).
2. Interview conducted for my story "Adu Looking to Impress at Youth Tourney," USATODAY.com, June 8, 2005, posted at http://www.usatoday.com/sports/

soccer/national/2005-06-08-adu-youth-championships_x.htm (accessed August 25, 2009). Part of the quote is used in the story.

Chapter 10: Hardball

1. Major League Soccer, "Houston Becomes New Home for Earthquakes," ML-Snet, December 15, 2005, posted at http://web.mlsnet.com/news/mls_news.jsp?ymd=20051215&content_id=49527&vkey=pr_mls&fext=.jsp (accessed August 25, 2009).
2. "Fans Betrayed by Quakes' Departure," editorial (San Jose) *Mercury News*, December 16, 2005.
3. David Pollak, "Seismic Shift: Quakes Leaving S.J.," (San Jose) *Mercury News*, December 16, 2005.
4. Ann Killion, "Earthquakes' Fans Are the Victims of This Joke," (San Jose) *Mercury News*, December 17, 2005.
5. Simon Romero, "What's in a Brand Name? Houston Just Found Out," *New York Times*, January 27, 2006, posted at http://query.nytimes.com/gst/fullpage.html?res=9401E2DD113FF934A15752C0A9609C8B63&sec=&spon=&&scp=1&sq=%22anschutz%20entertainment%20group%22%20houston&st=cse (accessed August 25, 2009).
6. John Ryan, "AEG up to Old Tricks," (San Jose) *Mercury News*, April 4, 2006, accessed through Knight Ridder/Tribune News Service.
7. "Build a Soccer Stadium at the County Fairgrounds," editorial, (San Jose) *Mercury News*, June 9, 2006.
8. Ann Killion, "Through the Looking Glass, MLS-style," (San Jose) *Mercury News*, May 25, 2006.
9. Ray Ratto, "Don't Fall for Quakes' Scam," *San Francisco Chronicle*, May 26, 2006, posted at http://www.sfgate.com/cgi-bin/article.cgi?f=/c/a/2006/05/26/SPGEOJ2GT81.DTL&feed=rss.sports (accessed August 25, 2009).
10. Derek P. Jensen, "RSL Done in Utah?" *Salt Lake Tribune*, July 12, 2006.
11. Ibid.
12. Dan Loney, column at *American Soccer News*, June 22, 2006, posted at http://www.americansoccernews.net/columnists/loney/060622loncy.shtml (accessed June 22, 2006).
13. Grant Wahl, "Entering a New Arena (pt. 5)," SI.com, August 15, 2006, posted at http://sportsillustrated.cnn.com/2006/writers/grant_wahl/08/15/arena.qa/4.html (accessed August 26, 2009).
14. Mark Zeigler, "Sidelines," *San Diego Union-Tribune*, November 9, 2005, posted at http://www.signonsandiego.com/uniontrib/20051109/news_lz1s9sideline.html (accessed August 26, 2009).
15. Terry Lefton, "MLS's $2 Million Man," *SportsBusiness Daily*, June 5, 2006, posted at http://www.sportsbusinessjournal.com/index.cfm?fuseaction=article.main&articleId=50763 (accessed August 26, 2009).

Chapter 11: Beckham and Blanco

1. Derek P. Jensen and Rosemary Winters, "Debt Committee Tells RSL No Way," *Salt Lake Tribune*, January 27, 2007.
2. Derek P. Jensen, "Stadium Deal Is Dead: Checketts May Sell RSL," *Salt Lake Tribune*, January 29, 2007.
3. Lisa Riley Roche, "Huntsman Gets Kudos for Working with Others," *Deseret News*, March 1, 2007, posted at http://www.deseretnews.com/article/1,5143, 660199744,00.html (accessed August 26, 2009).
4. Beau Dure, "Leftovers: Galaxy Makeover, Cobi's Retirement, Cold-Weather Fans," *USA Today* blog post, April 6, 2007, posted at http://www.usa today.com/community/profile.htm?UID=1e704431d89e7993&plck Controller=PersonaBlog&plckScript=personaScript&plckElement Id=personaDest&plckPersonaPage=BlogViewPost&plckPostId=Bl-og%3a1e704431d89e7993Post%3a8e5d5531-2039-46d9-bba7-8a7f8289ef7b (accessed August 26, 2009).
5. Beau Dure, "Q&A: Conrad on Beckham, Money, Rome, Diving," *USA Today*, March 30, 2008, posted at http://www.usatoday.com/sports/soccer/mls/2008-03-30-conrad-qa_N.htm (accessed August 26, 2009).
6. Original column no longer available online at http://www.cnbc.com/id/18276686/, though Rovell addresses it in a follow-up column at http://www.cnbc.com/id/18617338—several reports cite original language, including Grant Wahl at http://sportsillustrated.cnn.com/vault/article/magazine/MAG 1107715/index.htm and myself at http://www.usatoday.com/sports/soccer/mls/saltlake/2007-05-09-adu_N.htm.
7. Kevin Sherrington, "Beckham Takes Soccer's Shot and Whiffs," *Dallas Morning News*, August 1, 2007, posted at http://www.dallasnews.com/sharedcontent/dws/spt/columnists/ksherrington/stories/080107dnsposherrington.2e 5c943.html (accessed August 26, 2009).

Chapter 12: Beckham and Beyond

1. Grant Wahl, *The Beckham Experiment* (New York: Crown Publishers, 2009).
2. Fulham FC, "In McBride's Honour," June 17, 2009, posted at http://www.fulhamfc.com/Club/News/NewsArticles/2009/June/McBrides.aspx (accessed August 27, 2009).
3. I asked Beckham in an exclusive interview (July 18, 2008) if he had some sort of option for getting out if things weren't working out in MLS. He said no—once he makes a commitment, he honors it. Beckham may not have fully understood the question, and in any case, he was technically correct—he was committed to the Galaxy through the 2009 season.
4. Beau Dure, "MLS Lineup Could Soon See 20 Teams in Near Future," *USA Today*, March 25, 2009, posted at http://www.usatoday.com/sports/soccer/2009-

03-24-mls-lineup_N.htm (accessed August 28, 2009).

5. In informal conversations with players in MLS and WPS, I've never heard a positive word about artificial turf other than saying one kind is a slight improvement over another.

6. Beau Dure, "Red Bulls, Seeking Playoff Spot, Critique Themselves," *USA Today*, October 4, 2007, posted at http://www.usatoday.com/sports/soccer/mls/redbullny/2007-10-03-redbulls-mls_N.htm (accessed August 28, 2009—see online sidebar).

7. The *Daily Mail* reported in August 2009 that Pinton had finally sold the Cosmos brand for an undisclosed price to former Tottenham Hotspurs director Paul Kemsley. Charles Sale, "Kemsley Planning Rebirth of New York Cosmos," *Daily Mail*, August 29, 2009, posted at http://www.dailymail.co.uk/sport/article-1209787/CHARLES-SALE-Former-Tottenham-director-Paul-Kemsley-planning-rebirth-New-York-Cosmos.html (accessed October 16, 2009).

INDEX

ABOUT THE AUTHOR

Beau Dure, who grew up watching college football and baseball in Athens, Georgia, has covered Major League Soccer since 1999, including columns and a blog under the name "The Netminder." He graduated from Duke University in 1991 with majors in philosophy and music, then returned to Duke for a master's in liberal studies. Before joining *USA Today* in 1999, he worked at the *Morning Star* (Wilmington, North Carolina), the *News & Record* (Greensboro, North Carolina), and Knight Ridder Tribune News Service. As a writer and online editor at *USA Today*, he has contributed to the coverage of six Olympic Games and has written extensively on soccer and mixed martial arts. He lives in Vienna, Virginia, with his wife, two sons, and dog. This is his first book.